Visit classzone.com
and get conn[ected]

Online resources for students and parents

ClassZone resources provide instruction, practice, and learning support.

eEdition Plus ONLINE

This interactive version of the text encourages students to explore science.

Content Review Online

Interactive review reinforces the big idea and key concepts of each chapter.

SciLinks

NSTA-selected links provide relevant Web resources correlated to the text.

Chapter-Based Support

Math tutorials, news, resources, test practice, and a misconceptions database help students succeed.

Now it all clicks!™

CLASSZONE.COM

McDougal Littell

McDougal Littell Science

Earth's Atmosphere

TROPOSPHERE

UPDRAFT

CUMULUS

EARTH SCIENCE

A ▶ Earth's Surface
B ▶ The Changing Earth
C ▶ Earth's Waters
D ▶ Earth's Atmosphere
E ▶ Space Science

PHYSICAL SCIENCE

A ▶ Matter and Energy
B ▶ Chemical Interactions
C ▶ Motion and Forces
D ▶ Waves, Sound, and Light
E ▶ Electricity and Magnetism

LIFE SCIENCE

A ▶ Cells and Heredity
B ▶ Life Over Time
C ▶ Diversity of Living Things
D ▶ Ecology
E ▶ Human Biology

Acknowledgments: Excerpts and adaptations from *National Science Education Standards* by the National Academy of Sciences. Copyright © 1996 by the National Academy of Sciences. Reprinted with permission from the National Academies Press, Washington, D.C.

Excerpts and adaptations from *Benchmarks for Science Literacy: Project 2061.* Copyright © 1993 by the American Association for the Advancement of Science. Reprinted with permission.

ISBN-13: 978-0-618-84245-2   4500311983

ISBN-10: 0-618-84245-4   8 9   0914   13 12 11

Internet Web Site: http://www.mcdougallittell.com

Science Consultants

Chief Science Consultant

James Trefil, Ph.D. is the Clarence J. Robinson Professor of Physics at George Mason University. He is the author or co-author of more than 25 books, including *Science Matters* and *The Nature of Science*. Dr. Trefil is a member of the American Association for the Advancement of Science's Committee on the Public Understanding of Science and Technology. He is also a fellow of the World Economic Forum and a frequent contributor to *Smithsonian* magazine.

Rita Ann Calvo, Ph.D. is Senior Lecturer in Molecular Biology and Genetics at Cornell University, where for 12 years she also directed the Cornell Institute for Biology Teachers. Dr. Calvo is the 1999 recipient of the College and University Teaching Award from the National Association of Biology Teachers.

Kenneth Cutler, M.S. is the Education Coordinator for the Julius L. Chambers Biomedical Biotechnology Research Institute at North Carolina Central University. A former middle school and high school science teacher, he received a 1999 Presidential Award for Excellence in Science Teaching.

Instructional Design Consultants

Douglas Carnine, Ph.D. is Professor of Education and Director of the National Center for Improving the Tools of Educators at the University of Oregon. He is the author of seven books and over 100 other scholarly publications, primarily in the areas of instructional design and effective instructional strategies and tools for diverse learners. Dr. Carnine also serves as a member of the National Institute for Literacy Advisory Board.

Linda Carnine, Ph.D. consults with school districts on curriculum development and effective instruction for students struggling academically. A former teacher and school administrator, Dr. Carnine also co-authored a popular remedial reading program.

Donald Steely, Ph.D. serves as principal investigator at the Oregon Center for Applied Science (ORCAS) on federal grants for science and language arts programs. His background also includes teaching and authoring of print and multimedia programs in science, mathematics, history, and spelling.

Sam Miller, Ph.D. is a middle school science teacher and the Teacher Development Liaison for the Eugene, Oregon, Public Schools. He is the author of curricula for teaching science, mathematics, computer skills, and language arts.

Vicky Vachon, Ph.D. consults with school districts throughout the United States and Canada on improving overall academic achievement with a focus on literacy. She is also co-author of a widely used program for remedial readers.

Content Reviewers

John Beaver, Ph.D.
Ecology
Professor, Director of Science Education Center
College of Education and Human Services
Western Illinois University
Macomb, IL

Donald J. DeCoste, Ph.D.
Matter and Energy, Chemical Interactions
Chemistry Instructor
University of Illinois
Urbana-Champaign, IL

Dorothy Ann Fallows, Ph.D., MSc
Diversity of Living Things, Microbiology
Partners in Health
Boston, MA

Michael Foote, Ph.D.
The Changing Earth, Life Over Time
Associate Professor
Department of the Geophysical Sciences
The University of Chicago
Chicago, IL

Lucy Fortson, Ph.D.
Space Science
Director of Astronomy
Adler Planetarium and Astronomy Museum
Chicago, IL

Elizabeth Godrick, Ph.D.
Human Biology
Professor, CAS Biology
Boston University
Boston, MA

Isabelle Sacramento Grilo, M.S.
The Changing Earth
Lecturer, Department of the Geological Sciences
San Diego State University
San Diego, CA

David Harbster, MSc
Diversity of Living Things
Professor of Biology
Paradise Valley Community College
Phoenix, AZ

Richard D. Norris, Ph.D.
Earth's Waters
Professor of Paleobiology
Scripps Institution of Oceanography
University of California, San Diego
La Jolla, CA

Donald B. Peck, M.S.
Motion and Forces; Waves, Sound, and Light;
  Electricity and Magnetism
Director of the Center for Science Education (retired)
Fairleigh Dickinson University
Madison, NJ

Javier Penalosa, Ph.D.
Diversity of Living Things, Plants
Associate Professor, Biology Department
Buffalo State College
Buffalo, NY

Raymond T. Pierrehumbert, Ph.D.
Earth's Atmosphere
Professor in Geophysical Sciences (Atmospheric Science)
The University of Chicago
Chicago, IL

Brian J. Skinner, Ph.D.
Earth's Surface
Eugene Higgins Professor of Geology and Geophysics
Yale University
New Haven, CT

Nancy E. Spaulding, M.S.
Earth's Surface, The Changing Earth, Earth's Waters
Earth Science Teacher (retired)
Elmira Free Academy
Elmira, NY

Steven S. Zumdahl, Ph.D.
Matter and Energy, Chemical Interactions
Professor Emeritus of Chemistry
University of Illinois
Urbana-Champaign, IL

Susan L. Zumdahl, M.S.
Matter and Energy, Chemical Interactions
Chemistry Education Specialist
University of Illinois
Urbana-Champaign, IL

Safety Consultant

Juliana Texley, Ph.D.
Former K–12 Science Teacher and School Superintendent
Boca Raton, FL

English Language Advisor

Judy Lewis, M.A.
Director, State and Federal Programs for reading proficiency
and high risk populations
Rancho Cordova, CA

Teacher Panel Members

Carol Arbour
Tallmadge Middle School,
Tallmadge, OH

Patty Belcher
Goodrich Middle School,
Akron, OH

Gwen Broestl
Luis Munoz Marin Middle School,
Cleveland, OH

Al Brofman
Tehipite Middle School,
Fresno, CA

John Cockrell
Clinton Middle School,
Columbus, OH

Jenifer Cox
Sylvan Middle School,
Citrus Heights, CA

Linda Culpepper
Martin Middle School,
Charlotte, NC

Kathleen Ann DeMatteo
Margate Middle School,
Margate, FL

Melvin Figueroa
New River Middle School,
Ft. Lauderdale, FL

Doretha Grier
Kannapolis Middle School,
Kannapolis, NC

Robert Hood
Alexander Hamilton Middle School,
Cleveland, OH

Scott Hudson
Covedale Elementary School,
Cincinnati, OH

Loretta Langdon
Princeton Middle School,
Princeton, NC

Carlyn Little
Glades Middle School,
Miami, FL

Ann Marie Lynn
Amelia Earhart Middle School,
Riverside, CA

James Minogue
Lowe's Grove Middle School,
Durham, NC

Joann Myers
Buchanan Middle School,
Tampa, FL

Barbara Newell
Charles Evans Hughes Middle School,
Long Beach, CA

Anita Parker
Kannapolis Middle School,
Kannapolis, NC

Greg Pirolo
Golden Valley Middle School,
San Bernardino, CA

Laura Pottmyer
Apex Middle School,
Apex, NC

Lynn Prichard
Booker T. Washington Middle Magnet
School, Tampa, FL

Jacque Quick
Walter Williams High School,
Burlington, NC

Robert Glenn Reynolds
Hillman Middle School,
Youngstown, OH

Stacy Rinehart
Lufkin Road Middle School,
Apex, NC

Theresa Short
Abbott Middle School,
Fayetteville, NC

Rita Slivka
Alexander Hamilton Middle School,
Cleveland, OH

Marie Sofsak
B F Stanton Middle School,
Alliance, OH

Nancy Stubbs
Sweetwater Union Unified School District,
Chula Vista, CA

Sharon Stull
Quail Hollow Middle School,
Charlotte, NC

Donna Taylor
Okeeheelee Middle School,
West Palm Beach, FL

Sandi Thompson
Harding Middle School,
Lakewood, OH

Lori Walker
Audubon Middle School & Magnet Center,
Los Angeles, CA

Teacher Lab Evaluators

Andrew Boy
W.E.B. DuBois Academy,
Cincinnati, OH

Jill Brimm-Byrne
Albany Park Academy,
Chicago, IL

Gwen Broestl
Luis Munoz Marin Middle School,
Cleveland, OH

Al Brofman
Tehipite Middle School,
Fresno, CA

Michael A. Burstein
The Rashi School,
Newton, MA

Trudi Coutts
Madison Middle School,
Naperville, Il

Jenifer Cox
Sylvan Middle School,
Citrus Heights, CA

Larry Cwik
Madison Middle School,
Naperville, IL

Jennifer Donatelli
Kennedy Junior High School,
Lisle, IL

Melissa Dupree
Lakeside Middle School,
Evans, GA

Carl Fechko
Luis Munoz Marin Middle School,
Cleveland, OH

Paige Fullhart
Highland Middle School,
Libertyville, IL

Sue Hood
Glen Crest Middle School,
Glen Ellyn, IL

William Luzader
Plymouth Community Intermediate School,
Plymouth, MA

Ann Min
Beardsley Middle School,
Crystal Lake, IL

Aileen Mueller
Kennedy Junior High School,
Lisle, IL

Nancy Nega
Churchville Middle School,
Elmhurst, IL

Oscar Newman
Sumner Math and Science Academy,
Chicago, IL

Lynn Prichard
Booker T. Washington Middle Magnet
School, Tampa, FL

Jacque Quick
Walter Williams High School,
Burlington, NC

Stacy Rinehart
Lufkin Road Middle School,
Apex, NC

Seth Robey
Gwendolyn Brooks Middle School,
Oak Park, Il

Kevin Steele
Grissom Middle School,
Tinley Park, IL

Earth's Atmosphere

Unit Features

1 Earth's Changing Atmosphere   6

the **BIG** idea

Earth's atmosphere is a blanket of gases that supports and protects life.

2 Weather Patterns   40

the **BIG** idea

Some features of weather have predictable patterns.

What weather conditions do you see in the distance?
page 40

What types of weather can move a house? page 76

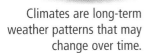

Features

Visual Highlights

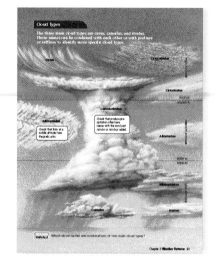

Internet Resources @ ClassZone.com

INVESTIGATIONS AND ACTIVITIES

Standards and Benchmarks

Each chapter in **Earth's Atmosphere** covers some of the learning goals that are described in the *National Science Education Standards* (NSES) and the Project 2061 *Benchmarks for Science Literacy.* Selected content and skill standards are shown below in shortened form. The following National Science Education Standards are covered on pages xii–xxvii, in Frontiers in Science, and in Timelines in Science, as well as in chapter features and laboratory investigations: Understandings About Scientific Inquiry (A.9), Understandings About Science and Technology (E.6), Science and Technology in Society (F.5), Science as a Human Endeavor (G.1), Nature of Science (G.2), and History of Science (G.3).

Content Standards

1 Earth's Changing Atmosphere

National Science Education Standards

D.1.h The atmosphere
- is a mixture of the gases nitrogen and oxygen
- has small amounts of water vapor and other gases
- has different properties at different heights

F.3.b Human activities can produce hazards and affect the speed of natural changes.

Project 2061 Benchmarks

4.B.6 The atmosphere can change suddenly when a volcano erupts or when Earth is struck by a huge rock from space. A small change in the substance of the atmosphere can have a big effect if the change lasts long enough.

4.E.3 Heat energy can move by the collision of particles, by the motion of particles, or by waves through space.

2 Weather Patterns

National Science Education Standards

D.1.f Water
- evaporates from Earth's surface
- rises, cools, and condenses in the atmosphere
- falls to the surface as rain or snow

D.1.i Clouds form when water vapor condenses. Clouds affect the weather.

D.1.j Global patterns have an effect on local weather and weather patterns.
- Global patterns of air motion affect the local weather.
- Oceans affect the weather patterns of a place.

Project 2061 Benchmarks

4.B.7 Water is important in the atmosphere. Water
- evaporates from Earth's surface
- rises and cools
- condenses into rain or snow
- falls back to the surface

4.B.4 Sunlight falls more intensely on different parts of Earth, and the pattern changes over the year. The differences in heating of Earth's surface produce seasons and other weather patterns.

Weather Fronts and Storms

National Science Education Standards

D.1.j | Global patterns of air motion and heat energy from oceans both have big effects on weather.

F.3.a | Processes of the Earth system, such as storms, can cause hazards that affect humans and wildlife.

Project 2061 Benchmarks

3.A.2 | Technologies are important in science because they let people gather large sets of data, put them together, analyze them, and share data and ideas.

11.B.1 | Models are often used to think about processes that cannot be observed directly or that are too vast or too dangerous to be changed directly. Models can be displayed on a computer and then changed to see what happens.

Climate and Climate Change

National Science Education Standards

D.1.j | The global patterns of motion in the atmosphere and the oceans affect the weather in different places.

D.2.a | The Earth processes we see today are similar to those that occurred in the past. Earth history is sometimes affected by catastrophes, such as the impact of an asteroid.

Project 2061 Benchmarks

4.B.6 | In the past, weather patterns have changed suddenly from events such as a volcano erupting or a large rock from space hitting Earth. Weather patterns around the world can be affected by even a small change in the atmosphere, if the change lasts long enough.

4.B.9 | Currents in the oceans move heat energy from place to place, so they affect the weather patterns in different locations.

Process and Skill Standards

National Science Education Standards

A.2 | Design and conduct a scientific investigation.

A.3 | Use appropriate tools and techniques to gather and interpret data.

A.4 | Use evidence to describe, predict, explain, and model.

A.5 | Use critical thinking to find relationships between results and interpretations.

A.7 | Communicate procedures, results, and conclusions.

A.8 | Use mathematics in scientific investigations.

E.2 | Design a solution or product.

E.3 | Implement the proposed solution.

E.4 | Evaluate the solution or design.

Project 2061 Benchmarks

12.B.5 | Estimate distances and travel times from maps.

12.C.3 | Using appropriate units, use and read instruments that measure length, volume, weight, time, rate, and temperature.

12.D.1 | Use tables and graphs to organize information and identify relationships.

12.D.2 | Read, interpret, and describe tables and graphs.

12.D.4 | Understand information that includes different types of charts and graphs, including circle charts, bar graphs, line graphs, data tables, diagrams, and symbols.

12.E.4 | Recognize more than one way to interpret a given set of findings.

Introducing Earth Science

Scientists are curious. Since ancient times, they have been asking and answering questions about the world around them. Scientists are also very suspicious of the answers they get. They carefully collect evidence and test their answers many times before accepting an idea as correct.

In this book you will see how scientific knowledge keeps growing and changing as scientists ask new questions and rethink what was known before. The following sections will help get you started.

What Is Earth Science?

Earth science is the study of Earth's interior, its rocks and soil, its atmosphere, its oceans, and outer space. For many years, scientists studied each of these topics separately. They learned many important things. More recently, however, scientists have looked more and more at the connections among the different parts of Earth—its oceans, atmosphere, living things, and rocks and soil. Scientists have also been learning more about other planets in our solar system, as well as stars and galaxies far away. Through these studies they have learned much about Earth and its place in the universe.

The text and pictures in this book will help you learn key concepts and important facts about earth science. A variety of activities will help you investigate these concepts. As you learn, it helps to have a big picture of earth science as a framework for this new information. The four unifying principles listed below will give you this big picture. Read the next few pages to get an overview of each of these principles and a sense of why they are so important.

- **Heat energy inside Earth and radiation from the Sun provide energy for Earth's processes.**

- **Physical forces, such as gravity, affect the movement of all matter on Earth and throughout the universe.**

- **Matter and energy move among Earth's rocks and soil, atmosphere, waters, and living things.**

- **Earth has changed over time and continues to change.**

the **BIG** idea

Each chapter begins with a big idea. Keep in mind that each big idea relates to one or more of the unifying principles.

Heat energy inside Earth and radiation from the Sun provide energy for Earth's processes.

The lava pouring out of this volcano in Hawaii is liquid rock that was melted by heat energy under Earth's surface. Another, much more powerful energy source constantly bombards Earth's surface with energy, heating the air around you, and keeping the oceans from freezing over. This energy source is the Sun. Everything that moves or changes on Earth gets its energy either from the Sun or from the inside of our planet.

What It Means

You are always surrounded by different forms of energy, such as heat energy or light. **Energy** is the ability to cause change. All of Earth's processes need energy to occur. A process is a set of changes that leads to a particular result. For example, **evaporation** is the process by which liquid changes into gas. A puddle on a sidewalk dries up through the process of evaporation. The energy needed for the puddle to dry up comes from the Sun.

Heat Energy Inside Earth

Underneath the cool surface layer of rock, Earth's interior is so hot that the solid rock there is able to flow very slowly—a few centimeters each year. In a process called **convection,** hot material rises, cools, then sinks until it is heated enough to rise again. Convection of hot rock carries heat energy up to Earth's surface, where it provides the energy to build mountains, cause earthquakes, and make volcanoes erupt.

Radiation from the Sun

Earth receives energy from the Sun as **radiation**—energy that travels across distances in the form of certain types of waves. Visible light is one type of radiation. Radiation from the Sun heats Earth's surface, making bright summer days hot. Different parts of Earth receive different amounts of radiation at different times of the year, causing seasons. Energy from the Sun also causes winds to blow, ocean currents to flow, and water to move from the ground to the atmosphere and back again.

Why It's Important

Understanding Earth's processes makes it possible to

- know what types of crops to plant and when to plant them
- know when to watch for dangerous weather, such as tornadoes and hurricanes
- predict a volcano's eruption in time for people to leave the area

Physical forces, such as gravity, affect the movement of all matter on Earth and throughout the universe.

The universe is everything that exists, and everything in the universe is governed by the same physical laws. The same laws govern the stars shown in this picture and the page on which the picture is printed.

What It Means

What do the stars in a galaxy, the planet Earth, and your body have in common? For one thing, they are all made of matter. **Matter** is anything that has mass and takes up space. Rocks are matter. You are matter. Even the air around you is matter. Matter is made of tiny particles called **atoms** that are too small to see through an ordinary microscope.

Everything in the universe is also affected by the same physical forces. A **force** is a push or a pull. Forces affect how matter moves everywhere in the universe.

- One force you experience every moment is **gravity,** which is the attraction, or pull, between two objects. Gravity is pulling you to Earth and Earth to you. Gravity is the force that causes objects to fall downward toward the center of Earth. Gravity is also the force that keeps objects in orbit around planets and stars.

- **Friction** is the force that resists motion between two surfaces that are pressed together. Friction can keep a rock on a hillside from sliding down to the bottom of the hill. If you lightly rub your finger across a smooth page in a book and then across a piece of sandpaper, you can feel how the different surfaces produce different frictional forces. Which is easier to do?

- There are many other forces at work on Earth and throughout the universe. For example, Earth has a magnetic field. A compass needle responds to the force exerted by Earth's magnetic field. Another example is the contact force between a rock and the ground beneath it. A contact force occurs when one object pushes or pulls on another object by touching it.

Why It's Important

Physical forces influence the movement of all matter, from the tiniest particle to you to the largest galaxy. Understanding forces allows people to

- predict how objects and materials move on Earth
- send spacecraft and equipment into space
- explain and predict the movements of Earth, the Moon, planets, and stars

Matter and energy move among Earth's rocks and soil, atmosphere, waters, and living things.

When a wolf eats a rabbit, matter and energy move from one living thing into another. When a wolf drinks water warmed by the Sun, matter and energy move from Earth's waters into one of its living things. These are just two examples of how energy and matter move among different parts of the Earth system.

What It Means

Think of Earth as a huge system, or an organized group of parts that work together. Within this system, matter and energy move among the different parts. The four major parts of Earth's system are the

- **atmosphere,** which includes all the air surrounding the solid planet
- **geosphere,** which includes all of Earth's rocks and minerals, as well as Earth's interior
- **hydrosphere,** which includes oceans, rivers, lakes, and every drop of water on or under Earth's surface
- **biosphere,** which includes all the living things on Earth

Matter in the Earth System

It's easy to see how matter moves within the Earth system. When water in the atmosphere falls as rain, it becomes part of the hydrosphere. When an animal drinks water from a puddle, the water becomes part of the biosphere. When rainwater soaks into the ground, it moves through the geosphere. As the puddle dries up, the water becomes part of the atmosphere again.

Energy in the Earth System

Most of the energy you depend on comes from the Sun and moves among the four major parts of the Earth system. Think again about the puddle that is drying up. Sunlight shines through the water and heats the soil, or geosphere, beneath the puddle. Some of this heat energy goes into the puddle, moving into the hydrosphere. As the water evaporates and becomes part of the atmosphere, it takes the energy that came from the Sun with it. The Sun provides energy for all weather and ocean currents. Without the Sun, life could not exist on Earth's surface.

Why It's Important

Understanding how matter and energy move through the Earth system makes it possible to

- predict how a temperature change in ocean water might affect the weather
- determine how clearing forests might affect rainfall
- explain where organisms on the ocean floor get energy to carry out life processes

Earth has changed over time and continues to change.

You see Earth changing all of the time. Rain turns dirt to mud, and a dry wind turns the mud to dust. Many changes are small and can take hundreds, thousands, or even millions of years to add up to much. Other changes are sudden and can destroy in minutes a house that had stood for many years.

What It Means

Events are always changing Earth's surface. Some events, such as the building or wearing away of mountains, occur over millions of years. Others, such as earthquakes, occur within seconds. A change can affect a small area or even the entire planet.

Records of Change

What was the distant past like? Think about how scientists learn about ancient people. They study what the people left behind and draw conclusions based on the evidence. In a similar way, scientists learn about Earth's past by examining the evidence they find in rock layers and by observing processes now occurring.

By observing that water breaks down rocks and carries the material away to other places, people learned that rivers can slowly carve deep valleys. Evidence from rocks and fossils along the edges of continents shows that all continents were once joined and then moved apart over time. A **fossil** is the trace of a once-living organism. Fossils also show that new types of plants and animals develop, and others, such as dinosaurs, die out.

Change Continues Today

Every year, earthquakes occur, volcanoes erupt, and rivers flood. Continents continue to move slowly. The Himalayan Mountains of Asia push a few millimeters higher. **Climate**—the long-term weather patterns of an area—may also change. Scientists are studying how changes in climates around the world might affect Earth even within this century.

Why It's Important

Understanding the changing Earth makes it possible to

- predict and prepare for events such as volcanic eruptions, landslides, floods, and climate changes
- design buildings to withstand shaking during earthquakes
- protect important environments for plants and animals

The Nature of Science

You may think of science as a body of knowledge or a collection of facts. More important, however, science is an active process that involves certain ways of looking at the world.

Scientific Habits of Mind

Scientists are curious. They ask questions. A scientist who finds an unusual rock by the side of a river would ask questions such as, "Did this rock form in this area?" or "Did this rock form elsewhere and get moved here?" Questions like these make a scientist want to investigate.

Scientists are observant. They look closely at the world around them. A scientist who studies rocks can learn a lot about a rock just by picking it up, looking at its color, and feeling how heavy it is.

Scientists are creative. They draw on what they know to form possible explanations for a pattern, an event, or an interesting phenomenon that they have observed. Then scientists put together a plan for testing their ideas.

Scientists are skeptical. Scientists don't accept an explanation or answer unless it is based on evidence and logical reasoning. They continually question their own conclusions as well as the conclusions suggested by other scientists. Scientists only trust evidence that can be confirmed by other people or other methods.

Scientists use seismographs to observe and measure vibrations that move through the ground.

This scientist is collecting a sample of melted rock from a hot lava flow in Hawaii.

Science Processes at Work

You can think of science as a continuous cycle of asking and seeking answers to questions about the world. Although there are many processes that scientists use, all scientists typically do the following:

- Observe and ask a question
- Determine what is known
- Investigate
- Interpret results
- Share results

Ask a question → Determine what is known → Investigate → Interpret results → Share results

Observe and Ask a Question

It may surprise you that asking questions is an important skill. A scientific investigation may start when a scientist asks a question. Perhaps scientists observe an event or a process that they don't understand, or perhaps answering one question leads to another.

Determine What Is Known

When beginning an inquiry, scientists find out what is already known about a question. They study results from other scientific investigations, read journals, and talk with other scientists. The scientist who is trying to figure out where an unusual rock came from will study maps that show what types of rocks are already known to be in the area where the rock was found.

Investigate

Investigating is the process of collecting evidence. Two important ways of doing this are experimenting and observing.

An **experiment** is an organized procedure to study something under controlled conditions. For example, the scientist who found the rock by the river might notice that it is lighter in color where it is chipped. The scientist might design an experiment to determine why the rock is a different color on the inside. The scientist could break off a small piece of the inside of the rock and heat it up to see if it becomes the same color as the outside. The scientist would need to use a piece of the same rock that is being studied. A different rock might react differently to heat.

A scientist may use photography to study fast events, such as multiple flashes of lightning.

Rocks, such as this one from the Moon, can be subjected to different conditions in a laboratory.

Observing is the act of noting and recording an event, characteristic, or anything else detected with an instrument or with the senses. A scientist makes observations while performing an experiment. However, some things cannot be studied using experiments. For example, streaks of light called meteors occur when small rocks from outer space hit Earth's atmosphere. A scientist might study meteors by taking pictures of the sky at a time when meteors are likely to occur.

Forming hypotheses and making predictions are two other skills involved in scientific investigations. A **hypothesis** is a tentative explanation for an observation or a scientific problem that can be tested by further investigation. For example, the scientist might make the following hypothesis about the rock from the beach:

The rock is a meteorite, which is a rock that fell to the ground from outer space. The outside of the rock changed color because it was heated up from passing through Earth's atmosphere.

A **prediction** is an expectation of what will be observed or what will happen. To test the hypothesis that the rock's outside is black because it is a meteorite, the scientist might predict that a close examination of the rock will show that it has many characteristics in common with rocks that are already known to be meteorites.

Interpret Results

As scientists investigate, they analyze their evidence, or data, and begin to draw conclusions. **Analyzing data** involves looking at the evidence gathered through observations or experiments and trying to identify any patterns that might exist in the data. Scientists often need to make additional observations or perform more experiments before they are sure of their conclusions. Many times scientists make new predictions or revise their hypotheses.

Scientists use computers to gather and interpret data.

Scientists make images such as this computer drawing of a landscape to help share their results with others.

Share Results

An important part of scientific investigation is sharing results of experiments. Scientists read and publish in journals and attend conferences to communicate with other scientists around the world. Sharing data and procedures gives scientists a way to test each others' results. They also share results with the public through newspapers, television, and other media.

The Nature of Technology

When you think of technology, you may think of cars, computers, and cell phones. Imagine having no refrigerator or radio. It's difficult to think of a world without the products of what we call technology. Technology, however, is more than just devices that make our daily activities easier. Technology is the process of using scientific knowledge to design solutions to real-world problems.

Science and Technology

Science and technology go hand in hand. Each depends upon the other. Even a device as simple as a thermometer is designed using knowledge of the ways different materials respond to changes in temperature. In turn, thermometers have allowed scientists to learn more about the world. Greater knowledge of how materials respond to changes in temperature helped engineers to build items such as refrigerators. They have also built thermometers that could be read automatically by computers. New technologies lead to new scientific knowledge and new scientific knowledge leads to even better technologies.

The Process of Technological Design

The process of technological design involves many choices. What, for example, should be done to protect the residents of an area prone to severe storms such as tornadoes and hurricanes? Build stronger homes that can withstand the winds? Try to develop a way to detect the storms long before they occur? Or learn more about hurricanes in order to find new ways to protect people from the dangers? The steps people take to solve the problem depend a great deal on what they already know about the problem as well as what can reasonably be done. As you learn about the steps in the process of technological design, think about the different choices that could be made at each step.

Identify a Need

To study hurricanes, scientists needed to know what happens inside the most dangerous parts of the storm. However, it was not safe for scientists to go near the centers of hurricanes because the winds were too strong and changed direction too fast. Scientists needed a way to measure conditions deep inside the storm without putting themselves in danger.

Design and Develop

One approach was to design a robotic probe to take the measurements. The probe and instruments needed to be strong enough to withstand the fast winds near the center of a hurricane. The scientists also needed a way to send the probe into the storm and to get the data from the instruments quickly.

Scientists designed a device called a dropsonde, which could be dropped from an airplane flying over the hurricane. A dropsonde takes measurements from deep inside the storm and radios data back to the scientists

Test and Improve

Even good technology can usually be improved. When scientists first used dropsondes, they learned about hurricanes. They also learned what things about the dropsondes worked well and what did not. For example, the scientists wanted better ways to keep track of where the probe moved. Newer dropsondes make use of the Global Positioning System, which is a way of pinpointing any position on Earth by using satellite signals.

Using McDougal Littell Science

Reading Text and Visuals

This book is organized to help you learn. Use these boxed pointers as a path to help you learn and remember the **Big Ideas** and **Key Concepts**.

Take notes.

Use the strategies on the **Getting Ready to Learn** page.

Read the Big Idea.

As you read **Key Concepts** for the chapter, relate them to the Big Idea.

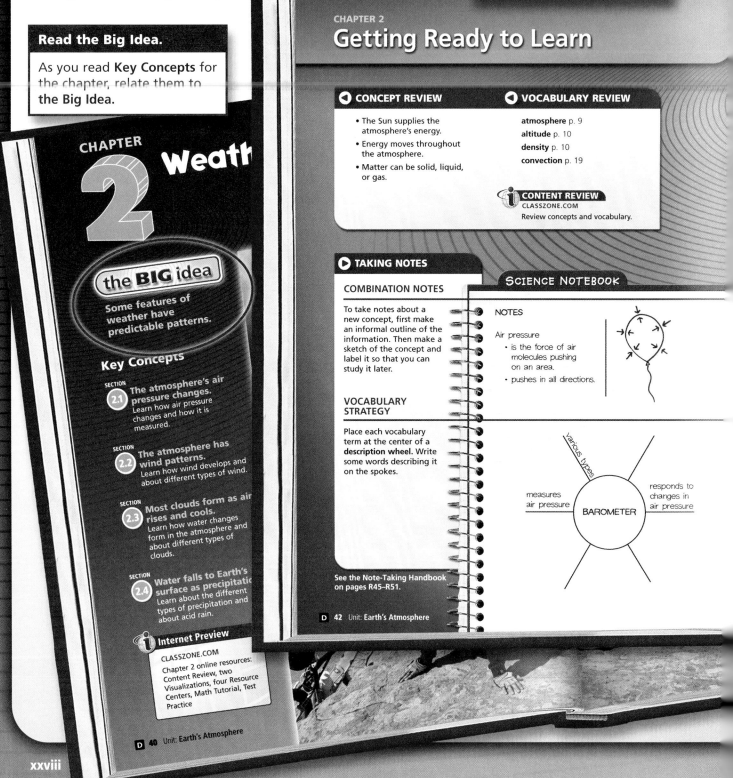

CHAPTER

2 **Weath**

the **BIG** idea

Some features of weather have predictable patterns.

Key Concepts

SECTION
2.1 The atmosphere's air pressure changes.
Learn how air pressure changes and how it is measured.

SECTION
2.2 The atmosphere has wind patterns.
Learn how wind develops and about different types of wind.

SECTION
2.3 Most clouds form as air rises and cools.
Learn how water changes form in the atmosphere and about different types of clouds.

SECTION
2.4 Water falls to Earth's surface as precipitatio
Learn about the different types of precipitation and about acid rain.

Internet Preview

CLASSZONE.COM
Chapter 2 online resources: Content Review, two Visualizations, four Resource Centers, Math Tutorial, Test Practice

D 40 Unit: Earth's Atmosphere

CHAPTER 2
Getting Ready to Learn

CONCEPT REVIEW

- The Sun supplies the atmosphere's energy.
- Energy moves throughout the atmosphere.
- Matter can be solid, liquid, or gas.

VOCABULARY REVIEW

atmosphere p. 9
altitude p. 10
density p. 10
convection p. 19

CONTENT REVIEW
CLASSZONE.COM
Review concepts and vocabulary.

TAKING NOTES

COMBINATION NOTES

To take notes about a new concept, first make an informal outline of the information. Then make a sketch of the concept and label it so that you can study it later.

VOCABULARY STRATEGY

Place each vocabulary term at the center of a **description wheel**. Write some words describing it on the spokes.

See the Note-Taking Handbook on pages R45–R51.

SCIENCE NOTEBOOK

NOTES

Air pressure
- is the force of air molecules pushing on an area.
- pushes in all directions.

various types

measures air pressure

BAROMETER

responds to changes in air pressure

D 42 Unit: Earth's Atmosphere

xxviii

KEY CONCEPT

2.1 The atmosphere's air pressure changes.

◀ BEFORE, you learned

- Density is the amount of mass in a given volume of a substance
- Air becomes less dense as altitude increases
- Differences in density cause air to rise and sink

▶ NOW, you will learn

- How the movement of air molecules causes air pressure
- How air pressure varies
- How differences in air pressure affect the atmosphere

VOCABULARY

air pressure p. 43
barometer p. 46

EXPLORE Air Pressure

What does air do to the egg?

PROCEDURE

1. Set a peeled hard-boiled egg in the mouth of a bottle. Make sure that the egg can't slip through.

2. Light the matches. Remove the egg, and drop the matches into the bottle. Quickly replace the egg.

3. Watch carefully, and record your observations.

MATERIALS

- peeled hard-boiled egg
- glass bottle
- 2 wooden matches

WHAT DO YOU THINK?

- What happened when you placed the egg back on top of the bottle?
- What can your observations tell you about the air in the bottle?

Air exerts pressure.

Air molecules move constantly. As they move, they bounce off each other like rubber balls. They also bounce off every surface they hit. As you read this book, billions of air molecules are bouncing off your body, the book, and everything else around you.

Each time an air molecule bounces off an object, it pushes, or exerts a force, on that object. When billions of air molecules bounce off a surface, the force is spread over the area of that surface. **Air pressure** is the force of air molecules pushing on an area. The greater the force, the higher the air pressure. Because air molecules move in all directions, air pressure pushes in all directions.

VOCABULARY
Add a description wheel for *air pressure* to your notebook.

CHECK YOUR READING How does the number of air molecules relate to air pressure?

Chapter 2: **Weather Patterns** 43 **D**

Reading Text and Visuals

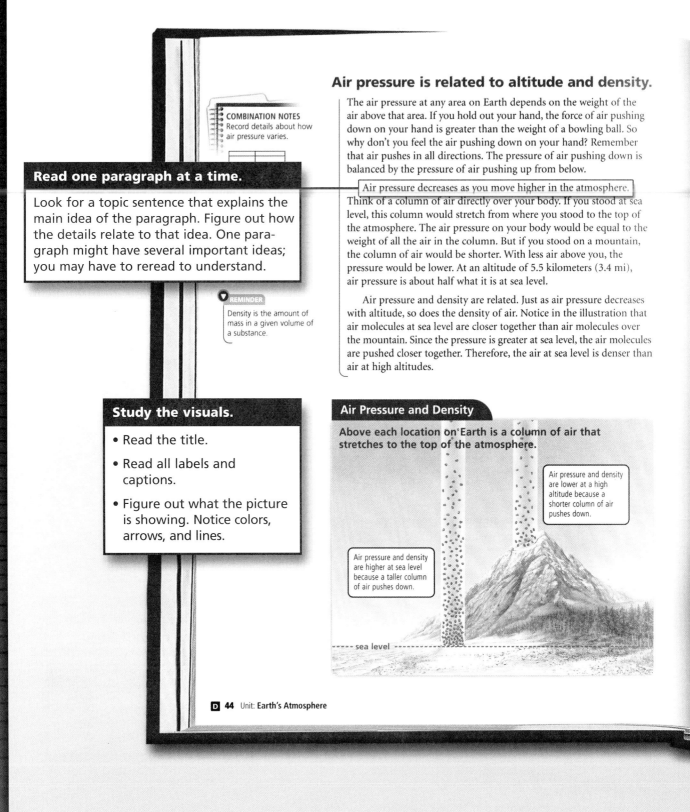

COMBINATION NOTES
Record details about how air pressure varies.

Read one paragraph at a time.

Look for a topic sentence that explains the main idea of the paragraph. Figure out how the details relate to that idea. One paragraph might have several important ideas; you may have to reread to understand.

REMINDER
Density is the amount of mass in a given volume of a substance.

Air pressure is related to altitude and density.

The air pressure at any area on Earth depends on the weight of the air above that area. If you hold out your hand, the force of air pushing down on your hand is greater than the weight of a bowling ball. So why don't you feel the air pushing down on your hand? Remember that air pushes in all directions. The pressure of air pushing down is balanced by the pressure of air pushing up from below.

Air pressure decreases as you move higher in the atmosphere.
Think of a column of air directly over your body. If you stood at sea level, this column would stretch from where you stood to the top of the atmosphere. The air pressure on your body would be equal to the weight of all the air in the column. But if you stood on a mountain, the column of air would be shorter. With less air above you, the pressure would be lower. At an altitude of 5.5 kilometers (3.4 mi), air pressure is about half what it is at sea level.

Air pressure and density are related. Just as air pressure decreases with altitude, so does the density of air. Notice in the illustration that air molecules at sea level are closer together than air molecules over the mountain. Since the pressure is greater at sea level, the air molecules are pushed closer together. Therefore, the air at sea level is denser than air at high altitudes.

Study the visuals.

- Read the title.
- Read all labels and captions.
- Figure out what the picture is showing. Notice colors, arrows, and lines.

Air Pressure and Density

Above each location on Earth is a column of air that stretches to the top of the atmosphere.

Air pressure and density are lower at a high altitude because a shorter column of air pushes down.

Air pressure and density are higher at sea level because a taller column of air pushes down.

----- sea level -----

Doing Labs

To understand science, you have to see it in action. Doing labs helps you understand how things really work.

① Read the entire lab first.

② Form a hypothesis.

③ Follow the procedure.

④ Record the data.

CHAPTER INVESTIGATION

Relative Humidity

OVERVIEW AND PURPOSE Finding out the relative humidity can help you predict how comfortable you will feel on a hot day or whether dew will form on the ground. You can use a psychrometer to measure relative humidity. A psychrometer is a device made from two thermometers—one with a wet bulb and the other with a dry bulb. In this activity you will
• make a milk-carton psychrometer
• use it to measure the relative humidity of the air at two locations in your school

▶ Problem
Write It Up

Which location will have the greater relative humidity?

▶ Hypothesize
Write It Up

Write a hypothesis in "If . . . , then . . . , because . . ." form to answer the problem.

▶ Procedure

MATERIALS
• 2 thermometers
• cotton or felt cloth
• 3 rubber bands
• plastic bowl
• water at room temperature
• scissors
• pint milk carton
• ruler
• relative humidity table

1. Make a table like the one shown on the sample notebook page to record your data.

2. Check the two thermometers that you are using in this experiment to make sure they read the same temperature. Wrap a piece of cotton or felt cloth around the bulb of one thermometer. Hold the cloth in place with a rubber band as shown in the photograph. Dip this wet-bulb thermometer into a bowl of room-temperature water until the cloth is soaked.

step 3

3. Use scissors to cut a small hole in one side of the milk carton, 2 centimeters from the bottom of the carton. Place the wet-bulb thermometer on the same side as the hole that you made in the milk carton, and attach it with a rubber band. Push the tail of the cloth through the hole. Attach the dry-bulb thermometer as shown.

4. Fill the carton with water to just below the hole so that the cloth will remain wet. Empty the bowl and place the completed psychrometer inside it.

5. Write "science room" under the heading "Location 1" in your data table. Take your first readings in the science classroom about 10 minutes after you set up your psychrometer. Read the temperatures on the two thermometers in degrees Celsius. Record the temperature readings for the first location in the first column of your table.

6. Choose a second location in your school, and identify it under the heading "Location 2" in the data table. Take a second set of temperature readings with your psychrometer in this location. Record the readings in the second column of your table.

7. Subtract the wet-bulb reading from the dry-bulb reading for each location. Record this information in the third row of your data table.

8. Use the relative humidity table your teacher provides to find each relative humidity (expressed as a percentage). In the left-hand column, find the dry-bulb reading for location 1 that you recorded in step 5. Then find in the top line the number you recorded in step 7 (the difference between the dry-bulb and wet-bulb readings). Record the relative humidity in the last row of your data table. Repeat these steps for location 2.

▶ Observe and Analyze
Write It Up

1. **RECORD OBSERVATIONS** Draw the setup of your psychrometer. Be sure your data table is complete.

2. **IDENTIFY** Identify the variables and constants in this experiment. List them in your **Science Notebook**.

3. **COMPARE** How do the wet-bulb readings compare with the dry-bulb readings?

4. **ANALYZE** If the difference between the temperature readings on the two thermometers is large, is the relative humidity high or low? Explain why.

▶ Conclude
Write It Up

5. **INTERPRET** Answer the question in the problem. Compare your results with your hypothesis.

6. **IDENTIFY LIMITS** Describe any possible errors that you made in following the procedure.

7. **APPLY** How would you account for the differences in relative humidity that you obtained for the two locations in your school?

▶ INVESTIGATE Further

CHALLENGE Use the psychrometer to keep track of the relative humidity in your classroom over a period of one week. Make a new chart to record your data. What do you notice about how the changes in relative humidity relate to the weather conditions outside?

Relative Humidity
Problem Which location will have the greater relative humidity?
Hypothesize
Observe and Analyze
Table 1. Relative Humidity at Two Locations

	Location 1	Location 2
Dry-bulb temperature		
Wet-bulb temperature		
Difference between dry-bulb and wet-bulb readings		
Relative humidity		

Conclude

Chapter 2: Weather Patterns **65** D

⑤ Analyze your results.

⑥ Write your lab report.

Using Technology

The Internet is a great source of information about up-to-date science.
The ClassZone Website and SciLinks have exciting sites for you to
explore. Video clips and simulations can make science come alive.

Look for red banners.

Go to **ClassZone.com** to see
simulations, visualizations,
resources centers, and
content review.

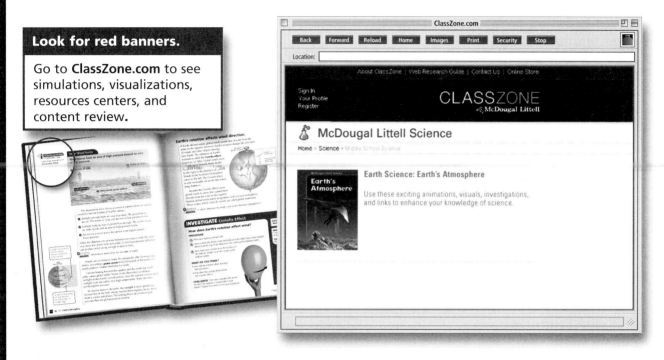

Watch the videos.

See science at work in
the **Scientific American
Frontiers video.**

Look up SciLinks.

Go to **scilinks.org** to explore
the topic.

Atmospheric Pressure and Winds **Code: MDL010**

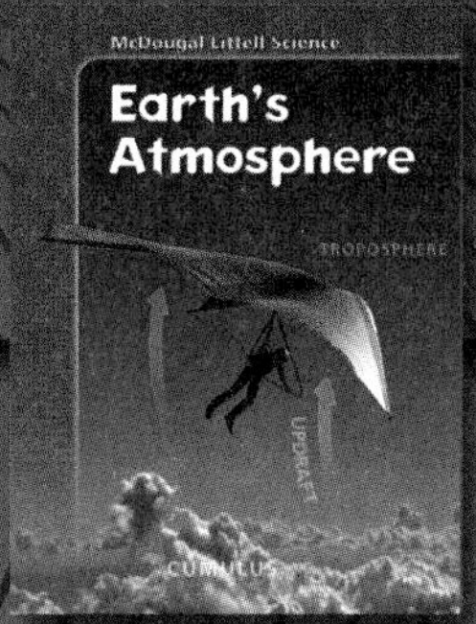

Earth's Atmosphere
Contents Overview

Unit Features

1 Earth's Changing Atmosphere   6

the **BIG** idea

Earth's atmosphere is a blanket of
gases that supports and protects life.

2 Weather Patterns   40

the **BIG** idea

Some features of weather have predictable patterns.

3 Weather Fronts and Storms   76

the **BIG** idea

The interaction of air masses causes
changes in weather.

4 Climate and Climate Change   114

the **BIG** idea

Climates are long-term weather patterns
that may change over time.

DUST
in the AIR

What happens around this beautiful
island in the Caribbean when dust from
an African storm travels thousands of
kilometers across the ocean?

SCIENTIFIC
AMERICAN
FRONTIERS

Learn more about the
scientists studying dust in
the atmosphere. See the
video "Dust Busting."

This map shows the path that dust travels from Africa, across the Atlantic Ocean, to the Caribbean—a distance of about 5000 kilometers (3000 mi).

A Problem to Solve

Images from space show gigantic clouds of dust traveling from Africa thousands of kilometers across the Atlantic Ocean. Weather reports in the Caribbean warn listeners about African dust storms. Coral and manatees in Caribbean waters show signs of disease. Are these events connected?

Each year, natural events and human activities together send as much as 2 billion metric tons of material into the skies. Once dust enters the atmosphere, it moves with the other materials in the air.

But how do Earth's surface processes and the movement of air relate to diseased coral? Teams of scientists studied diseases in living things around the Caribbean. In addition, they examined satellite photographs and recorded when dust storms occurred. After analyzing these data, they hypothesized that materials in African dust were affecting living things in the Caribbean.

Satellite images show us how far dust can travel in the atmosphere. Experiments on air samples let scientists look at dust up close. Tests reveal that atmospheric dust includes many substances, including living material. As often happens in science, this new knowledge raises more questions. Could the living material in dust grow in a distant location? Could a fungus that lives in African soil end up in Caribbean waters?

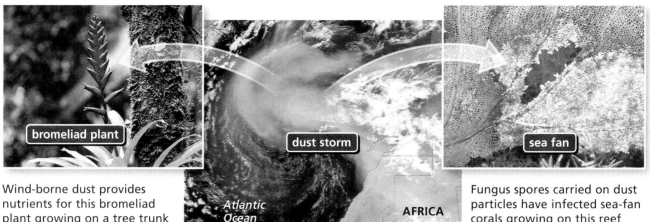

bromeliad plant

dust storm

sea fan

Atlantic Ocean

AFRICA

Wind-borne dust provides nutrients for this bromeliad plant growing on a tree trunk high in the rain forest of South America.

The huge dust storm shown in this satellite image carries both destructive fungus spores and life-sustaining nutrients across the Atlantic.

Fungus spores carried on dust particles have infected sea-fan corals growing on this reef near the island of St. John in the Caribbean Sea.

Answers Hidden in Dust

To explore these questions, scientists in the Caribbean gather air samples during dust storms. They collect dust from high in the air and from locations closer to Earth's surface. To collect the samples, scientists pull air through a paper filter, trapping the dust. Once they have caught the dust, the scientists are ready to perform tests to see what's really in the tiny particles.

In the laboratory, researchers place dust samples on top of nutrients in petri dishes. Then they see if anything in the dust grows. Recent studies have shown that dust samples collected over the Caribbean contained African fungi and bacteria. More importantly, scientists saw that, even after their long voyage through the atmosphere, the living materials were able to grow.

SCIENTIFIC AMERICAN FRONTIERS

View the "Dust Busting" segment of your *Scientific American Frontiers* video to learn about the detective work that went into solving the mystery of sea-fan disease.

IN THIS SCENE FROM THE VIDEO ▶ Biologist Ginger Garrison shows diseased coral to host Alan Alda.

MYSTERY SOLVED Sea fans are an important part of the Caribbean coral-reef community, but in the 1970s they began to die off. Recently marine biologist Garriet Smith was surprised to discover that a common soil fungus, called aspergillus, was killing the sea fans. But how could a soil fungus reach an undersea reef?

The answer came from geologist Gene Shinn, who knew that global winds carry dust from Africa to the Caribbean. When Shinn read about Smith's research, he hypothesized that aspergillus might be arriving with African dust. Shinn teamed up with Smith and biologist Ginger Garrison to test the hypothesis. They collected Caribbean air samples during an African dust event and cultured dust from the samples. Aspergillus grew in their very first cultures.

Dust from Africa also contains tiny bits of metals, such as iron. The soil and atmosphere in the Caribbean are enriched by iron carried in African dust. Beautiful plants called bromeliads get the iron they need directly from the atmosphere.

Unfortunately, some of the materials found in the dust samples could be harmful to living things, such as manatees and corals. One of the fungi found in Caribbean dust samples is *Aspergillus sydowii,* which may cause diseases in sea fans and other corals. In addition, the dust contains bacteria that may speed the growth of toxic red algae, which can be harmful to manatees and other ocean animals.

Strong Connections

Dust storms affect the entire planet. On April 6–8, 2001, soils from the Gobi Desert in Mongolia and China blew into the air, creating a massive dust cloud. Satellite images showed the cloud traveling eastward. A few days later people in the western United States saw the sky turn a chalky white.

Such observations of atmospheric dust show us how events in one part of the planet can affect living and nonliving things thousands of kilometers away in ways we might not have imagined.

UNANSWERED Questions

Tiny particles of atmospheric dust may have huge effects. Yet the more we learn about the makeup and nature of dust, the more questions we have.

- How do dust storms affect human health?
- What can dust tell us about climate change?
- How can we use information about dust storms to predict climate change?
- How do materials in dust change ecosystems?

UNIT PROJECTS

As you study this unit, work alone or with a group on one of these projects.

TV News Report

Prepare a brief news report on recent dust storms, using visuals and a script.

- Research dust storms that have occurred recently. Find out how they were related to the weather.
- Copy or print visuals, and write and practice delivering your report. Then make your presentation.

Map the Dust

Make a map showing how dust arrives in your area or another location.

- Find out what the dust contains and how it moved there. Collect information from atlases, the Internet, newspapers, and magazines.
- Prepare your map, including all the areas you need to show. Include a key, a title, and a compass rose.

Design an Experiment

Design an experiment to explore how the atmosphere has changed in the past or how it is changing today. Research the forms of evidence scientists gather about the state of our atmosphere.

- Pick one question to investigate in an experiment. Write a hypothesis.
- List and assemble materials for your experiment. Create a data table and write up your procedure.
- Demonstrate or describe your experiment for the class.

CAREER CENTER
CLASSZONE.COM

Learn about careers in meteorology.

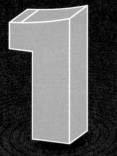

Earth's Changing Atmosphere

the **BIG** idea

Earth's atmosphere is a blanket of gases that supports and protects life.

What will make this kite soar?

Key Concepts

SECTION

1.1 Earth's atmosphere supports life.
Learn about the materials that make up the atmosphere.

SECTION

1.2 The Sun supplies the atmosphere's energy.
Learn how energy from the Sun affects the atmosphere.

SECTION

1.3 Gases in the atmosphere absorb radiation.
Learn about the ozone layer and the greenhouse effect.

SECTION

1.4 Human activities affect the atmosphere.
Learn about pollution, global warming, and changes in the ozone layer.

Internet Preview

CLASSZONE.COM
Chapter 1 online resources: Content Review, two Visualizations, two Resource Centers, Math Tutorial, Test Practice

How Heavy Is Paper?

Put a ruler on a table with one end off the edge. Tap on the ruler lightly and observe what happens. Then cover the ruler with a sheet of paper as shown. Tap again on the ruler and observe what happens.

Observe and Think
What happened to the ruler when you tapped lightly on it with and without the sheet of paper? Was the paper heavy enough by itself to hold the ruler down?

How Does Heating Affect Air?

Stretch the lip of a balloon over the neck of a small bottle. Next, fill a bowl with ice water and a second bowl with hot tap water. Place the bottle upright in the hot water. After 5 minutes, move the bottle to the cold water.

Observe and Think What changes did you observe in the balloon? What might have caused these changes?

Internet Activity: Atmosphere

Go to **ClassZone.com** to learn about Earth's atmosphere.

Observe and Think How does the thickness of the atmosphere compare with the height of a mountain or the altitude of the space shuttle in orbit?

NSTA SCiLINKS
scilinks.org
Composition of the Atmosphere **Code: MDL009**

Getting Ready to Learn

◀ **CONCEPT REVIEW**

- Matter is made up of atoms.
- All things on or near Earth are pulled toward Earth by its gravity.
- Heating or cooling any material changes some of its properties.

◀ **VOCABULARY REVIEW**

See Glossary for definitions.

atom   **mass**

gas   **molecule**

gravity

CONTENT REVIEW
CLASSZONE.COM
Review concepts and vocabulary.

▶ **TAKING NOTES**

SUPPORTING MAIN IDEAS

Make a chart to show main ideas and the information that supports them. Write each blue heading from the chapter in a separate box. In boxes below it, add supporting information, such as reasons, explanations, and examples.

VOCABULARY STRATEGY

Write each new vocabulary term in the center of a **frame game** diagram. Decide what information to frame the term with. Use examples, descriptions, pictures, or sentences in which the term is used in context. You can change the frame to fit each term.

See the Note-Taking Handbook on pages R45–R51.

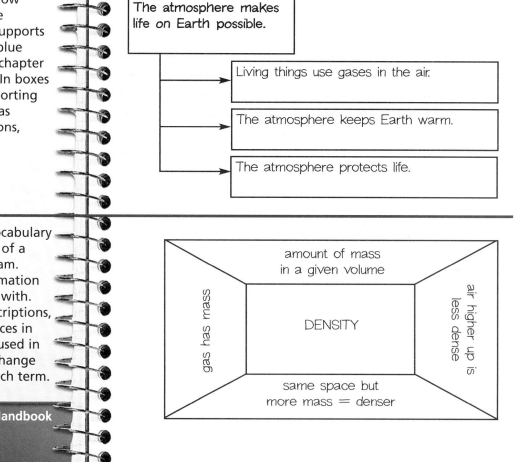

SCIENCE NOTEBOOK

The atmosphere makes life on Earth possible.

Living things use gases in the air.

The atmosphere keeps Earth warm.

The atmosphere protects life.

amount of mass in a given volume

gas has mass

DENSITY

air higher up is less dense

same space but more mass = denser

1.1 Earth's atmosphere supports life.

BEFORE, you learned

- Living things need food, water, and air
- Matter can be solid, liquid, or gas

NOW, you will learn

- Why the atmosphere is important to living things
- What the atmosphere is made of
- How natural cycles affect the atmosphere

VOCABULARY

atmosphere p. 9
altitude p. 10
density p. 10
cycle p. 12

EXPLORE Air Resistance

How does air affect falling objects?

PROCEDURE

1. Drop the washer from shoulder height.

2. Tape the metal washer to the center of the coffee filter. The filter will act as a parachute.

3. Drop the washer with the parachute from shoulder height.

WHAT DO YOU THINK?

- What difference did the parachute make?
- What do your results tell you about air?

MATERIALS

- metal washer
- coffee filter
- tape

The atmosphere makes life on Earth possible.

VOCABULARY
Remember to make a frame game diagram for the term *atmosphere*.

Every time you breathe in, your lungs fill with air, which is a mixture of gases. Your body uses materials from the air to help you stay alive. The **atmosphere** is a whole layer of air that surrounds Earth. The atmosphere supports life and protects it. The gases of the atmosphere keep Earth warm and transport energy to different regions of the planet. Without the atmosphere, the oceans would not exist, life would not survive, and the planet would be a cold, lifeless rock.

Even though the atmosphere is very important to life, it is surprisingly thin. If the solid part of Earth were the size of a peach, most of the atmosphere would be no thicker than the peach fuzz surrounding the fruit. The atmosphere is a small but important part of the Earth system.

CHECK YOUR READING How does the atmosphere make life possible? Find three examples in the text above.

 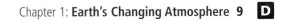

Characteristics of the Atmosphere

In 1862 two British balloonists reached the highest **altitude,** or distance above sea level, any human had ever reached. As their balloon rose to 8.8 kilometers (5.5 mi), one balloonist fainted and the other barely managed to bring the balloon back down. They found that the air becomes thinner as altitude increases.

The thickness or thinness of air is measured by its density. **Density** is the amount of mass in a given volume of a substance. If two objects take up the same amount of space, then the object with more mass has a greater density than the one with less mass. For example, a bowling ball has a higher density than a soccer ball.

The atmosphere's density decreases as you travel upward. The air on top of a mountain is less dense than the air at sea level. A deep breath of mountain air fills your lungs but contains less mass—less gas—than a deep breath of air at sea level. Higher up, at altitudes where jets fly, a breath of air would contain only about one-tenth the mass of a breath of air at sea level. The air farther above Earth's surface contains even less mass. There is no definite top to the atmosphere. It just keeps getting less dense as you get farther from Earth's surface. However, altitudes 500 kilometers (300 mi) or more above Earth's surface can be called outer space.

The decrease of density with greater altitude means that most of the mass of the atmosphere is close to Earth's surface. In fact, more than 99 percent of the atmosphere's mass is in the lowest 30 kilometers (20 mi).

INFER This climber has reached the top of Mount Everest, 8850 m (29,000 ft) above sea level in Nepal. Why does he need an oxygen mask?

INVESTIGATE Gas in the Air

How do you know that air has different gases?

PROCEDURE

1. Put a spoonful of limewater into each jar. Limewater is clear, but turns milky in the presence of carbon dioxide.

2. Cover one jar. Add extra carbon dioxide to the second jar by exhaling gently into it before you cover it. Tighten the lids carefully to seal the jars.

3. Predict what will happen, then shake each jar.

WHAT DO YOU THINK?

- What happened to the limewater in each jar?
- How do you know that air is made of different gases?

CHALLENGE How would you test a different gas in the air?

SKILL FOCUS
Predicting

MATERIALS
- limewater
- 2 jars
- spoon

TIME
10 minutes

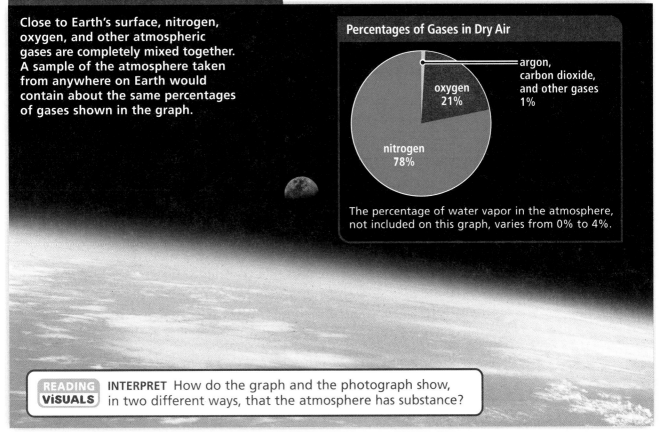

Gases of Earth's Atmosphere

Close to Earth's surface, nitrogen, oxygen, and other atmospheric gases are completely mixed together. A sample of the atmosphere taken from anywhere on Earth would contain about the same percentages of gases shown in the graph.

Percentages of Gases in Dry Air

argon, carbon dioxide, and other gases 1%

oxygen 21%

nitrogen 78%

The percentage of water vapor in the atmosphere, not included on this graph, varies from 0% to 4%.

READING VISUALS INTERPRET How do the graph and the photograph show, in two different ways, that the atmosphere has substance?

Materials in the Atmosphere

Most of the materials in the atmosphere are gases. However, the atmosphere also contains tiny particles of solid or liquid material such as dust, sea salt, and water droplets. Perhaps you have sat by an open window and noticed some of these particles on the window sill.

If you were to write a recipe for air, you would include nitrogen gas as the main ingredient. In dry air, about 78 percent of the gas is nitrogen. The next most common ingredient is oxygen gas, which makes up about 21 percent of the atmosphere. Argon, carbon dioxide, and other gases make up about 1 percent of the atmosphere. Unlike the amounts of nitrogen and other gases, the amount of water vapor varies a great deal. In some places at some times, water vapor can make up as much as 4 percent of the air.

The atmosphere's gases provide materials essential for living things. Nitrogen promotes plant growth and is an important ingredient in the chemicals that make up living things. Oxygen is necessary for animals and plants to perform life processes. Plants use carbon dioxide and water to make food.

READING TiP
As you read about the amounts of gases, find each gas on the graph above.

CHECK YOUR READING Which gas is the most common material in the air around you?

Natural processes modify the atmosphere.

The exact amounts of some gases in the air change depending on location, time of day, season, and other factors. Water vapor, carbon dioxide, and other gases in the atmosphere are affected by both ongoing processes and sudden changes.

Ongoing Processes

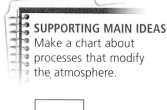

SUPPORTING MAIN IDEAS
Make a chart about processes that modify the atmosphere.

You and all other living things participate in ongoing processes. For example, each day you breathe in and out about 13,000 liters (3,000 gal) of air—about as much air as would fill five school buses. When you breathe, your body exchanges gases with the atmosphere. The air you inhale is a slightly different mixture of gases than the air you exhale.

Living things take part in a repeated process of gas exchange with the atmosphere. In addition, living things continually exchange materials in solid and liquid form with the environment. Processes like these that repeat over and over are called **cycles.**

Three of the most important cycles that affect the atmosphere are the carbon cycle, the nitrogen cycle, and the water cycle.

❶ The Carbon Cycle Carbon dioxide (CO_2) and oxygen (O_2) gases constantly circulate, or cycle, among plants, animals, and the atmosphere. For example,

- Animals inhale air, use some of its oxygen, and exhale air that has less oxygen but more carbon dioxide and water
- Plants take in carbon dioxide and release oxygen as they make food in the process of photosynthesis

❷ The Nitrogen Cycle Different forms of nitrogen cycle among the atmosphere, the soil, and living organisms. For example,

- Tiny organisms remove nitrogen gas (N_2) from the air and transform it into other chemicals, which then enter the soil
- Plants and animals use solids and liquids that contain nitrogen, which returns to the soil when the organisms die and decay
- The soil slowly releases nitrogen back into the air as nitrogen gas

❸ The Water Cycle Different forms of water (H_2O) cycle between Earth's surface and the atmosphere. For example,

- Liquid water from oceans and lakes changes into gas and enters the atmosphere
- Plants release water vapor from their leaves
- Liquid water falls from the atmosphere as rain

READING TIP

In the diagrams on page 13, color is used to show particular materials.

O_2 is red.

CO_2 is purple.

N_2 is aqua.

H_2O is blue.

Cycles and the Atmosphere

A tiger breathing, leaves decaying, trees growing—all are involved in cycles that affect our atmosphere. The diagrams to the right show how materials move in three important cycles.

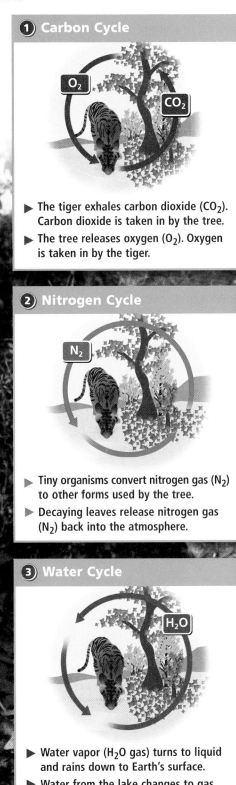

① Carbon Cycle

▶ The tiger exhales carbon dioxide (CO_2). Carbon dioxide is taken in by the tree.

▶ The tree releases oxygen (O_2). Oxygen is taken in by the tiger.

② Nitrogen Cycle

▶ Tiny organisms convert nitrogen gas (N_2) to other forms used by the tree.

▶ Decaying leaves release nitrogen gas (N_2) back into the atmosphere.

③ Water Cycle

▶ Water vapor (H_2O gas) turns to liquid and rains down to Earth's surface.

▶ Water from the lake changes to gas and returns to the atmosphere.

READING ViSUALS **COMPARE AND CONTRAST** How are the three cycles similar? How are they different?

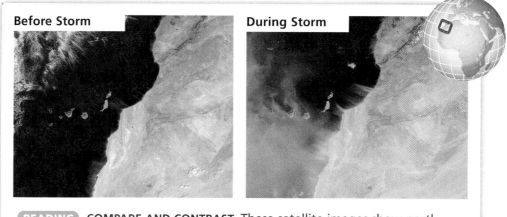

Before Storm

During Storm

READING VISUALS **COMPARE AND CONTRAST** These satellite images show north-western Africa before and during a dust storm. How does the second image differ from the first?

Sudden Changes

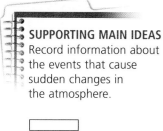
In addition to ongoing processes, dramatic events may cause changes in the atmosphere. When sudden events occur, it takes time before the atmosphere is able to restore balance.

- **Volcanic Eruptions** Volcanoes shoot gases and huge amounts of ash into the atmosphere. Certain gases produce a haze that may affect the air for many months and lower temperatures worldwide.

- **Forest Fires** When forests burn, the carbon that makes up each tree combines with oxygen and enters the atmosphere as carbon dioxide. Wood ash also enters the atmosphere.

- **Dust Storms** Wind, water, or drought can loosen soil. Powerful windstorms may then raise clouds of this eroded soil, as in the second picture above. These storms add huge amounts of particles to the air for a time.

1.1 Review

KEY CONCEPTS

1. How is the atmosphere important to living things?

2. What substances make up air?

3. Draw a diagram to show how one natural cycle affects the atmosphere.

CRITICAL THINKING

4. **Apply** Give three examples from everyday life of how the atmosphere supports and protects life.

5. **Predict** How would the atmosphere in your area change if a disease killed all the plants?

CHALLENGE

6. **Compare** Carbon dioxide enters the oceans from the air. Some carbon becomes stored in shells, and then in rocks. Eventually, it can be released back into the air by volcanoes in the form of carbon dioxide. How are these slow processes similar to the cycles shown on page 13?

Carbon Cycle Chemistry

The atmosphere is keeping you alive. Every time you breathe, you take in the oxygen that you need to live. But that's not the end of the story. The food you eat would not exist without the carbon dioxide in the air that you, and every other animal on Earth, breathe out.

A Closer Look at Oxygen and Carbon Dioxide

Gases in air are tiny molecules that are much too small to see, even if you look through a microscope. Chemists use diagrams to represent these molecules. Oxygen gas (O_2) is made of two atoms of oxygen, so a diagram of an oxygen gas molecule shows two red balls stuck together. A diagram of a carbon dioxide molecule (CO_2) looks similar, but it has one black carbon atom in addition to two red oxygen atoms.

oxygen

carbon dioxide

The Carbon Connection

1 The orange tree takes in carbon dioxide from the air. Molecules of carbon dioxide are broken apart, and some carbon atoms become part of other more complex molecules in the growing orange.

2 You take carbon-containing molecules into your body when you eat the orange. Later, your body uses the food to carry out life processes. Some of the carbon atoms become part of carbon dioxide molecules, which you exhale into the air.

The carbon dioxide you exhale may be taken in again by the tree. This time, the carbon may become part of the trunk of the tree, and then return to the air when the tree dies and decays. Carbon keeps going around and around among living things and the atmosphere.

The Carbon Cycle

1 The tree takes carbon from the air.

carbon in food

oxygen in air

carbon dioxide in air

2 You move carbon from food back into the air.

EXPLORE

1. **COMPARE AND CONTRAST** What is the difference between a carbon dioxide molecule and an oxygen molecule?

2. **CHALLENGE** Draw a diagram showing how carbon can move into and out of the air when a tree grows and then later dies and decays.

1.2 The Sun supplies the atmosphere's energy.

BEFORE, you learned

- The atmosphere supports and protects life
- The atmosphere contains a mixture of gases
- The atmosphere is affected by natural processes

NOW, you will learn

- How solar energy heats Earth's surface and atmosphere
- How the atmosphere moves heat energy around
- About the layers of the atmosphere

VOCABULARY

radiation p. 17
conduction p. 18
convection p. 19

THINK ABOUT

Can you feel sunlight?

If you have been on a hot beach, you have felt energy from sunlight. Perhaps you felt sunlight warming your skin or hot sand underneath your feet. It is easy to notice the energy of sunlight when it makes the ground or your skin warm. Where else does the energy from sunlight go?

Energy from the Sun heats the atmosphere.

SUPPORTING MAIN IDEAS
Write the blue heading into your notes to begin a new chart. Add supporting details.

It may seem hard to believe, but almost all the energy around you comes from the Sun. That means that food energy, fires, and even the warmth of your own body can be traced back to energy from the Sun. A lot of this energy reaches Earth in a form you can see—visible light.

Two main things happen to the sunlight that reaches Earth. Some is reflected, or sent in a new direction. You see most of the objects around you by reflected light. The sand in the picture above looks light in color because it reflects much of the sunlight that hits it. Some of the sunlight that reaches Earth's surface is absorbed. The energy from this light heats the substance that absorbs it. The sand can become warm or even hot as it absorbs some of the sunlight that hits it. Some objects, such as the striped shirts above, have bright parts that reflect more light and dark parts that absorb more light.

 CHECK YOUR READING What two things happen to the sunlight that reaches Earth?

The light that you can see is one type of radiation. **Radiation** (RAY-dee-AY-shuhn) is energy that travels across distances in the form of certain types of waves. Visible light and other types of radiation can be absorbed or reflected.

The diagram shows the average amounts of solar radiation, or radiation from the Sun, that are absorbed and reflected by Earth's atmosphere, clouds, and surface. Each arrow in the diagram represents 5 percent of the solar radiation that reaches Earth. As you can see, about 30 percent of the solar energy that reaches Earth is reflected. Clouds and snow-covered ground are white, so they reflect a lot of the radiation that hits them. Air also reflects some radiation. The energy of the reflected radiation goes back into outer space.

The other 70 percent of solar radiation that reaches Earth is absorbed. Most of this energy is absorbed by oceans, landforms, and living things. The absorbed energy heats Earth's surface. In the same way, energy that is absorbed by gas molecules, clouds, and dust particles heats the atmosphere.

Solar Radiation

Arrows show the average global reflection and absorption of solar radiation.

About 5% of solar energy is reflected by Earth's surface.

About 25% of solar energy is reflected by clouds and Earth's atmosphere.

About 20% of solar energy is absorbed by clouds and the atmosphere.

About 50% of solar energy is absorbed by Earth's surface.

The atmosphere is much smaller than shown.

INVESTIGATE Solar Radiation

How does reflection affect temperature?

PROCEDURE

1. Cover the top of one cup with plastic wrap. Cover the second cup with paper. Secure the plastic wrap and paper with tape.

2. Poke a small slit in each cup's cover. Insert a thermometer through each slit.

3. Place the cups in direct sunlight. Record their temperature every minute for 15 minutes.

WHAT DO YOU THINK?

• How did the temperature change inside each cup?

• How did the coverings contribute to these changes?

CHALLENGE What does the paper represent in this model?

SKILL FOCUS
Measuring

MATERIALS
• 2 cups
• plastic wrap
• white paper
• tape
• 2 short thermometers
• watch

TIME
25 minutes

The atmosphere moves energy.

If you walk along a sunny beach, you may be comfortably warm except for the burning-hot soles of your feet. The sand may be much hotter than the air. The sand absorbs solar energy all day and stores it in one place. The air also absorbs solar energy but moves it around and spreads it out. Radiation, conduction, and convection are processes that move energy from place to place.

Radiation You have already read that solar radiation warms a sandy beach. You may be surprised to learn that radiation also transfers energy from the sand to the air. Earth's surface gives off a type of invisible radiation, called infrared radiation, that can be absorbed by certain gases. The energy from the radiation warms the air. The air also gives off infrared radiation. You will read more about this cycle of radiation in Section 1.3.

Conduction Another way that sand warms the air is through conduction. When you walk barefoot on a hot beach, rapidly moving molecules in the hot sand bump against molecules in your feet. This process transfers energy to your feet, which get hot. **Conduction** is the transfer of heat energy from one substance to another by direct contact. Earth's surface transfers energy to the atmosphere by conduction, such as when hot beach sand warms the air above it. Molecules of air can

VOCABULARY
Add new terms to your notebook.

Transfer of Energy

Radiation, conduction, and convection move energy from place to place.

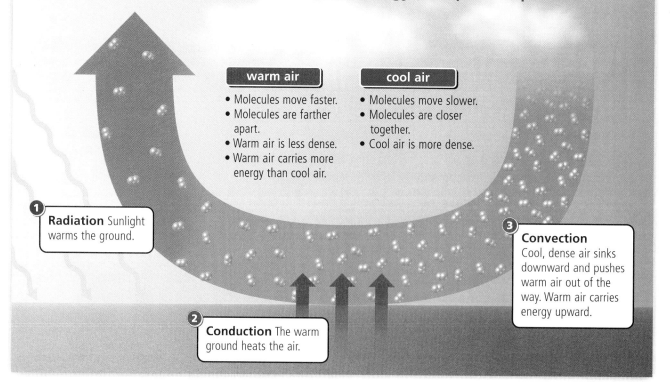

warm air
- Molecules move faster.
- Molecules are farther apart.
- Warm air is less dense.
- Warm air carries more energy than cool air.

cool air
- Molecules move slower.
- Molecules are closer together.
- Cool air is more dense.

1 **Radiation** Sunlight warms the ground.

2 **Conduction** The warm ground heats the air.

3 **Convection** Cool, dense air sinks downward and pushes warm air out of the way. Warm air carries energy upward.

gain energy when they collide with molecules in grains of hot sand. The air just above the sand gets warm. Energy can also spread slowly through the air by conduction as air molecules bump into one another.

Convection Heated air can move easily from place to place. When a heated liquid or gas moves, it carries energy along with it. **Convection** is the transfer of energy from place to place by the motion of gas or liquid. When scientists talk about convection in the atmosphere, they usually mean the motion of gases up and down rather than side to side. The heat energy comes from below and is moved upward. Think once more about the beach. First, radiation from the Sun warms the sand. Second, the hot sand conducts energy to the air. Third, the warm air carries energy upward in convection. Follow this cycle of radiation, conduction, and convection in the diagram on page 18.

Moving hot air near the flames makes the mountain behind appear distorted.

CHECK YOUR READING Compare conduction and convection. How are they similar?

Differences in density produce the motion of air convection. You have read that the atmosphere is less dense at higher altitudes. At any particular altitude, however, the density of air depends mostly on its temperature. Warm air has more energy, so the molecules move faster than they do in cool air. The motion makes the molecules collide more, so they stay farther apart. When there is more space between molecules, the air is less dense.

Imagine a box full of warm air and another box of the same size full of cool air. If you could see air molecules, you would find more molecules—more mass—in the box of cool air. Cool, dense air is heavier, so it tends to sink and push warm, less dense air upward.

As it moves upward, warm air carries energy away from the ground. The air can cool as it rises. Eventually, the air can become cool enough—dense enough—to sink back to the ground, where it may heat up again.

REMINDER

Density is the amount of mass in a given volume of a substance.

VISUALIZATION
CLASSZONE.COM

See radiation, conduction, and convection in action.

The atmosphere has temperature layers.

Density is not the only characteristic of the atmosphere that changes with altitude. Different parts of the atmosphere absorb and move energy in different ways. As a result, the air's temperature changes with altitude. Scientists use the patterns of these temperature changes to define four layers of the atmosphere. To explore these layers, turn the page and ride an imaginary elevator up through the atmosphere.

Temperature Layers

Explore the atmosphere's temperature layers by riding an imaginary elevator up from the ground.

Thermosphere
Continue through the thermosphere. The air thins out until you reach outer space.

Mesosphere
Reach the mesosphere after rising 50 km (31 mi) off the ground. You are now above 99.9% of the molecules of Earth's air.

Stratosphere
Pass through the stratosphere, which includes the ozone layer. The air gets thinner as you move up through the atmosphere.

Troposphere
Board the elevator at ground level, which is also the bottom of the troposphere.

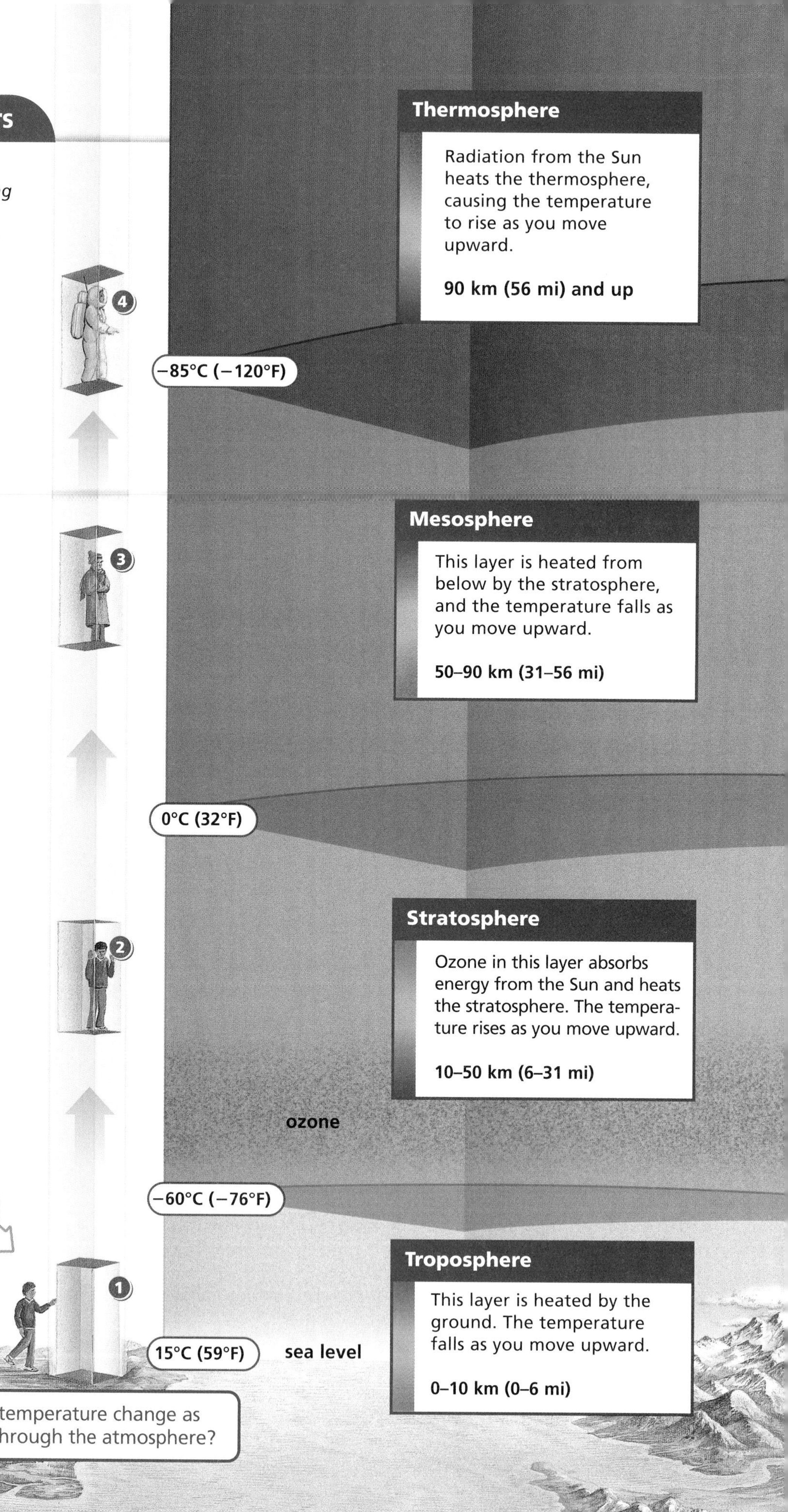

4

3

2

START HERE

1

−85°C (−120°F)

0°C (32°F)

−60°C (−76°F)

15°C (59°F)   sea level

Thermosphere

Radiation from the Sun heats the thermosphere, causing the temperature to rise as you move upward.

90 km (56 mi) and up

Mesosphere

This layer is heated from below by the stratosphere, and the temperature falls as you move upward.

50–90 km (31–56 mi)

Stratosphere

Ozone in this layer absorbs energy from the Sun and heats the stratosphere. The temperature rises as you move upward.

10–50 km (6–31 mi)

ozone

Troposphere

This layer is heated by the ground. The temperature falls as you move upward.

0–10 km (0–6 mi)

READING VISUALS How does the temperature change as you move up through the atmosphere?

①　Troposphere (TROH-puh-SFEER) The layer of the atmosphere nearest Earth's surface is called the troposphere because convection seems to turn the air over. This layer contains about 80 percent of the total mass of the atmosphere, including almost all of the water vapor present in the atmosphere. The troposphere is warmed from below by the ground. The temperature is highest at ground level and generally decreases about 6.5°C for each kilometer you rise.

②　Stratosphere (STRAT-uh-SFEER) Above the troposphere lies a clear, dry layer of the atmosphere called the stratosphere. Within the stratosphere are molecules of a gas called ozone. These molecules absorb a type of solar radiation that is harmful to life. The energy from the radiation raises the temperature of the air. The temperature increases as you rise high in the stratosphere.

③　Mesosphere (MEHZ-uh-SFEER) The air in the mesosphere is extremely thin. In fact, this layer contains less than 0.1 percent of the atmosphere's mass. Most meteors that enter the atmosphere burn up within the mesosphere. The mesosphere, like the troposphere, is heated from below, so the temperature in the mesosphere decreases as you rise.

④　Thermosphere (THUR-muh-SFEER) The thermosphere starts about 90 kilometers (56 mi) above Earth's surface. It grows less and less dense over hundreds of kilometers until it becomes outer space. The air high in this layer becomes very hot because the molecules absorb a certain type of solar radiation. However, even the hottest air in this layer would feel cold to you because the molecules are so spread out that they would not conduct much energy to your skin. The temperature in the thermosphere increases as you rise.

READING TIP
You can use the word parts to help you recall the temperature layers.
tropo-"turning"
strato-"spreading out"
meso-"middle"
thermo-"heat"

⬥ **CHECK YOUR READING**　How does the temperature change in each layer of the atmosphere?

1.2 Review

KEY CONCEPTS

1. What two things happen to solar radiation that reaches Earth?

2. Describe the three processes that transport energy.

3. What characteristic do scientists use to define four layers of Earth's atmosphere?

CRITICAL THINKING

4. **Draw Conclusions** How might a thick, puffy cloud reflect a different amount of the Sun's radiation than a thin, wispy one?

5. **Apply** Jet planes fly near the top of the troposphere. Is it more important to heat or to cool the passenger cabins? Explain your reasoning.

⬥ CHALLENGE

6. **Analyze** Earth loses about the same amount of energy as it absorbs from the Sun. If it did not, Earth's temperature would increase. Does the energy move from Earth's surface and atmosphere out to space through radiation, conduction, or convection? Give your reasons.

1.3 Gases in the atmosphere absorb radiation.

◀ BEFORE, you learned

- Solar radiation heats Earth's surface and atmosphere
- Earth's surface and atmosphere give off radiation
- The ozone layer is in the stratosphere

▶ NOW, you will learn

- More about how radiation and gases affect each other
- About the ozone layer and ultraviolet radiation
- About the greenhouse effect

VOCABULARY

ultraviolet radiation p. 23
infrared radiation p. 23
ozone p. 23
greenhouse effect p. 24
greenhouse gas p. 24

EXPLORE Radiation

Can you feel radiation?

PROCEDURE

① Turn on the lamp and wait for it to become warm. It gives off visible and infrared radiation.

② Hold one hand a short distance from the bulb. Record your observations.

③ Turn the lamp off. The bulb continues to give off infrared radiation. Hold your other hand a short distance from the bulb.

WHAT DO YOU THINK?
- What did you see and feel?
- How did radiation affect each hand?

MATERIALS
- lamp

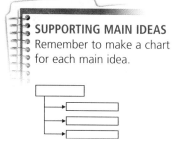

Gases can absorb and give off radiation.

SUPPORTING MAIN IDEAS
Remember to make a chart for each main idea.

On a sunny day, objects around you look bright. Earth's atmosphere reflects or absorbs some sunlight, but allows most of the visible light to pass through to Earth's surface. A cloudy day is darker because clouds reflect and absorb much of the sunlight, so less light passes through to the ground.

The atmosphere can affect light in four ways. It can absorb light, reflect it, or let it pass through. Air can also emit, or give off, light. Although air does not emit much visible light, certain gases absorb and emit radiation that is similar to visible light.

CHECK YOUR READING List four ways that the atmosphere can affect light.

Just as there are sounds humans cannot hear, there are forms of radiation that humans cannot see. Sounds can be too high to hear. In a similar way, waves of **ultraviolet radiation** (UHL-truh-VY-uh-liht) have more energy than the light you can see. Ultraviolet radiation can cause sunburn and other types of damage. Sounds can also be too low for humans to hear. In a similar way, waves of **infrared radiation** (IHN-fruh-REHD) have less energy than visible light. Infrared radiation usually warms the materials that absorb it. Different gases in the atmosphere absorb these two different types of radiation.

The ozone layer protects life from harmful radiation.

In Section 1.2, you read about a gas called ozone that forms in the stratosphere. An **ozone** molecule (O_3) is made of three atoms of the element oxygen. Your body uses regular oxygen gas (O_2), which has two atoms of oxygen. In the stratosphere, ozone and regular oxygen gases break apart and form again in a complex cycle. The reactions that destroy and form ozone normally balance each other, so the cycle can repeat endlessly. Even though ozone is mixed with nitrogen and other gases, the ozone in the stratosphere is called the ozone layer.

The ozone layer protects life on Earth by absorbing harmful ultraviolet radiation from the Sun. Too much ultraviolet radiation can cause sunburn, skin cancer, and damaged eyesight. Ultraviolet radiation can harm crops and materials such as plastic or paint. Ozone absorbs ultraviolet radiation but lets other types of radiation, such as visible light, pass through.

READING **TiP**

In this section, wavy arrows represent different types of radiation.

ultraviolet

visible

infrared

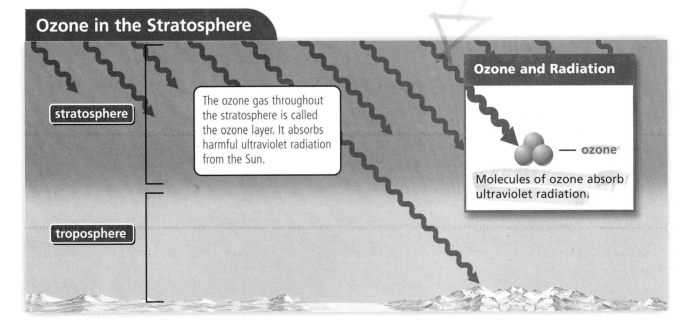

Ozone in the Stratosphere

stratosphere

The ozone gas throughout the stratosphere is called the ozone layer. It absorbs harmful ultraviolet radiation from the Sun.

troposphere

Ozone and Radiation

— ozone

Molecules of ozone absorb ultraviolet radiation.

The greenhouse effect keeps Earth warm.

VISUALIZATION
CLASSZONE.COM

See how the greenhouse effect works.

REMINDER

Ozone absorbs ultraviolet radiation in the stratosphere. Greenhouse gases absorb and emit infrared radiation in the troposphere.

A jacket helps keep you warm on a cool day by slowing the movement of heat energy away from your body. In a similar way, certain gases in the atmosphere slow the movement of energy away from Earth's surface. The gases absorb and emit infrared radiation, which keeps energy in Earth's system for a while. This process was named the **greenhouse effect** because it reminded scientists of the way glass traps warmth inside a greenhouse.

Carbon dioxide, methane, water vapor, nitrous oxide, and other gases that absorb and give off infrared radiation are known as **greenhouse gases.** Unlike the glass roof and walls of a greenhouse, the greenhouse gases do not form a single layer. They are mixed together with nitrogen, oxygen, and other gases in the air. The atmosphere is densest in the troposphere—the lowest layer—so most of the greenhouse gas molecules are also in the troposphere.

Radiation from the Sun, including visible light, warms Earth's surface, which then emits infrared radiation. If the atmosphere had no greenhouse gases, the infrared radiation would go straight through the atmosphere into outer space. Earth's average surface temperature would be only about –18°C (0°F). Water would freeze, and it would be too cold for most forms of life on Earth to survive.

INVESTIGATE Greenhouse Gases

How have levels of greenhouse gases changed?

Scientists have used ice cores from Antarctica to calculate prehistoric carbon dioxide levels and temperatures. The CO_2 data table has the results for you to plot.

PROCEDURE

(1) Plot the CO_2 levels on the graph sheet using a regular pencil. Draw line segments to connect the points.

(2) Plot the temperatures on the same graph using a red pencil. Draw red line segments to connect the points.

WHAT DO YOU THINK?

• How many times during the past 400,000 years were average temperatures in Antarctica above –56°C?

• Do these changes seem to be connected to changes in levels of carbon dioxide? Explain.

CHALLENGE Is it possible to tell from the graph whether temperature affected carbon dioxide levels or carbon dioxide levels affected temperature? Why or why not?

SKILL FOCUS
Graphing

MATERIALS
• Carbon Dioxide Table
• regular pencil
• red pencil

TIME
30 minutes

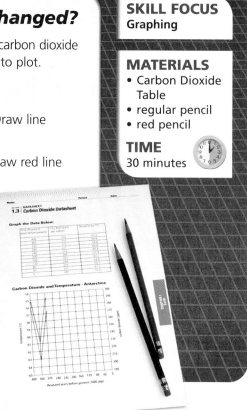

The Greenhouse Effect

Greenhouse gas molecules absorb and emit infrared radiation.

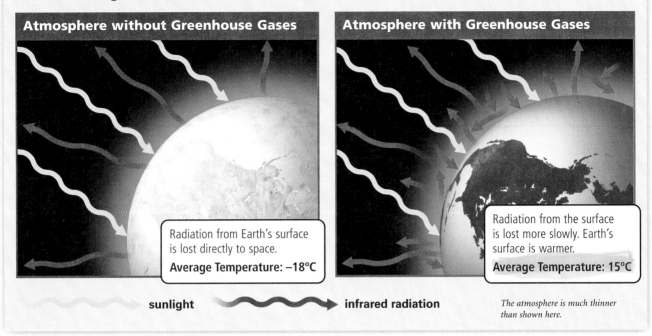

Atmosphere without Greenhouse Gases

Radiation from Earth's surface is lost directly to space.
Average Temperature: −18°C

Atmosphere with Greenhouse Gases

Radiation from the surface is lost more slowly. Earth's surface is warmer.
Average Temperature: 15°C

sunlight → infrared radiation

The atmosphere is much thinner than shown here.

Earth's atmosphere does have greenhouse gases. These gases absorb some of the infrared radiation emitted by Earth's surface. The greenhouse gases can then give off this energy as infrared radiation. Some of the energy is absorbed again by the surface, while some of the energy goes out into space. The greenhouse effect keeps Earth's average surface temperature around 15°C (59°F). The energy stays in Earth's system longer with greenhouse gases than without them. In time, all the energy ends up back in outer space. If it did not, Earth would grow warmer and warmer as it absorbed more and more solar radiation.

1.3 Review

KEY CONCEPTS

1. Name and describe two of the ways gases can affect radiation.

2. What type of radiation does the ozone layer affect?

3. How do greenhouse gases keep Earth warm?

CRITICAL THINKING

4. **Infer** What would happen if gases in the atmosphere absorbed visible light?

5. **Compare and Contrast** How are ozone and greenhouse gases alike? How are they different?

⬢ CHALLENGE

6. **Predict** How would the temperature on Earth be affected if the amount of greenhouse gases in the atmosphere changed?

MATH TUTORIAL
CLASSZONE.COM
Click on Math Tutorial for
more help with equations.

Solar Radiation

The amount of sunlight that reaches Earth's surface varies from day to day. On a cloudy day, for example, clouds may absorb or reflect most of the sunlight before it reaches Earth's surface. You can use equations to determine how much incoming solar radiation is absorbed by Earth's surface on each day.

Example

On a particular cloudy day, 50% of the solar radiation coming into Earth is reflected by clouds and the atmosphere, 40% is absorbed by clouds and the atmosphere, and 1% is reflected by Earth's surface. How much is absorbed by Earth's surface?

Write a verbal model:

radiation reflected by clouds & atmosphere	+	radiation absorbed by clouds & atmosphere	+	radiation reflected by Earth's surface	+	radiation absorbed by Earth's surface	=	total incoming radiation

Substitute into the model: **50% + 40% + 1% + x = 100%**

Simplify the left side: $91\% + x = 100\%$

Subtract: $-91\% \qquad -91\%$

Simplify: $x = 9\%$

ANSWER 9% of the incoming solar radiation is absorbed by Earth's surface.

Determine the amount of incoming solar radiation that is absorbed by Earth's surface on each day.

1. On a sunny day, 15% is reflected by clouds and the atmosphere, 20% is absorbed by clouds and the atmosphere, and 10% is reflected by Earth's surface.

sunny day

2. On a partly cloudy day, 25% is reflected by clouds and the atmosphere, 20% is absorbed by clouds and the atmosphere, and 5% is reflected by Earth's surface.

CHALLENGE On a particular day, how much incoming solar radiation is absorbed by Earth's surface if 60% is reflected (either by clouds and the atmosphere or by Earth's surface), and half that amount is absorbed by the atmosphere?

partly cloudy day

1.4 Human activities affect the atmosphere.

◀ **BEFORE, you learned**

- The atmosphere has gases that absorb and give off radiation
- The ozone layer absorbs ultraviolet radiation
- The greenhouse effect keeps Earth warm

▶ **NOW, you will learn**

- What the types and effects of pollution are
- About the effect of human activities on greenhouse gases
- How the ozone layer is changing

VOCABULARY

air pollution p. 27
particulate p. 28
fossil fuel p. 28
smog p. 28

EXPLORE Air Pollution

Where does smoke go?

PROCEDURE

① Light the candle and let it burn for a minute or two. Observe the air around the candle.

② Blow out the candle and observe the smoke until you cannot see it anymore.

WHAT DO YOU THINK?

- How far did the smoke from the candle travel?
- A burning candle produces invisible gases. Where do you think they went?

MATERIALS
- candle in holder
- matches

Human activity can cause air pollution.

SUPPORTING MAIN IDEAS
Remember to start a new chart for each main idea.

If someone in your kitchen burns a piece of toast, and if a fan is blowing in the hallway, everyone in your home will smell the smoke. That means that everyone will breathe some air containing smoke. Smoke and other harmful materials that are added to the air are called **air pollution.** Outdoors, wind can spread air pollution from place to place the way a fan does within your home.

When toast burns, you may be able to see smoke. If smoke drifts in from another room, it may be too thin to see, but you may be able to smell it. There are other types of air pollution that you cannot see or smell. Like smoke, they can be spread around by wind. Air pollution from one place can affect a wide area. However, most types of pollution leave the air or become thin enough to be harmless after a time.

CHECK YOUR READING How is air pollution moved around?

Types of Pollution

READING TIP

Pollution and *pollutant* have the same root, *pollute*—"to make unfit."

Scientists classify the separate types of air pollution, called pollutants, as either gases or particles. Gas pollutants include carbon monoxide, methane, ozone, sulfur oxides, and nitrogen oxides. Some of these gases occur naturally in the atmosphere. These gases are considered pollutants only when they are likely to cause harm. For example, ozone gas is good in the stratosphere but is harmful to breathe. When ozone is in the troposphere, it is a pollutant.

Particle pollutants can be easier to see than gas pollutants. **Particulates** are tiny particles or droplets that are mixed in with air. Smoke contains particulates. The wind can pick up other particulates, such as dust and dirt, pollen, and tiny bits of salt from the oceans. Some sources of pollutants are listed below.

CHECK YOUR READING What are the two types of pollutants? Give an example of each.

In cities and suburbs, most air pollution comes from the burning of fossil fuels such as oil, gasoline, and coal. **Fossil fuels** are fuels formed from the remains of prehistoric animals and plants. In London in the 1800s, burning coal provided much of the heat and energy for homes and factories. The resulting smoke and local weather conditions often produced a thick fog or cloud. The word **smog** describes this combination of smoke and fog. A newer type of air pollution is also called smog. Sunlight causes the fumes from gasoline, car exhaust, and other gases to react chemically. The reactions form new pollutants, such as ozone, which together are called smog. In cities, there can be enough smog to make a brownish haze.

Sources of Pollution

The burning of fossil fuels in power plants, cars, factories, and homes is a major source of pollution in the United States.

Human Activities

- fossil fuels: gases and particles
- unburned fuels: smog
- manufacturing: gases and particles
- tractors/construction equipment: dust and soil
- farming: fertilizers and pesticides

Natural Sources

- dust, pollen, soil, salt
- volcanoes and forest fires: gases and particles

Effects of Pollution

Air pollution can cause health problems. Polluted air may irritate your eyes, nose, throat, and lungs. It can smell bad or make it hard to breathe. Gases or chemicals from particulates can move from your lungs to other parts of your body. Exercising in polluted air can be dangerous because you take more air into your lungs when you exercise. Over time, people who breathe polluted air can develop lung disease and other health problems. Air pollution can cause extra problems for young children, older adults, and people who suffer from asthma.

A man in Mexico City wears a gas mask while he sells newspapers. The green sign behind him warns people of a high ozone level.

 CHECK YOUR READING Describe three of the ways in which pollution can affect people.

Particulates can stick to surfaces and damage plants, buildings, and other objects outdoors. Dusty air or a dust storm can darken the day and make it difficult to see. Particulates can be carried high into the atmosphere, where they can reflect or absorb sunlight and even affect the weather. Rain clears the air by removing particles and some polluting gases from the air. However, some pollutants are still harmful when rain moves them from the air to the ground, lakes, and oceans.

Controlling Pollution

You may have experienced a smog or ozone alert. In some cities, smog becomes so bad that it is dangerous to exercise outdoors. Weather reports may include smog alerts so that people will know when to be careful. Cities may ask people not to drive cars when the weather conditions are likely to produce smog.

National, state, and local governments work together to reduce air pollution and protect people from its effects. Countries may come to agreements when the air pollution from one country affects another. Within the United States, Congress has passed laws to reduce air pollution. The Clean Air Act limits the amount of air pollution that factories and power plants are allowed to release. The act also sets rules for making car exhaust cleaner. The Environmental Protection Agency measures air pollution and works to enforce the laws passed by Congress.

Human activities are increasing greenhouse gases.

A source of air pollution usually affects areas close to it. In contrast, some natural processes and human activities change the amounts of gases throughout Earth's atmosphere.

Sources of Greenhouse Gases

REMINDER

Plants remove carbon dioxide from the air and store the carbon in solid forms.

You read in Section 1.1 how natural cycles move gases into and out of the atmosphere. Plant growth, forest fires, volcanoes, and other natural processes affect the amounts of carbon dioxide and other greenhouse gases in the atmosphere. The amounts of greenhouse gases then affect temperatures on Earth. In turn, the temperatures affect plant growth and other processes that produce or reduce greenhouse gases.

CHECK YOUR READING How do life and the atmosphere affect each other?

Most greenhouse gases occur naturally. They have helped keep temperatures within a range suitable for the plants and animals that live on Earth. However, human activities are producing greenhouse gases faster than natural processes can remove these gases from the

Greenhouse Gases from Human Activities

Carbon dioxide (CO_2)

Carbon dioxide comes largely from the use of fossil fuels in power plants, cars, factories, and homes.

Methane (CH_4)

Methane comes from cattle and other livestock, bacteria in rice fields, and landfills (waste disposal).

Nitrous oxide (N_2O)

Nitrous oxide comes from fertilizers and chemical factories.

atmosphere. Some activities that produce greenhouse gases are shown on page 30. Water vapor is also a greenhouse gas, but the amount of water vapor in the air depends more on weather than on human activity.

Global Warming

Many people are concerned about the amounts of greenhouse gases that humans are adding to the air. Carbon dioxide, for example, can stay in the atmosphere for more than 100 years, so the amounts keep adding up. The air contains about 30 percent more carbon dioxide than it did in the mid-1700s, and the level of carbon dioxide is now increasing about 0.4 percent per year.

CHECK YOUR READING How are carbon dioxide levels changing?

As the graph below shows, temperatures have risen in recent decades. Earth's atmosphere, water, and other systems work together in complex ways, so it is hard to know exactly how much greenhouse gases change the temperature. Scientists make computer models to understand the effects of greenhouse gases and explore what might happen in the future. The models predict that the average global temperature will continue to rise another 1.4–5.8°C (2.5–10.4°F) by the year 2100. This may not seem like a big change in temperature, but it can have big effects. Global warming can affect sources of food, the amount of water and other resources available, and even human health. You will read more about the possible effects of global warming in Chapter 4.

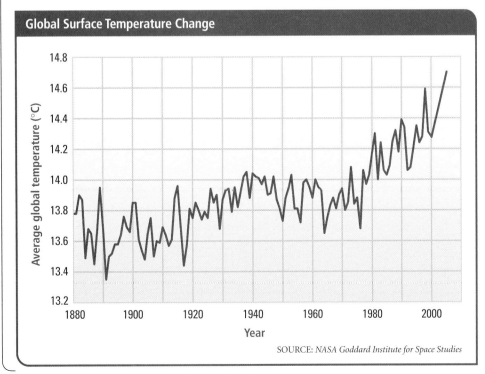

Global Surface Temperature Change

SOURCE: *NASA Goddard Institute for Space Studies*

Earth's average temperature has risen over the last century.

Reducing Greenhouse Gases

Global warming is not a local issue. It affects the atmosphere around the entire planet. An international agreement to limit the amounts of greenhouse gases, called the Kyoto Protocol, requires developed nations to reduce greenhouse gases emitted by 5.2% compared to 1990. The Kyoto Protocol took effect in 2005 after 166 nations releasing the most greenhouse gases accepted the agreement. In 1990, more than one-third of the amount of greenhouse gases released came from the United States, which did not accept the agreement.

New technologies may help fight the problem of global warming. Scientists are developing ways to heat and cool buildings, transport people and goods, and make products using less energy. Using less energy saves resources and money and it also reduces greenhouse gases. Scientists are also developing ways to produce energy without using any fossil fuels at all.

This commuter is traveling to work without burning fossil fuels.

 CHECK YOUR READING How can technology help reduce global warming?

Human activities produce chemicals that destroy the ozone layer.

 **RESOURCE CENTER**
CLASSZONE.COM

Examine the current state of the ozone layer.

At ground level, ozone is a pollutant, but at higher altitudes it benefits life. The ozone layer in the stratosphere protects living things by absorbing harmful ultraviolet radiation. You read in Section 1.3 that ozone is constantly being formed and broken apart in a natural cycle.

In the 1970s, scientists found that certain chemicals were disrupting this cycle. An atom of chlorine (Cl), for example, can start a series of chemical reactions that break apart ozone (O_3) and form regular oxygen gas (O_2). The same atom of chlorine can repeat this process thousands of times. No new ozone is formed to balance the loss.

 CHECK YOUR READING What does chlorine do to the amount of ozone in the stratosphere?

Some natural processes put chlorine into the stratosphere, but about 85 percent of the chlorine there comes from human activity. Chemicals called chlorofluorocarbons (KLAWR-oh-FLUR-oh-KAHR-buhnz) have been manufactured for use in cooling systems, spray cans, and foam for packaging. These chemicals break down in the stratosphere and release chlorine and other ozone-destroying chemicals.

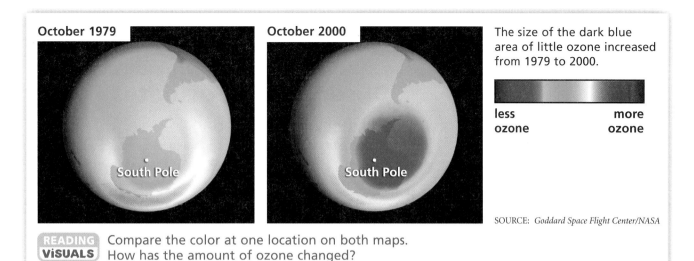

October 1979

October 2000

The size of the dark blue area of little ozone increased from 1979 to 2000.

less ozone   more ozone

SOURCE: *Goddard Space Flight Center/NASA*

South Pole

South Pole

READING VISUALS Compare the color at one location on both maps. How has the amount of ozone changed?

The amount of ozone in the stratosphere varies from place to place and changes with the seasons. Cold temperatures and sunshine make the ozone over Antarctica—the South Pole—especially sensitive to the chemicals that destroy ozone. The amount of ozone over Antarctica decreased by half from the 1970s to the mid-1990s. The maps above show the loss of ozone over Antarctica. Smaller but important changes were measured in other regions.

The ozone layer affects the whole world. Since 1987, more than 180 nations have signed an agreement called the Montreal Protocol. They have agreed on a plan to stop making and using chemicals that harm the ozone layer. Experts study the ozone layer and recommend changes to the agreement. The Montreal Protocol has been updated several times. Less harmful chemicals are now used instead of chlorofluorocarbons, but gases from past human activities are still in the ozone layer. If countries continue to follow the Montreal Protocol, ozone levels will return to normal in about 50 years.

1.4 Review

KEY CONCEPTS

1. Describe two of the sources of air pollution.

2. What are three human activities that increase the levels of greenhouse gases?

3. How do human activities affect the ozone layer?

CRITICAL THINKING

4. **Classify** List the following pollutants as either gases or particles: dust, ozone, pollen, carbon monoxide, methane.

5. **Predict** How might global warming affect the way you live in the future?

◆ CHALLENGE

6. **Synthesize** In North America, winds typically blow from west to east. Where might pollution from your community end up? Use a map to help you answer the question.

CHAPTER INVESTIGATION

Observing Particulates

OVERVIEW AND PURPOSE Many of us go through life unaware of particulates in the air, but allergy or asthma sufferers may become uncomfortably aware of high particulate levels. Certain particles, such as dust mite casings, can trigger asthma attacks. Particles that cling to surfaces can make them look dirty or even damage them. Some colors of surfaces may hide the dirt. In this investigation you will

- compare the number and types of particles that settle to surfaces in two different locations
- learn a method of counting particles

▶ Problem

How do the types and numbers of particles in two different locations compare?

▶ Hypothesize

You should decide on the locations in step 3 before writing your hypothesis. Write a hypothesis to explain how particulates collected at two different locations might differ. Your hypothesis should take the form of an "If . . . , then . . . , because . . ." statement.

MATERIALS
- 2 index cards
- ruler
- scissors
- transparent packing tape
- magnifying glass
- white paper
- black paper
- graph paper
- calculator

▶ Procedure

1. Use the ruler to mark on each index card a centered square that is 3 cm per side. Carefully cut out each square.

2. On each card, place a piece of tape so that it covers the hole. Press the edges of the tape to the card, but do not let the center of the tape stick to anything. You should have a clean sticky window when you turn the card over.

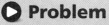

3. Choose two different collecting locations where you can safely leave your cards—sticky side up—undisturbed overnight. You might place them on outside and inside windowsills, on the ground and in a tree, or in different rooms.

4. Mark each card with your name, the date, and the location. Tape the cards in place or weigh them down so they will not blow away. Write your hypothesis. Collect your cards the next day.

▶ Observe and Analyze

1. **OBSERVE** Use the magnifying glass to inspect each card closely. Can you identify any of the particles? Try using white paper and black paper behind the card to help you see dark and light particles better. Describe and draw in your **Science Notebook** the types of particles from each card. How does the background affect the type or number of particles you see?

2. **RECORD** Make a data table like the one shown on the notebook page below. Then, place each card onto a piece of graph paper. Line up the top and left edges of each card's center square with the grid on the graph paper and tape the card down. Choose four graph-paper squares and count the number of visible particles in each square. Use the magnifying glass. Record your results on the data table.

3. **CALCULATE**

    AVERAGE Calculate the average number of particles per square for each card.

    $$\text{average} = \frac{\text{sum of particles in 4 squares}}{4}$$

    CONVERT Use the formula below to convert from particles per square to particles per square centimeter. If your squares were half a centimeter wide, then use 0.5 cm in the denominator below.

    $$\begin{array}{c}\text{particles} \\ \text{per cm}^2\end{array} = \begin{array}{c}\text{particles} \\ \text{per} \\ \text{square}\end{array} \times \left(\frac{1 \text{ square}}{\text{width (in cm) of square}}\right)^2$$

▶ Conclude | Write It Up

1. **COMPARE** Compare the types of particles found on the cards. List similarities and differences. Compare the numbers of particles found on the cards.

2. **INTERPRET** Compare your results with your hypothesis. Do your data support your hypothesis?

3. **INFER** What can you infer about where the particles came from or how they reached each location? What evidence did you find to support these inferences?

4. **IDENTIFY LIMITS** What possible limitations or sources of error might have affected your results? Why was it necessary to average the number of particles from several squares?

5. **EVALUATE** Do you think the color of the graph paper affected the number of particles you were able to count?

6. **APPLY** What color would you choose for playground equipment in your area? Explain your choice.

▶ INVESTIGATE Further

CHALLENGE Design an experiment to find out how fast particles in one location are deposited.

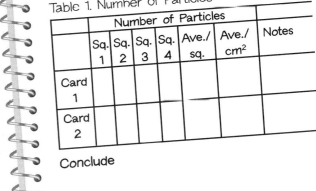

Observing Particulates

Problem How do the types and numbers of particles in two different locations compare?

Hypothesize

Observe and Analyze

Table 1. Number of Particles

	Number of Particles						Notes
	Sq. 1	Sq. 2	Sq. 3	Sq. 4	Ave./ sq.	Ave./ cm²	
Card 1							
Card 2							

Conclude

Chapter Review

the **BIG** idea

Earth's atmosphere is a blanket of gases that supports and protects life.

CONTENT REVIEW
CLASSZONE.COM

KEY CONCEPTS SUMMARY

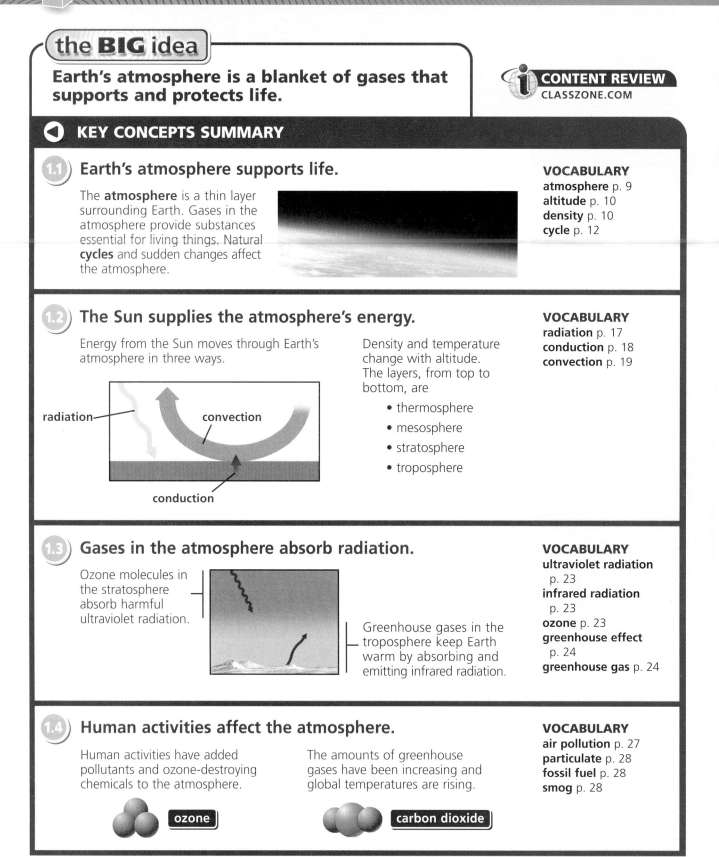

1.1 **Earth's atmosphere supports life.**

The **atmosphere** is a thin layer surrounding Earth. Gases in the atmosphere provide substances essential for living things. Natural **cycles** and sudden changes affect the atmosphere.

VOCABULARY
atmosphere p. 9
altitude p. 10
density p. 10
cycle p. 12

1.2 **The Sun supplies the atmosphere's energy.**

Energy from the Sun moves through Earth's atmosphere in three ways.

radiation — convection

conduction

Density and temperature change with altitude. The layers, from top to bottom, are

- thermosphere
- mesosphere
- stratosphere
- troposphere

VOCABULARY
radiation p. 17
conduction p. 18
convection p. 19

1.3 **Gases in the atmosphere absorb radiation.**

Ozone molecules in the stratosphere absorb harmful ultraviolet radiation.

Greenhouse gases in the troposphere keep Earth warm by absorbing and emitting infrared radiation.

VOCABULARY
ultraviolet radiation
  p. 23
infrared radiation
  p. 23
ozone p. 23
greenhouse effect
  p. 24
greenhouse gas p. 24

1.4 **Human activities affect the atmosphere.**

Human activities have added pollutants and ozone-destroying chemicals to the atmosphere.

The amounts of greenhouse gases have been increasing and global temperatures are rising.

ozone

carbon dioxide

VOCABULARY
air pollution p. 27
particulate p. 28
fossil fuel p. 28
smog p. 28

Reviewing Vocabulary

Draw a word triangle for each of the vocabulary terms listed below. Define the term, use it in a sentence, and draw a picture to help you remember the term. A sample is shown below.

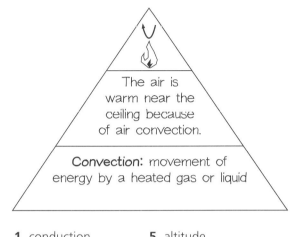

The air is warm near the ceiling because of air convection.

Convection: movement of energy by a heated gas or liquid

1. conduction
2. atmosphere
3. density
4. air pollution
5. altitude
6. radiation
7. cycle
8. particulate

Reviewing Key Concepts

Multiple Choice *Choose the letter of the best answer.*

9. Which of the following represents a sudden change in Earth's atmosphere?
   a. the carbon cycle   c. a rain shower
   b. the nitrogen cycle   d. a dust storm

10. The gas that makes up the largest percentage of the atmosphere's substance is
    a. nitrogen   c. water vapor
    b. oxygen   d. carbon dioxide

11. Which of the cycles below involves oxygen gas?
    a. the carbon cycle   c. the density cycle
    b. the water cycle   d. the argon cycle

12. What process moves energy from Earth's surface to high in the troposphere?
    a. solar energy   c. convection
    b. conduction   d. the nitrogen cycle

13. In which of the atmosphere's layers does temperature decrease as the altitude increases?
    a. the troposphere and the stratosphere
    b. the troposphere and the mesosphere
    c. the stratosphere and the mesosphere
    d. the stratosphere and the thermosphere

14. What keeps Earth's surface warm?
    a. conduction   c. convection
    b. the ozone layer   d. the greenhouse effect

15. Which gas absorbs ultraviolet radiation?
    a. carbon dioxide   c. ozone
    b. methane   d. water vapor

16. Which type of pollution includes harmful droplets?
    a. particulate   c. dust
    b. gas   d. smoke

Short Answer *Write a short answer to each question.*

17. Explain why ozone is helpful to life in the stratosphere but harmful in the troposphere.

18. Describe three of the ways human activities affect the atmosphere.

19. Write a brief paragraph describing how the photograph below provides evidence that Earth's atmosphere is in motion.

Use the photographs to answer the next two questions.

cold water   hot water

In the demonstration pictured above, hot water has been tinted red with food coloring, and cold water has been tinted blue. View B shows the results after the divider has been lifted and the motion of the water has stopped.

20. OBSERVE Describe how the hot water and the cold water moved when the divider was lifted.

21. APPLY Use your understanding of density to explain the motion of the water.

22. CALCULATE The top of Mount Everest is 8850 meters above sea level. Which layer of the atmosphere contains the top of this mountain? Use the information from page 20 and convert the units.

23. APPLY Why is radiation from Earth's surface and atmosphere important for living things?

24. PREDICT Dust is often light in color, while soot from fires is generally dark. What would happen to the amounts of solar radiation reflected and absorbed if a large amount of light-colored dust was added to the air? What if a large amount of dark soot was added?

25. IDENTIFY EFFECT When weather conditions and sunlight are likely to produce smog, cities may ask motorists to refuel their cars at night instead of early in the day. Why would this behavior make a difference?

26. COMPARE How are the processes in the diagram on page 18 similar to those in the illustration below?

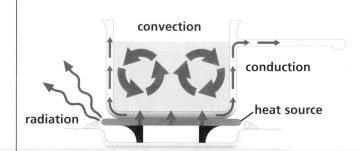

27. CONNECT Give an example from everyday life that shows that the atmosphere has substance.

28. EVALUATE If you had a choice between burning natural gas to cook or using electricity from a power plant, which would you choose? Explain the issues involved. **Hint:** Where does the power plant get energy?

the BIG idea

29. SYNTHESIZE Write one or more paragraphs describing the specific ways that the atmosphere supports and protects life. In your description, use each of the terms below. Underline each term in your answer.

carbon dioxide	solar radiation
water	ozone
oxygen	stratosphere
cycle	

30. APPLY Look again at the photograph on pages 6–7. Now that you have finished the chapter, how would you change or add details to your answer to the question on the photograph?

UNIT PROJECTS

If you are doing a unit project, make a folder for your project. Include in your folder a list of the resources you will need, the date on which the project is due, and a schedule to track your progress. Begin gathering data.

Interpreting Graphs

The following three graphs show the amounts of three types of air pollutants released into the atmosphere in the United States each year from 1950 to 1990. Study the graphs closely and use the information to answer the first four questions.

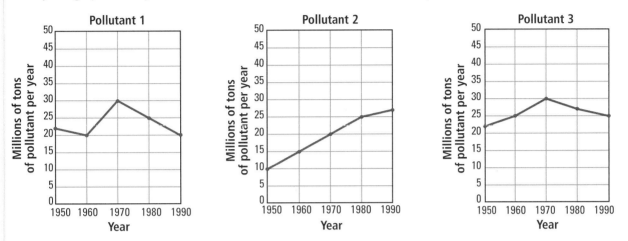

1. What conclusion can you make about pollutant 1?

   a. The release of pollutant 1 has steadily decreased since 1970.

   b. More pollutant 1 has been released since 1990.

   c. More pollutant 1 has been released since 1970.

   d. The release of pollutant 1 has not changed.

2. Based on the graph for pollutant 2, which of the following is true?

   a. The release of pollutant 2 declined after 1950.

   b. The release of pollutant 2 has increased since 1970.

   c. The release of pollutant 2 declined and then rose.

   d. About 15 million tons of pollutant 2 were released in 1990.

3. Compare the graphs for pollutants 1 and 2. Which of the following statements is supported by the graphs?

   a. In 1950, more pollutant 1 was released than pollutant 2.

   b. Since 1980, no pollutant 1 has been released.

   c. In 1990, twice as much pollutant 2 was released as pollutant 1.

   d. Since 1950, no pollutant 1 has been released.

4. About how many million tons of pollutant 3 entered the atmosphere in the United States in 1990?

   a. 10   **c.** 25

   b. 15   **d.** 30

Extended Response

Answer the next two questions in detail. Use in your answers some of the terms from the word box. In your answer, underline each term you use.

oxygen	nitrogen	energy
water	air density	carbon dioxide
altitude	absorption	

5. Luz builds a terrarium for her class science fair. She puts her pet slug in with the plants. She covers the terrarium with clear plastic that has vent holes. She places it in a sunlit window. How do the soil, plants, slug, sunlight, and plastic affect the air in Luz's terrarium?

6. Mile High Stadium in Denver, Colorado, makes bottled oxygen available to its players. Players at lower altitudes do not need extra oxygen. Explorers pack bottled oxygen when they climb tall mountains, such as Mount Everest. Explain why extra oxygen might be necessary for players in Mile High Stadium and climbers on tall mountains.

CHAPTER 2
Weather Patterns

the **BIG** idea

Some features of weather have predictable patterns.

> **What weather conditions do you see in the distance?**

Key Concepts

SECTION 2.1
The atmosphere's air pressure changes.
Learn how air pressure changes and how it is measured.

SECTION 2.2
The atmosphere has wind patterns.
Learn how wind develops and about different types of wind.

SECTION 2.3
Most clouds form as air rises and cools.
Learn how water changes form in the atmosphere and about different types of clouds.

SECTION 2.4
Water falls to Earth's surface as precipitation.
Learn about the different types of precipitation and about acid rain.

Internet Preview

CLASSZONE.COM
Chapter 2 online resources: Content Review, two Visualizations, four Resource Centers, Math Tutorial, Test Practice

EXPLORE (the BIG idea)

Are You Stronger Than Air?

Line a wide-mouthed jar with a plastic bag. Secure the bag tightly with a rubber band. Reach in and try to pull the bag out of the jar.

Observe and Think
How easy was it to move the plastic bag? What was holding the bag in place?

How Does Air Motion Affect Balloons?

Tie two balloons to a pencil 5 centimeters apart as shown. Gently blow air between the balloons.

Observe and Think
How did the balloons move? Why did the air make them move this way?

Internet Activity: Wind

Go to **ClassZone.com** to explore how breezes blowing over land and water change over the course of an entire day.

Observe and Think
What patterns can you see in winds that occur near water?

NSTA
scilinks.org
SCiLINKS

Atmospheric Pressure and Winds **Code: MDL010**

Getting Ready to Learn

◀ CONCEPT REVIEW

- The Sun supplies the atmosphere's energy.
- Energy moves throughout the atmosphere.
- Matter can be solid, liquid, or gas.

◀ VOCABULARY REVIEW

atmosphere p. 9

altitude p. 10

density p. 10

convection p. 19

ⓘ CONTENT REVIEW
CLASSZONE.COM
Review concepts and vocabulary.

▶ TAKING NOTES

COMBINATION NOTES

To take notes about a new concept, first make an informal outline of the information. Then make a sketch of the concept and label it so that you can study it later.

VOCABULARY STRATEGY

Place each vocabulary term at the center of a **description wheel.** Write some words describing it on the spokes.

See the Note-Taking Handbook on pages R45–R51.

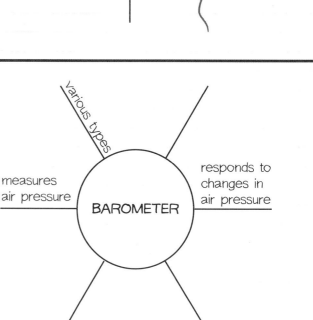

SCIENCE NOTEBOOK

NOTES

Air pressure
- is the force of air molecules pushing on an area
- pushes in all directions

various types

measures air pressure

BAROMETER

responds to changes in air pressure

The atmosphere's air pressure changes.

◀ BEFORE, you learned

- Density is the amount of mass in a given volume of a substance
- Air becomes less dense as altitude increases
- Differences in density cause air to rise and sink

▶ NOW, you will learn

- How the movement of air molecules causes air pressure
- How air pressure varies
- How differences in air pressure affect the atmosphere

VOCABULARY

air pressure p. 43
barometer p. 46

EXPLORE Air Pressure

What does air do to the egg?

PROCEDURE

① Set a peeled hard-boiled egg in the mouth of a bottle. Make sure that the egg can't slip through.

② Light the matches. Remove the egg, and drop the matches into the bottle. Quickly replace the egg.

③ Watch carefully, and record your observations.

WHAT DO YOU THINK?

- What happened when you placed the egg back on top of the bottle?
- What can your observations tell you about the air in the bottle?

MATERIALS

- peeled hard-boiled egg
- glass bottle
- 2 wooden matches

Air exerts pressure.

Air molecules move constantly. As they move, they bounce off each other like rubber balls. They also bounce off every surface they hit. As you read this book, billions of air molecules are bouncing off your body, the book, and everything else around you.

Each time an air molecule bounces off an object, it pushes, or exerts a force, on that object. When billions of air molecules bounce off a surface, the force is spread over the area of that surface. **Air pressure** is the force of air molecules pushing on an area. The greater the force, the higher the air pressure. Because air molecules move in all directions, air pressure pushes in all directions.

VOCABULARY
Add a description wheel for *air pressure* to your notebook.

 CHECK YOUR READING How does the number of air molecules relate to air pressure?

Air pressure is related to altitude and density.

COMBINATION NOTES
Record details about how air pressure varies.

The air pressure at any area on Earth depends on the weight of the air above that area. If you hold out your hand, the force of air pushing down on your hand is greater than the weight of a bowling ball. So why don't you feel the air pushing down on your hand? Remember that air pushes in all directions. The pressure of air pushing down is balanced by the pressure of air pushing up from below.

Air pressure decreases as you move higher in the atmosphere. Think of a column of air directly over your body. If you stood at sea level, this column would stretch from where you stood to the top of the atmosphere. The air pressure on your body would be equal to the weight of all the air in the column. But if you stood on a mountain, the column of air would be shorter. With less air above you, the pressure would be lower. At an altitude of 5.5 kilometers (3.4 mi), air pressure is about half what it is at sea level.

Air pressure and density are related. Just as air pressure decreases with altitude, so does the density of air. Notice in the illustration that air molecules at sea level are closer together than air molecules over the mountain. Since the pressure is greater at sea level, the air molecules are pushed closer together. Therefore, the air at sea level is denser than air at high altitudes.

REMINDER

Density is the amount of mass in a given volume of a substance.

Air Pressure and Density

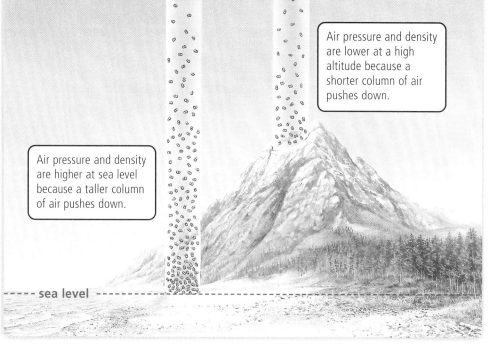

Above each location on Earth is a column of air that stretches to the top of the atmosphere.

Air pressure and density are lower at a high altitude because a shorter column of air pushes down.

Air pressure and density are higher at sea level because a taller column of air pushes down.

sea level

Pressure and Air Motion

You've read that air pressure decreases as you move to higher altitudes. Air pressure also often varies in two locations at the same altitude. You can observe how such pressure differences affect air when you open a new can of tennis balls. You may hear a hiss as air rushes into the can. The air inside the sealed can of tennis balls is at a lower pressure than the air outside the can. When you break the seal, air moves from outside the can toward the lower pressure inside it.

Air pressure differences in the atmosphere affect air in a similar way. If the air pressure were the same at all locations, air wouldn't move much. Because of differences in pressure, air starts to move from areas of higher pressure toward areas of lower pressure. The air may move only a short distance, or it may travel many kilometers. You will learn more about how air moves in response to pressure differences in Section 2.2.

RESOURCE CENTER
CLASSZONE.COM

Find out more about air pressure.

CHECK YOUR READING How do differences in air pressure affect the movement of air?

INVESTIGATE Air Pressure

How can you measure changes in air pressure?

PROCEDURE

1. Cut open a balloon along one side until you get close to the end. Stretch the balloon across the open top of the can. Secure it tightly in place with a rubber band.

2. Cut the straw on an angle to make a pointer. Tape the other end of the straw to the center of the balloon.

3. Tape a ruler against a wall or a box so that the end of the pointer almost touches the ruler. Record the position of the pointer against the ruler.

4. Record the position of the pointer at least once a day for the next five days. Look for small changes in its position. For each day, record the air pressure printed in a local newspaper.

WHAT DO YOU THINK?

- In what direction did the pointer move when the air pressure went up? when the air pressure went down?
- Explain how your instrument worked.

CHALLENGE Predict what would happen to the pointer if you repeated this experiment but poked some small holes in the balloon.

SKILL FOCUS
Collecting data

MATERIALS
- scissors
- round balloon
- metal can
- rubber band
- thin straw
- tape
- ruler

TIME
15 minutes

How a Barometer Works

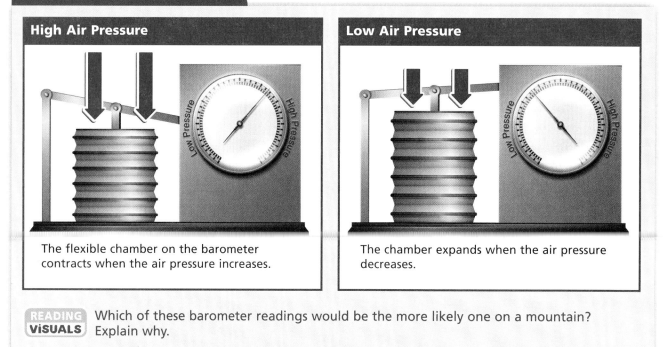

High Air Pressure

The flexible chamber on the barometer contracts when the air pressure increases.

Low Air Pressure

The chamber expands when the air pressure decreases.

READING VISUALS Which of these barometer readings would be the more likely one on a mountain? Explain why.

Barometers and Air Pressure

Air pressure can be measured in different ways. A **barometer** is any instrument that measures air pressure. The illustrations above show a simplified version of a common type of barometer. This type contains a sealed flexible chamber that has little air inside. The chamber contracts when the outside air pressure is high and expands when the air pressure is low. A series of levers or other devices turns the motion of the chamber into something that can be read—the movement of a needle on a dial or a jagged line on a strip of graph paper.

2.1 Review

KEY CONCEPTS

1. How does the movement of air molecules cause pressure?
2. How does altitude affect air pressure?
3. How is air density related to air pressure?

CRITICAL THINKING

4. **Apply** Would you expect the air pressure in a valley that's below sea level to be higher or lower than air pressure at sea level? Explain.
5. **Predict** Two barometers are placed one kilometer apart. One shows higher pressure than the other. What will happen to air between them?

⚠ CHALLENGE

6. **Infer** The eardrum is a thin sheet of tissue that separates air in the middle part of your ear from air outside your ear. What could cause your eardrum to make a popping sound as you ride up a tall building in an elevator?

2.2 The atmosphere has wind patterns.

◀ BEFORE, you learned

- Solar energy heats Earth's surface and atmosphere
- Differences in density cause air to move
- Air pressure differences set air in motion

▶ NOW, you will learn

- About forces that affect wind
- About global winds
- About patterns of heating and cooling

VOCABULARY

weather p. 47
wind p. 47
global wind p. 48
Coriolis effect p. 49
jet stream p. 52
monsoon p. 54

EXPLORE Solar Energy

How does Earth's shape affect solar heating?

PROCEDURE

1. Place a globe on a desk in a darkened room.

2. Point a flashlight at the equator on the globe from a distance of about 15 centimeters. Keep the flashlight level. Observe the lighted area on the globe.

3. Keeping the flashlight level, raise it up and point it at the United States. Observe the lighted area.

WHAT DO YOU THINK?

- How were the two lighted areas different?
- What might have caused the difference?

MATERIALS
- globe
- flashlight
- ruler

Uneven heating causes air to move.

On local news broadcasts, weather forecasters often spend several minutes discussing what the weather will be like over the next few days. **Weather** is the condition of Earth's atmosphere at a particular time and place. Wind is an important part of weather. You will read about other weather factors later in this chapter.

Wind is air that moves horizontally, or parallel to the ground. Remember that air pressure can differ from place to place at the same altitude. Uneven heating of Earth's surface causes such pressure differences, which set air in motion. Over a short distance, wind moves directly from higher pressure toward lower pressure.

▼ REMINDER

Remember that air pressure is the force that air molecules exert on an area.

 CHECK YOUR READING What is the relationship between air pressure and wind?

VISUALIZATION
CLASSZONE.COM
View an animation of
the Coriolis effect.

How Wind Forms

Wind moves from an area of high pressure toward an area of low pressure.

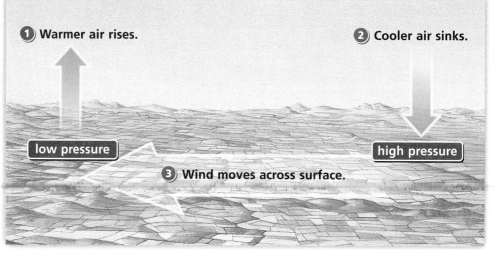

① **Warmer air rises.**

② **Cooler air sinks.**

low pressure

high pressure

③ **Wind moves across surface.**

The illustration above shows a common pattern of air circulation caused by uneven heating of Earth's surface:

① Sunlight strongly heats an area of ground. The ground heats the air. The warm air rises, and an area of low pressure forms.

② Sunlight heats an area of ground less strongly. The cooler, dense air sinks slowly, and an area of high pressure forms.

③ Air moves as wind across the surface, from higher toward lower pressure.

When the difference in pressure between two areas is small, the wind may move too slowly to be noticeable. A very large pressure difference can produce wind strong enough to uproot trees.

CHECK YOUR READING What factor determines the strength of wind?

The distance winds travel varies. Some winds die out quickly after blowing a few meters. In contrast, **global winds** travel thousands of kilometers in steady patterns. Global winds last for weeks.

Uneven heating between the equator and the north and south poles causes global winds. Notice in the illustration at left how sunlight strikes Earth's curved surface. Near the equator, concentrated sunlight heats the surface to a high temperature. Warm air rises, producing low pressure.

In regions closer to the poles, the sunlight is more spread out. Because less of the Sun's energy reaches these regions, the air above them is cooler and denser. The sinking dense air produces high pressure that sets global winds in motion.

Sunlight is concentrated near the equator because it strikes the surface directly.

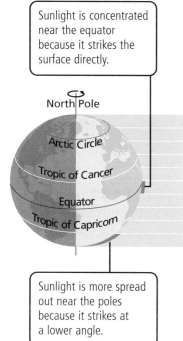

North Pole

Arctic Circle

Tropic of Cancer

Equator

Tropic of Capricorn

Sunlight is more spread out near the poles because it strikes at a lower angle.

Earth's rotation affects wind direction.

If Earth did not rotate, global winds would flow directly from the poles to the equator. However, Earth's rotation changes the direction of winds and other objects moving over Earth. The influence of Earth's rotation is called the **Coriolis effect** (KAWR-ee-OH-lihs). Global winds curve as Earth turns beneath them. In the Northern Hemisphere, winds curve to the right in the direction of motion. Winds in the Southern Hemisphere curve to the left. The Coriolis effect is noticeable only for winds that travel long distances.

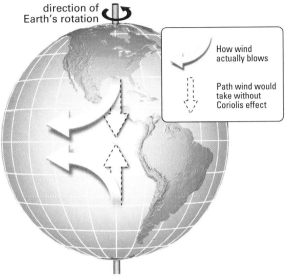

direction of Earth's rotation

How wind actually blows

Path wind would take without Coriolis effect

Because the Coriolis effect causes global winds to curve, they cannot flow directly from the poles to the equator. Instead, global winds travel along three routes in each hemisphere. These routes, which circle the world, are called global wind belts.

CHECK YOUR READING In which direction do winds curve in the Northern Hemisphere?

INVESTIGATE Coriolis Effect

How does Earth's rotation affect wind?

PROCEDURE

1. Blow up a balloon and tie it off.

2. Have a classmate slowly rotate the balloon to the right. Draw a line straight down from the top of the balloon to the center as the balloon rotates.

3. Now draw a line from the bottom of the balloon straight up to the center as the balloon rotates.

WHAT DO YOU THINK?

- How did the rotation affect the lines that you drew?

- How does this activity demonstrate the Coriolis effect?

CHALLENGE How might changing the speed at which the balloon is rotated affect your results? Repeat the activity to test your prediction.

SKILL FOCUS
Modeling

MATERIALS
- round balloon
- felt-tip pen

TIME
10 minutes

Bands of calm air separate global wind belts.

RESOURCE CENTER
CLASSZONE.COM

Learn more about global winds.

Earth's rotation and the uneven heating of its surface cause a pattern of wind belts separated by calm regions. Each calm region is a zone of either high pressure or low pressure. The illustration on page 51 shows how each wind belt and the calm regions that border it form a giant loop of moving air. These loops are called circulation cells. The section of a cell that flows along Earth's surface is global wind. Notice that the direction of airflow changes from one circulation cell to the next.

Calm Regions

READING TiP

As you read about each region or wind belt, locate it in the diagram on page 51.

The air usually stays calm in high-pressure and low-pressure zones. Winds are light, and they often change direction.

1 The doldrums are a low-pressure zone near the equator. There, warm air rises to the top of the troposphere, which is the atmosphere's lowest layer. Then the air spreads out toward the poles. The rising, moist air produces clouds and heavy rain. During the hottest months, heavy evaporation from warm ocean water in the region fuels tropical storms.

2 The horse latitudes are high-pressure zones located about 30° north and 30° south of the equator. Warm air traveling away from the equator cools and sinks in these regions. The weather tends to be clear and dry.

Wind Belts

As dense air sinks to Earth's surface in the horse latitudes and other high-pressure zones, it flows out toward regions of low pressure. This pattern of air movement produces three global wind belts in each hemisphere. Because of the Coriolis effect, the winds curve toward the east or toward the west. Some global winds are named for the directions from which they blow. The westerlies, for example, blow from west to east.

3 The trade winds blow from the east, moving from the horse latitudes toward the equator. These strong, steady winds die out as they come near the equator.

4 The westerlies blow from the west, moving from the horse latitudes toward the poles. They bring storms across much of the United States.

5 The easterlies blow from the east, moving from the polar regions toward the mid-latitudes. Stormy weather often occurs when the cold air of the easterlies meets the warmer air of the westerlies.

Global Winds

Belts of global wind circle Earth. Because of the Coriolis effect, the winds in these belts curve to the east or the west. Between the global wind belts are calm areas of rising or falling air.

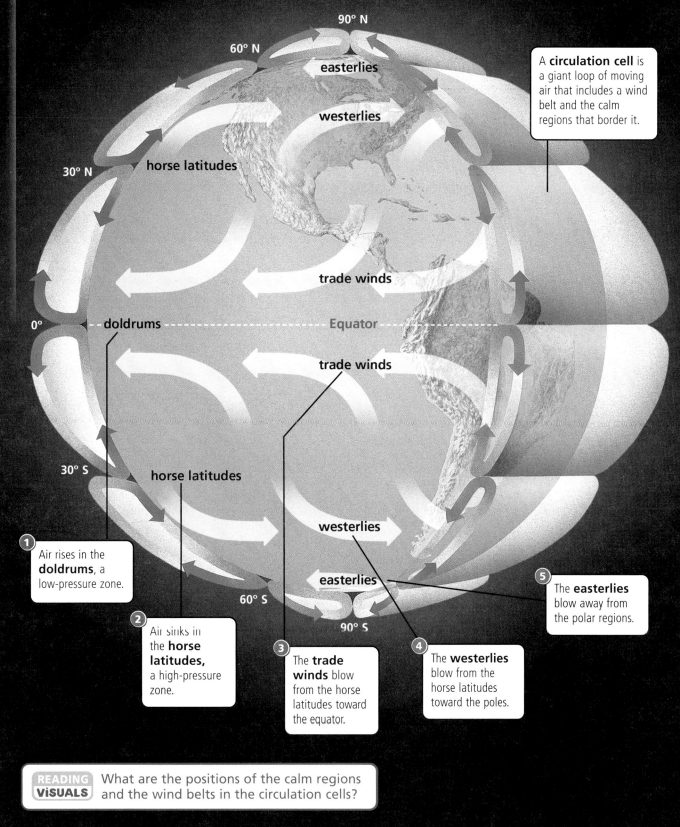

A **circulation cell** is a giant loop of moving air that includes a wind belt and the calm regions that border it.

90° N

60° N

easterlies

westerlies

30° N

horse latitudes

0°   doldrums   Equator

trade winds

trade winds

30° S

horse latitudes

westerlies

60° S

easterlies

90° S

1 Air rises in the **doldrums**, a low-pressure zone.

2 Air sinks in the **horse latitudes,** a high-pressure zone.

3 The **trade winds** blow from the horse latitudes toward the equator.

4 The **westerlies** blow from the horse latitudes toward the poles.

5 The **easterlies** blow away from the polar regions.

READING VISUALS What are the positions of the calm regions and the wind belts in the circulation cells?

Effects of Wind on Travel

Before the invention of steam engines, sailors used to dread traveling through the doldrums and the horse latitudes. There often wasn't enough wind to move their sailing ships. A ship might stall for days or even weeks, wasting precious supplies of food and fresh water.

To avoid the calm regions, sailors sought out global wind belts. The trade winds got their name because traders used them to sail from east to west. For centuries, sailors relied on the trade winds to reach North America from Europe. They would return by sailing north to catch the westerlies and ride them across the Atlantic.

Jet streams flow near the top of the troposphere.

COMBINATION NOTES
Record information about how jet streams flow and their effects on weather and travel.

Not all long-distance winds travel along Earth's surface. **Jet streams** usually flow in the upper troposphere from west to east for thousands of kilometers. Air often moves in jet streams at speeds greater than 200 kilometers per hour (124 mi/hr). Like global winds, jet streams form because Earth's surface is heated unevenly. Instead of following a straight line, jet streams loop north and south, as shown on the globe below.

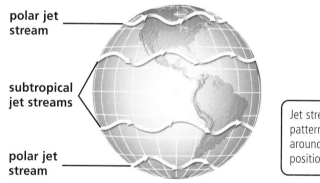

polar jet stream

subtropical jet streams

polar jet stream

Jet streams flow in a wavy pattern from west to east around the world. They change positions during the year.

Each hemisphere usually has two jet streams, a polar jet stream and a subtropical jet stream. The polar jet streams flow closer to the poles in summer than in winter.

The polar jet stream has a strong influence on weather in North America. It can pull cold air down from Canada into the United States and pull warm air up toward Canada. In addition, strong storms tend to form along its loops. Scientists must know where the jet stream is flowing to make accurate weather predictions.

Jet streams also affect air-travel times. They usually flow 10 to 15 kilometers (6–9 mi) above Earth's surface. Since airplanes often fly at these altitudes, their travel times can be lengthened or shortened by the strong wind of a jet stream.

Patterns of heating and cooling cause local winds and monsoons.

Have you ever noticed how the wind can change in predictable ways? For example, at the beach on a hot day you will often feel a cool breeze coming off the water. At night a breeze will flow in the opposite direction. The change in the breeze occurs because water and land heat up and cool down at different rates.

Local Winds

Some winds change daily in a regular pattern. These local winds blow within small areas.

- Sea breezes and land breezes occur near shorelines. During the day, land heats up faster than water. The air over the land rises and expands. Denser ocean air moves into the area of low pressure, producing a sea breeze. As the illustration below shows, this pattern is reversed at night, when land cools faster than water. Warm air rises over the ocean, and cooler air flows in, producing a land breeze.

Sea Breeze

Warmer air rises over land during the day.

Cooler air blows in from water.

Land Breeze

Cooler air blows out from land.

Warmer air rises over water at night.

> **REMINDER**
> Red arrows stand for warmer air. Blue arrows stand for cooler air.

- Valley breezes and mountain breezes are caused by a similar process. Mountain slopes heat up and cool faster than the valleys below them. During the day, valley breezes flow up mountains. At night mountain breezes flow down into valleys.

CHECK YOUR READING How do mountains and bodies of water affect patterns of heating and cooling?

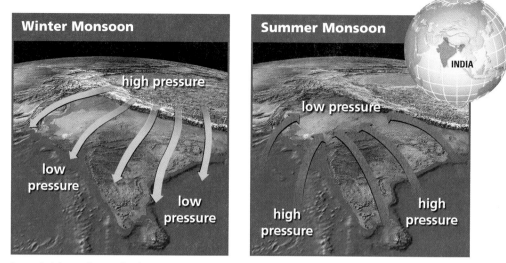

Winter Monsoon

high pressure

low pressure

low pressure

Dry air blows from the high-pressure area over the continent to the low-pressure areas over the ocean.

Summer Monsoon

INDIA

low pressure

high pressure

high pressure

Moist air blows from the high pressure areas over the ocean to the low-pressure area over the continent.

Monsoons

VOCABULARY
Add a description wheel for *monsoon* to your notebook.

Winds that change direction with the seasons are called **monsoons.** Like sea breezes and land breezes, monsoons are caused by the different heating and cooling rates of land and sea. However, monsoons flow longer distances and affect much larger areas.

Winter monsoons occur in regions where the land becomes much cooler than the sea during winter. High pressure builds over the land, and cool, dry wind blows out toward the sea. During summer this pattern reverses as the land becomes much warmer than the sea. Moist wind flows inland, often bringing heavy rains. The most extreme monsoons occur in South Asia and Southeast Asia. Farmers there depend on rain from the summer monsoon to grow crops.

 CHECK YOUR READING How do monsoon winds affect rainfall?

2.2 Review

KEY CONCEPTS

1. How does the uneven heating of Earth's surface cause winds to flow?

2. How does Earth's rotation influence the movement of global winds?

3. Why do some winds change direction in areas where land is near water?

CRITICAL THINKING

4. **Compare and Contrast** How are global winds and local winds similar? How are they different?

5. **Analyze** Make a table that shows the causes and effects of local winds and monsoons.

○ CHALLENGE

6. **Predict** Suppose that a city is located in a valley between the sea and a mountain range. What kind of wind pattern would you predict for this area?

SKILL: ADDING MEASUREMENTS

 MATH TUTORIAL
CLASSZONE.COM

Click on Math Tutorial for more help with adding measures of time.

High clouds show the location of the jet stream in this satellite image.

Navigate the Jet Stream

When an airplane is flying in the same direction as a jet stream, the airplane gets a boost in its speed. Pilots can save an hour or more if they fly with the jet stream. On the other hand, flying against the jet stream can slow an airplane down.

Example

To determine the total flight time between San Francisco and Chicago, with a stop in Denver, you need to add the hours and minutes separately. Set up the problem like this:

San Francisco to Denver:	2 h	10 min
Denver to Chicago:	1 h	45 min
Total flight time:	3 h	55 min

ANSWER The total flight time is 3 hours 55 minutes.

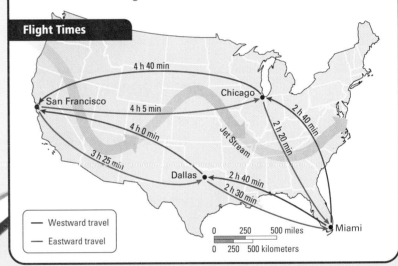

Flight Times

- 4 h 40 min
- San Francisco
- 4 h 5 min
- Chicago
- 2 h 40 min
- 4 h 0 min
- 2 h 20 min
- 3 h 25 min
- Jet Stream
- Dallas — 2 h 40 min
- 2 h 30 min
- Miami

— Westward travel
— Eastward travel

0 250 500 miles
0 250 500 kilometers

Use the map to answer the following questions.

1. What is the total flight time for an airliner flying from San Francisco to Miami through Chicago?

2. What is the total flight time for an airliner flying from San Francisco to Miami through Dallas?

3. How much time will the fastest possible trip from Miami to San Francisco take?

4. Compare the flight time from Chicago to San Francisco with the flight time from San Francisco to Chicago.

CHALLENGE What is the total flight time from Miami to San Francisco through Chicago? Convert minutes to hours if necessary.

2.3 Most clouds form as air rises and cools.

BEFORE, you learned

- Water vapor circulates from Earth to the atmosphere
- Warm air is less dense than cool air and tends to rise

NOW, you will learn

- How water in the atmosphere changes
- How clouds form
- About the types of clouds

VOCABULARY

evaporation p. 56
condensation p. 56
precipitation p. 57
humidity p. 58
saturation p. 58
relative humidity p. 58
dew point p. 58

EXPLORE Condensation

How does condensation occur?

PROCEDURE

① Observe the air as a classmate breathes out.

② Observe a mirror as a classmate breathes onto it.

WHAT DO YOU THINK?

- What changes did you observe on the mirror?
- Why could you see water on the mirror but not in the air when your classmate breathed out?

MATERIALS
hand mirror

Temperature affects water in the air.

Water is always in the atmosphere. You may see water in solid form, such as falling snow. Water may also be present as liquid water droplets. Even if you can't see any water, it is still part of the air as water vapor, an invisible gas. When temperatures change, water changes its form.

- **Evaporation** is the process by which a liquid changes into a gas. For water to evaporate, it needs extra energy.

- **Condensation** is the process by which a gas, such as water vapor, changes into a liquid. Condensation occurs when moist air cools.

The picture on the left shows the processes of evaporation and condensation at work. Water in a teakettle absorbs heat. It gets enough energy to evaporate into water vapor. The invisible water vapor rises and escapes from the kettle. When the vapor hits the cooler air outside the kettle, it cools and condenses into tiny but visible water droplets.

droplets

vapor

Water in the Air

Vast amounts of Earth's water are recycled. The oceans hold most of the water. Water is also stored in lakes, rivers, and ice sheets; in plants; and underground. Energy from sunlight causes molecules to evaporate from the surface of a body of water. These molecules become part of the air in the form of water vapor.

As air rises in the atmosphere, it cools. The loss of heat causes water vapor to condense into tiny water droplets or ice crystals. If the droplets or crystals grow and become heavy enough, they fall as rain, snow, sleet, or hail. Any type of liquid or solid water that falls to Earth's surface is called **precipitation.** Earth's water goes through a never-ending cycle of evaporation, condensation, and precipitation.

Water vapor can also condense on solid surfaces. Have you ever gotten your shoes wet while walking on grass in the early morning? The grass was covered with dew, which is water that has condensed on cool surfaces at night. If the temperature is cold enough, water vapor can change directly into a covering of ice, called frost.

VOCABULARY
Add a description wheel for *precipitation* to your notebook.

 CHECK YOUR READING Summarize the way water moves in the water cycle. For each part of the cycle, specify whether water exists as a gas, liquid, or solid.

Water Cycle

1 Water evaporates from bodies of water.

2 Water vapor condenses to form clouds.

3 Water falls to Earth's surface as precipitation.

Humidity and Relative Humidity

On a warm summer day, evaporation of moisture from your skin can help you feel comfortable. However, a lot of water vapor in the air can cause less moisture to evaporate from your skin. With less evaporation, the air will seem hotter and damper. **Humidity** is the amount of water vapor in air. Humidity varies from place to place and from time to time.

The illustration shows how humidity increases in a sealed container. As water molecules evaporate into the air, some start to condense and return to the water. For a while the air gains water vapor because more water evaporates than condenses. But eventually the air reaches **saturation,** a condition in which the rates of evaporation and condensation are equal. Any additional water that evaporates is balanced by water that condenses.

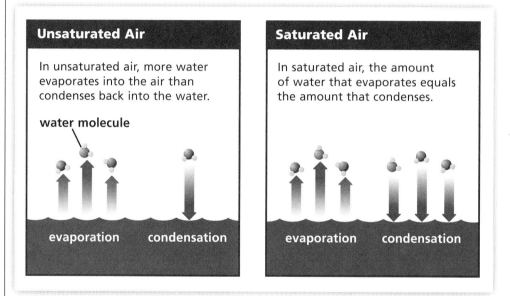

Unsaturated Air

In unsaturated air, more water evaporates into the air than condenses back into the water.

water molecule

evaporation   condensation

Saturated Air

In saturated air, the amount of water that evaporates equals the amount that condenses.

evaporation   condensation

READING TiP

Relative means "considered in comparison with something else."

The amount of water vapor in air at saturation depends on the temperature of the air. The warmer air is, the more water vapor it takes to saturate it. Scientists use this principle to describe the humidity of air in two different ways: relative humidity and dew point.

Relative humidity compares the amount of water vapor in air with the maximum amount of water vapor that can be present at that temperature. For example, air with 50 percent relative humidity has half the amount of water needed for saturation. If the amount of water vapor in air stays the same, relative humidity will decrease as the air heats up and increase as the air cools.

Dew point is the temperature at which air with a given amount of water vapor will reach saturation. For example, air with a dew point of 26°C (79°F) will become saturated if it cools to 26°C. The higher the dew point of air, the more water vapor the air contains.

Water vapor condenses and forms clouds.

Clouds are made of condensed water vapor. As warm air rises in the atmosphere, it cools. When the air cools to its dew point—the temperature at which air reaches saturation—water vapor condenses into tiny droplets or ice crystals. These droplets and crystals are so light that they either float as clouds on rising air or fall very slowly.

level where condensation begins

Rising warm air can produce clouds. Water vapor begins to condense when the air cools to its dew point.

Recall how dew condenses on grass. Water must condense on something solid. There are no large solid surfaces in the air. However, the air is filled with tiny particles such as dust, smoke, and salt from the ocean. Water vapor condenses on these particles.

INVESTIGATE Condensation

How does a cloud form?

PROCEDURE

1. Add a spoonful of water to the bottle to increase the humidity inside it.

2. Lay the bottle on its side. Light a match, blow it out, and then stick the match into the bottle for a few seconds to let smoke flow in. Replace the cap.

3. Squeeze the bottle quickly and then release it. Observe what happens when the bottle is allowed to expand.

WHAT DO YOU THINK?

- What happened to the water vapor inside the bottle when you squeezed the bottle and then let it expand?
- How did the smoke affect what happened to the water vapor?

CHALLENGE How would the cloud change if you raised or lowered the temperature inside the bottle?

SKILL FOCUS
Observing

MATERIALS
- clear 1-liter plastic bottle with cap
- water at room temperature
- tablespoon
- matches

TIME
10 minutes

Characteristics of Clouds

If you watch the sky over a period of time, you will probably observe clouds that do not look alike. Clouds have different characteristics because they form under different conditions. The shapes and sizes of clouds are mainly determined by air movement. For example, puffy clouds form in air that rises sharply or moves straight up and down. Flat, smooth clouds covering large areas form in air that rises gradually.

Location affects the composition of clouds. Since the troposphere gets colder with altitude, clouds that form at high altitudes are made of tiny ice crystals. Closer to Earth's surface, clouds are made of water droplets or a mixture of ice crystals and water droplets.

CHECK YOUR READING How are clouds that form at high altitudes different from clouds that form close to Earth's surface?

COMBINATION NOTES
Record information about the three main cloud types.

In the illustration on page 61, notice that some cloud names share word parts. That is because clouds are classified and named according to their altitudes, the ways they form, and their general characteristics. The three main types of clouds are cirrus, cumulus, and stratus. These names come from Latin words that suggest the clouds' appearances.

- **Cirrus** (SEER-uhs) means "curl of hair." Cirrus clouds appear feathery or wispy.
- **Cumulus** (KYOOM-yuh-luhs) means "heap" or "pile." Cumulus-type clouds can grow to be very tall.
- **Stratus** (STRAT-uhs) means "spread out." Stratus-type clouds form in flat layers.

Word parts are used to tell more about clouds. For example, names of clouds that produce precipitation contain the word part *nimbo-* or *nimbus*. Names of clouds that form at a medium altitude have the prefix *alto-*.

cirrus clouds

Cirrus Clouds

Cirrus clouds form in very cold air at high altitudes. Made of ice crystals, they have a wispy or feathery appearance. Strong winds often blow streamers or "tails" off cirrus clouds. These features show the direction of the wind in the upper troposphere. You will usually see cirrus clouds in fair weather. However, they can be a sign that a storm is approaching.

Cloud Types

The three main cloud types are cirrus, cumulus, and stratus. These names can be combined with each other and with other word parts to identify more specific cloud types.

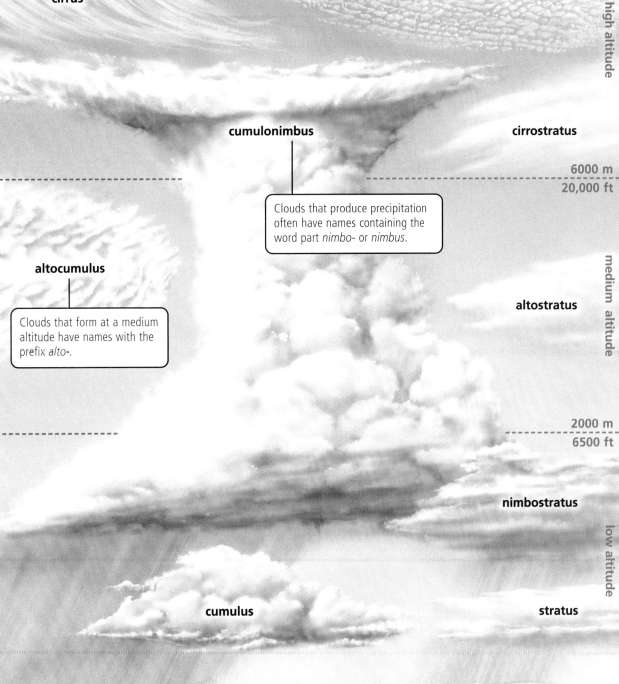

cirrus

cirrocumulus

high altitude

cumulonimbus

cirrostratus

6000 m
20,000 ft

Clouds that produce precipitation often have names containing the word part *nimbo-* or *nimbus*.

altocumulus

medium altitude

altostratus

Clouds that form at a medium altitude have names with the prefix *alto-*.

2000 m
6500 ft

nimbostratus

low altitude

cumulus

stratus

READING VISUALS Which cloud names are combinations of names of two main cloud types?

READING TiP

As you read each description of a main cloud type, look back at the visual on page 61. Notice the different clouds that have the main cloud type as part of their names.

Cumulus Clouds

Cumulus clouds are puffy white clouds with darker bases. They look like cotton balls floating in the sky. There are several varieties of cumulus clouds. Usually they appear in the daytime in fair weather, when warm air rises and its water vapor condenses. Cooler air sinks along the sides of the clouds, keeping cumulus clouds separate from one another.

cumulus clouds

If cumulus clouds keep growing taller, they can produce showers. The precipitation usually lasts less than half an hour because there are spaces between the clouds. The tallest clouds are cumulonimbus clouds, or thunderheads. These clouds produce thunderstorms that drop heavy rainfall. A cumulonimbus cloud can tower 18 kilometers (11 mi) above Earth's surface. By comparison, jet planes usually fly at about 10 kilometers (6 mi). Strong high-altitude winds often cause the top of the cloud to jut out sharply.

cumulonimbus clouds

 CHECK YOUR READING   How are cumulonimbus clouds different from other cumulus clouds?

Stratus Clouds

Have you ever noticed on some days that the whole sky looks gray? You were looking at stratus clouds. They form in layers when air cools over a large area without rising or when the air is gently lifted. Stratus clouds are smooth because they form without strong air movement.

stratus clouds

Some low stratus clouds are so dark that they completely block out the Sun. These clouds produce steady, light precipitation—unlike the brief showers that come from cumulus clouds. Stratus clouds that form at high altitudes are much thinner than low stratus clouds. You can see the Sun and the Moon through them. The ice crystals in high stratus clouds can make it seem as if there's a circle of colored light around the Sun or the Moon.

This fog formed around Castleton Tower in Utah. The land cooled overnight, causing water vapor in the air above it to condense.

Fog

Fog is a cloud that rests on the ground or a body of water. Like stratus clouds, fog has a smooth appearance. It usually forms when a surface is colder than the air above it. Water vapor in the air condenses as it cools, forming a thick mist. Fog on land tends to be heaviest at dawn, after the ground has cooled overnight. It clears as the ground is heated up by sunlight.

Fog can look beautiful rolling over hills or partly covering structures such as bridges. However, it often makes transportation dangerous by limiting visibility. In the United States close to 700 people die each year in automobile accidents that occur in dense fog.

2.3 Review

KEY CONCEPTS

1. Describe the three forms in which water is present in the atmosphere.
2. How does altitude affect the composition of clouds?
3. How are clouds classified?

CRITICAL THINKING

4. **Summarize** Describe the main characteristics of cirrus, cumulus, and stratus clouds.
5. **Draw Conclusions** Why might cumulonimbus clouds be more likely to form on sunny days than on days with little sunlight?

⬤ CHALLENGE

6. **Apply** Imagine that the sky has turned very cloudy after a hot morning. You notice that the bread in your sandwich is soggy and the towels on the towel rack won't dry. Explain why these things are happening. Use the following terms in your answer: *condensation, evaporation, relative humidity.*

CHAPTER INVESTIGATION

Relative Humidity

OVERVIEW AND PURPOSE Finding out the relative humidity can help you predict how comfortable you will feel on a hot day or whether dew will form on the ground. You can use a psychrometer to measure relative humidity. A psychrometer is a device made from two thermometers—one with a wet bulb and the other with a dry bulb. In this activity you will

- make a milk-carton psychrometer
- use it to measure the relative humidity of the air at two locations in your school

MATERIALS
- 2 thermometers
- cotton or felt cloth
- 3 rubber bands
- plastic bowl
- water at room temperature
- scissors
- pint milk carton
- ruler
- Relative Humidity Chart

▶ Problem

Which location will have the greater relative humidity?

▶ Hypothesize

Write a hypothesis in "If . . . , then . . . , because . . ." form to answer the problem.

▶ Procedure

1. Make a table like the one shown on the sample notebook page to record your data.

2. Check the two thermometers that you are using in this experiment to make sure they read the same temperature. Wrap a piece of cotton or felt cloth around the bulb of one thermometer. Hold the cloth in place with a rubber band as shown in the photograph. Dip this wet-bulb thermometer into a bowl of room-temperature water until the cloth is soaked.

   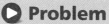
   step 3

3. Use scissors to cut a small hole in one side of the milk carton, 2 centimeters from the bottom of the carton. Place the wet-bulb thermometer on the same side as the hole that you made in the milk carton, and attach it with a rubber band. Push the tail of the cloth through the hole. Attach the dry-bulb thermometer as shown.

4 Fill the carton with water to just below the hole so that the cloth will remain wet. Empty the bowl and place the completed psychrometer inside it.

5 Write "science room" under the heading "Location 1" in your data table. Take your first readings in the science classroom about 10 minutes after you set up your psychrometer. Read the temperatures on the two thermometers in degrees Celsius. Record the temperature readings for the first location in the first column of your table.

6 Choose a second location in your school, and identify it under the heading "Location 2" in the data table. Take a second set of temperature readings with your psychrometer in this location. Record the readings in the second column of your table.

7 Subtract the wet-bulb reading from the dry-bulb reading for each location. Record this information in the third row of your data table.

8 Use the relative humidity table your teacher provides to find each relative humidity (expressed as a percentage). In the left-hand column, find the dry-bulb reading for location 1 that you recorded in step 5. Then find in the top line the number you recorded in step 7 (the difference between the dry-bulb and wet-bulb readings). Record the relative humidity in the last row of your data table. Repeat these steps for location 2.

▶ Observe and Analyze [Write It Up]

1. **RECORD OBSERVATIONS** Draw the setup of your psychrometer. Be sure your data table is complete.

2. **IDENTIFY** Identify the variables and constants in this experiment. List them in your **Science Notebook.**

3. **COMPARE** How do the wet-bulb readings compare with the dry-bulb readings?

4. **ANALYZE** If the difference between the temperature readings on the two thermometers is large, is the relative humidity high or low? Explain why.

▶ Conclude

1. **INTERPRET** Answer the question in the problem. Compare your results with your hypothesis.

2. **IDENTIFY LIMITS** Describe any possible errors that you made in following the procedure.

3. **APPLY** How would you account for the differences in relative humidity that you obtained for the two locations in your school?

▶ INVESTIGATE Further

CHALLENGE Use the psychrometer to keep track of the relative humidity in your classroom over a period of one week. Make a new chart to record your data. What do you notice about how the changes in relative humidity relate to the weather conditions outside?

Relative Humidity

Problem Which location will have the greater relative humidity?

Hypothesize

Observe and Analyze

Table 1. Relative Humidity at Two Locations

	Location 1	Location 2
Dry-bulb temperature		
Wet-bulb temperature		
Difference between dry-bulb and wet-bulb readings		
Relative humidity		

Conclude

2.4 Water falls to Earth's surface as precipitation.

◀ **BEFORE**, you learned

- Water moves between Earth's surface and the atmosphere
- Water vapor condenses into clouds

▶ **NOW**, you will learn

- How precipitation forms
- How precipitation is measured
- About acid rain

VOCABULARY

freezing rain p. 68
sleet p. 68
hail p. 68
acid rain p. 70

THINK ABOUT

Why does steam from a shower form large drops?

When you run a hot shower, the bathroom fills up with water vapor. The vapor condenses into tiny droplets that make it seem as if you are standing in fog. You may also see larger drops running down cool surfaces, such as a mirror. Why do some drops fall while others remain suspended?

Precipitation forms from water droplets or ice crystals.

All precipitation comes from clouds. For example, rain occurs when water droplets in a cloud fall to the ground. Then why doesn't every cloud produce precipitation? Cloud droplets are much smaller than a typical raindrop. They weigh so little that it takes only a slight upward movement of air to hold them up. In order for rain to fall from a cloud and reach Earth's surface, the cloud droplets must become larger and heavier.

One way that precipitation can form is through the combining of cloud droplets. The tiny droplets of water move up and down in clouds. Some collide with each other and combine, forming slightly bigger droplets. As the droplets continue to combine, they grow larger and larger. Eventually they become heavy enough to fall. It takes about a million droplets to make a single raindrop.

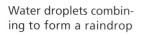

Water droplets combining to form a raindrop

Another way that precipitation can form is through the growth of ice crystals. When the temperature inside a cloud is below freezing, water vapor changes into tiny ice crystals. The crystals grow by collecting more water vapor or by colliding and merging with one another. When the crystals become heavy enough, they fall from the cloud. Snow isn't the only type of precipitation that forms this way. Most rain in the United States actually starts out as falling ice crystals. Before the crystals reach the ground, they melt in a layer of warm air.

 CHECK YOUR READING How do cloud droplets become large enough to fall as precipitation?

Measuring Precipitation

Scientists use a rain gauge to measure rainfall. A funnel or opening at the top of the gauge allows rain to flow into a cylinder. By measuring the water collected, you can find out how much rain fell in a storm or over a period of time.

Snow depth can be measured with a long ruler. Because the amount of water in snow varies, scientists use a special gauge to find out how much water the snow contains. A built-in heater melts the snow so that it can be measured just like rain.

 READING TIP

A gauge (gayj) is an instrument used for measuring or testing.

INVESTIGATE Precipitation

How much rain falls during a storm?

PROCEDURE

1. Cut off the top third of the bottle. Set this part aside.

2. Put some gravel at the bottom of the bottle to keep it from tipping over. Add water to cover the gravel. Draw a horizontal line on the bottle at the top of the water. Use a ruler to mark off centimeters on the bottle above the line that you drew. Now take the part of the bottle that you set aside and turn it upside down. Fit it inside the bottle to create a funnel.

3. Place the bottle outside when a rainstorm is expected. Make sure that nothing will block rain from entering it. Check your rain gauge after 24 hours. Observe and record the rainfall.

WHAT DO YOU THINK?

- How much rain fell during the time period?
- How do the measurements compare with your observations?

CHALLENGE Do you think you would measure the same amount of rain if you used a wider rain gauge? Explain.

SKILL FOCUS
Measuring

MATERIALS
- scissors
- 1-liter plastic bottle
- gravel
- water
- permanent marker
- ruler

TIME
15 minutes

When you watch weather reports on television, you often see storm systems passing across a weather map. Some of these images are made with Doppler radar. The radar shows which areas are getting precipitation and how fast it is falling. Forecasters use this information to estimate the total amount of precipitation an area will receive.

Types of Precipitation

Precipitation reaches Earth's surface in various forms. Some precipitation freezes or melts as it falls through the atmosphere.

❶ Rain and Drizzle Rain is the most common type of precipitation. Raindrops form from liquid cloud droplets or from ice crystals that melt as they fall. A light rain with very small drops is called drizzle. Drizzle usually comes from stratus clouds, which don't have enough air movement to build up larger raindrops.

❷ Freezing Rain Raindrops may freeze when they hit the ground or other surfaces in cold weather. **Freezing rain** covers surfaces with a coating of ice. During an ice storm, roads become slippery and dangerous. The weight of ice can also bring down trees and power lines.

❸ Sleet When rain passes through a layer of cold air, it can freeze before hitting the ground. The small pellets of ice that form are called **sleet.**

❹ Snow As ice crystals grow and merge in clouds, they become snowflakes. Snowflakes come in many different shapes and sizes. Usually they have six sides or branches. When snow falls through moist air that is near freezing, the flakes tend to join together in clumps. When snow falls through colder and drier air, snowflakes don't join together, and the snow is powdery.

❺ Hail Surprisingly, the largest type of frozen precipitation often arrives in warm weather. Lumps or balls of ice that fall from cumulonimbus clouds are called **hail.** During a thunderstorm, violent air currents hurl ice pellets around the cloud. These pellets grow as water droplets freeze onto them at high elevations. Some start to fall and then are pushed back up again. They may repeat this process several times, adding a layer of ice each time. Eventually they fall to the ground.

Large hailstones can damage property and injure people and animals. The biggest hailstone ever found in the United States weighed 1.7 pounds and was about as wide as a compact disc.

Most snowflakes have six branches or sides.

 CHECK YOUR READING Which forms of precipitation undergo a change after they leave a cloud?

How Precipitation Forms

All precipitation forms from water droplets or ice crystals in clouds. Some precipitation freezes or melts after it falls from the clouds.

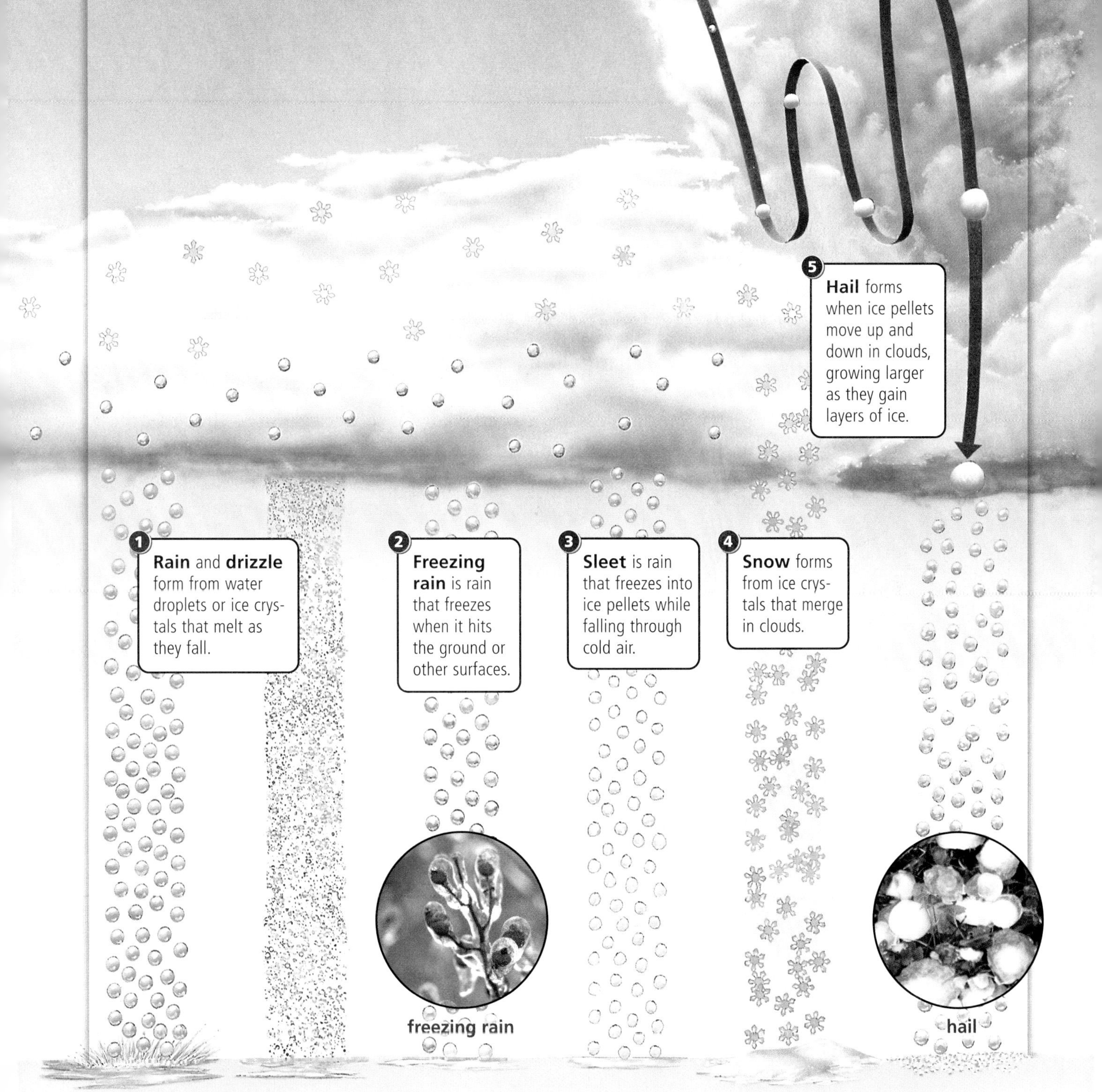

5 **Hail** forms when ice pellets move up and down in clouds, growing larger as they gain layers of ice.
1 **Rain** and **drizzle** form from water droplets or ice crystals that melt as they fall.
2 **Freezing rain** is rain that freezes when it hits the ground or other surfaces.
3 **Sleet** is rain that freezes into ice pellets while falling through cold air.
4 **Snow** forms from ice crystals that merge in clouds.
freezing rain
hail

READING VISUALS What forms of precipitation occur most often where you live?

These trees have few needles because acid rain has damaged the trees.

Precipitation can carry pollution.

VOCABULARY
Add a description wheel for *acid rain* to your notebook.

Rainwater is naturally a little acidic. **Acid rain** is rain that has become much more acidic than normal because of pollution. Factories, power plants, automobiles, and some natural sources release sulfur dioxide and nitrogen oxides into the air. These gases can combine with water vapor to form sulfuric acid and nitric acid. The acids mix with cloud droplets or ice crystals that eventually fall to Earth's surface as precipitation.

Because wind can blow air pollution hundreds of kilometers, acid rain may fall far from the source of the pollution. Acid rain harms trees and raises the acidity of lakes, making it difficult for fish to live in them. Acid rain also damages the surfaces of buildings and sculptures.

CHECK YOUR READING How does acid rain form? Your answer should mention water vapor.

2.4 Review

KEY CONCEPTS

1. What are the two ways that rain can form?

2. How are rain and snow measured?

3. What human activities cause acid rain?

CRITICAL THINKING

4. **Compare and Contrast** How are sleet and freezing rain similar? How are they different?

5. **Draw Conclusions** When a large hailstone is cut open, four layers can be seen. What conclusions can you draw about the formation of the hailstone?

▲ CHALLENGE

6. **Predict** Temperatures in a cloud and on the ground are below freezing. A warmer layer of air lies between the cloud and the ground. What type of precipitation do you predict will occur? Explain.

EXTREME SCIENCE

Caught Inside a Thunderhead

In 1959, engine failure forced Lieutenant Colonel William Rankin to eject from his plane at a high altitude. When his parachute opened, he thought he was out of danger. However, he soon realized that he was caught inside a cumulonimbus cloud during a fierce thunderstorm.

As Rankin hung by his parachute, violent air movement inside the cloud tossed him "up, down, sideways, clockwise." The rain was so heavy that he feared he would drown in midair. Lightning flashed all around him. Rankin finally landed 40 minutes after his adventure began. He had many injuries, including bruises from hailstones. Fortunately, none of the storm's lightning had struck him.

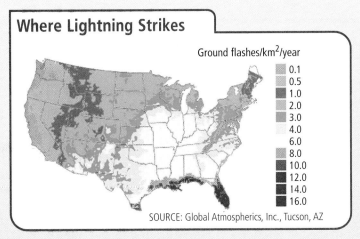

Where Lightning Strikes

Ground flashes/km²/year

	0.1
	0.5
	1.0
	2.0
	3.0
	4.0
	6.0
	8.0
	10.0
	12.0
	14.0
	16.0

SOURCE: Global Atmospherics, Inc., Tucson, AZ

Water, Wind, Hail, and Lightning

- A cumulonimbus cloud, or thunderhead, can rise to over 18 kilometers above Earth's surface. That's about twice the elevation of Mount Everest.

- A cumulonimbus cloud may contain 500,000 tons of water.

- Thunderstorm clouds cause 8 million lightning flashes each day.

EXPLORE

1. **ANALYZE** Find where you live on the map. Use the color key to figure out how often lightning strikes each square kilometer in your area.

2. **CHALLENGE** Use information from the Resource Center to propose an explanation for the pattern of lightning frequencies shown on the map.

RESOURCE CENTER
CLASSZONE.COM
Learn more about lightning.

Lightning flashes to the ground from a thunderhead, or cumulonimbus cloud.

Chapter Review

the BIG idea

Some features of weather have predictable patterns.

CONTENT REVIEW
CLASSZONE.COM

KEY CONCEPTS SUMMARY

2.1 **The atmosphere's air pressure changes.**

Air pressure is the force of air molecules pushing on an area. Air pressure decreases as you move higher in the atmosphere. Air pressure can also differ in two locations at the same altitude.

VOCABULARY
air pressure p. 43
barometer p. 46

2.2 **The atmosphere has wind patterns.**

Wind blows from areas of high pressure toward areas of low pressure. Earth's rotation causes long-distance winds to curve.

area of
high pressure   *wind direction*   area of
                                                         low pressure

VOCABULARY
weather p. 47
wind p. 47
global wind p. 48
Coriolis effect p. 49
jet stream p. 52
monsoon p. 54

2.3 **Most clouds form as air rises and cools.**

Clouds are made of tiny water droplets or ice crystals that condense from water vapor in rising air.

VOCABULARY
evaporation p. 56
condensation p. 56
precipitation p. 57
humidity p. 58
saturation p. 58
relative humidity p. 58
dew point p. 58

2.4 **Water falls to Earth's surface as precipitation.**

Water droplets in clouds merge to form raindrops.

Ice crystals in clouds can form snow, rain, and other types of precipitation.

VOCABULARY
freezing rain p. 68
sleet p. 68
hail p. 68
acid rain p. 70

Reviewing Vocabulary

Write a definition of each term. Use the meaning of the underlined root to help you.

Word	Root Meaning	Definition
EXAMPLE air <u>pressure</u>	to apply force	the force of air molecules pushing on an area
1. <u>baro</u>meter	weight	
2. <u>satura</u>tion	to fill	
3. <u>glob</u>al wind	sphere	
4. <u>monsoon</u>	season	
5. <u>evapor</u>ation	steam	
6. con<u>dens</u>ation	thick	
7. <u>humid</u>ity	moist	
8. <u>precipit</u>ation	thrown down	

Reviewing Key Concepts

Multiple Choice *Choose the letter of the best answer.*

9. The movement of air molecules causes
- **a.** air density
- **b.** air pressure
- **c.** humidity
- **d.** relative humidity

10. Winds curve as they move across Earth's surface because of
- **a.** the Coriolis effect
- **b.** air pressure
- **c.** humidity
- **d.** relative humidity

11. Jet streams generally flow toward the
- **a.** north
- **b.** south
- **c.** east
- **d.** west

12. Condensation increases with greater
- **a.** relative humidity
- **b.** air temperature
- **c.** air pressure
- **d.** wind speed

13. Any type of liquid or solid water that falls to Earth's surface is called
- **a.** precipitation
- **b.** dew
- **c.** a monsoon
- **d.** humidity

14. What are low-altitude clouds composed of?
- **a.** snowflakes
- **b.** raindrops
- **c.** water droplets
- **d.** water vapor

15. Clouds made of ice crystals form under conditions of
- **a.** strong winds
- **b.** high altitude
- **c.** low humidity
- **d.** high pressure

16. Which type of cloud is most likely to bring thunderstorms?
- **a.** stratus
- **b.** altostratus
- **c.** cumulonimbus
- **d.** cirrus

17. Over short distances wind blows toward areas of
- **a.** high pressure
- **b.** high density
- **c.** low temperature
- **d.** low pressure

18. The doldrums and the horse latitudes are both regions of
- **a.** high air pressure
- **b.** light winds
- **c.** heavy rains
- **d.** low temperatures

19. As altitude increases, air pressure usually
- **a.** decreases
- **b.** increases
- **c.** varies more
- **d.** varies less

Short Answer *Write a short answer to each question.*

20. What causes land breezes to flow at night?

21. Why does hair take longer to dry after a shower on days with high relative humidity?

22. How does air pressure affect air density?

23. Why are dust and other particles necessary for precipitation?

24. How did global wind belts and calm regions affect transportation in the past?

Thinking Critically

The soil in this terrarium was soaked with water two weeks ago. Then the box was sealed so that no moisture could escape. Use the diagram to answer the next six questions.

25. IDENTIFY EFFECTS How does sunlight affect conditions inside the terrarium?

26. ANALYZE Draw a diagram of the water cycle inside the terrarium.

27. INFER What do the water drops on the glass indicate about the temperatures inside and outside the terrarium?

28. PREDICT Explain how long you think the plants will live without being watered.

29. PREDICT What would happen if you placed the terrarium on top of a block of ice?

30. HYPOTHESIZE How would conditions inside the terrarium change if there were a hole in one side of it?

31. COMPARE AND CONTRAST How are sea breezes and monsoon winds alike, and how are they different?

32. PREDICT A cumulus cloud is growing taller. What will happen to the density of the air beneath it? Explain.

33. INFER Imagine that a group of factories and power plants lies 200 kilometers to the west of a forest where trees are dying. Describe three steps in a process that could be causing the trees to die.

IDENTIFY EFFECTS Write the type of precipitation that would form under each set of conditions.

Conditions	Precipitation
34. above-freezing air inside a cloud and freezing air beneath it	
35. above-freezing air beneath a cloud and freezing temperatures on the ground	
36. below-freezing air inside a cloud and above-freezing temperatures in the air beneath it and on the ground	
37. below-freezing air inside a cloud and beneath it	
38. ice pellets hurled around by air currents inside a cloud	

the **BIG** idea

39. APPLY Look again at the photograph on pages 40–41. Now that you have finished the chapter, how would you change your response to the question on the photograph?

40. WRITE Write one or more paragraphs explaining how energy from the Sun influences the weather. In your discussion, include at least three of the following topics:

- global wind belts
- high- and low-pressure areas
- local winds
- monsoons
- the water cycle
- cloud formation

UNIT PROJECTS

If you need to do an experiment for your unit project, gather the materials. Be sure to allow enough time to observe results before the project is due.

Standardized Test Practice

Analyzing a Diagram

This diagram shows the water cycle. Use it to answer the questions below.

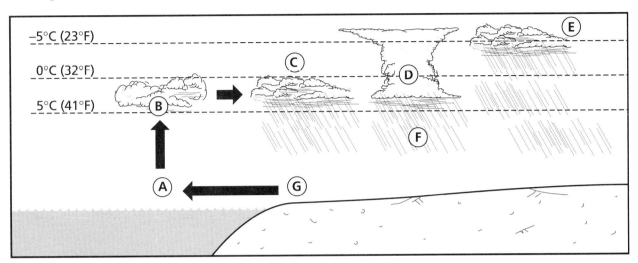

1. Where is evaporation occurring?

a. A   **c.** F

b. D   **d.** G

2. Where is condensation occurring?

a. A   **c.** F

b. B   **d.** G

3. Where is precipitation shown?

a. A   **c.** E

b. C   **d.** F

4. Where is hail most likely to form?

a. C   **c.** E

b. D   **d.** F

5. From which cloud will precipitation fall as snow and then turn to rain?

a. B   **c.** D

b. C   **d.** E

6. Which is the best estimate for the temperature in B?

a. 8°C (46°F)   **c.** −3°C (27°F)

b. 3°C (37°F)   **d.** −8°C (17°F)

7. What does the arrow pointing up between A and B indicate?

a. the movement of moisture

b. the direction of the wind

c. a low pressure area

d. a reflection off the water

Extended Response

Answer the two questions below in detail. Include some of the terms shown in the word box. In your answers underline each term you use.

low air pressure	cool air	west
high air pressure	warm air	east
Coriolis effect		

8. Whenever Richard rides in an elevator to the top of a skyscraper, he feels a pop inside his ears. Explain what is happening in the air to produce the pop in Richard's ears.

9. Winds tend to blow from west to east across the United States. If Earth spun in the other direction, how might the winds across the United States be different? Use the terms *east, west,* and *Coriolis effect* in your answer.

Weather Fronts and Storms

the **BIG** idea

The interaction of air masses causes changes in weather.

What types of weather can move a house?

Key Concepts

SECTION

3.1 Weather changes as air masses move.
Learn about air masses, fronts, and high- and low-pressure systems.

SECTION

3.2 Low-pressure systems can become storms.
Learn about hurricanes and winter storms.

SECTION

3.3 Vertical air motion can cause severe storms.
Learn about thunderstorms, lightning, and tornadoes.

SECTION

3.4 Weather forecasters use advanced technologies.
Learn about different types of weather data and how forecasters predict weather.

Internet Preview

CLASSZONE.COM

Chapter 3 online resources: Content Review, two Visualizations, two Resource Centers, Math Tutorial, Test Practice

EXPLORE (the BIG idea)

How Does Cold Air Move?

Hold one hand near the top of a refrigerator door and the other hand near the bottom. Open the refrigerator door just a little bit.

Observe and Think
How did each hand feel before and after you opened the door? How did the air move?

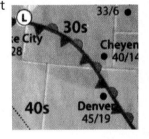

How Does Weather Move?

Collect newspaper weather maps for three consecutive days. Identify at least one flagged line on a map (identifying a weather front) and track the line's movement over the three days.

Observe and Think
What type of weather did you find each day where the line passed? Why did this line move the way it did?

Internet Activity: Weather Safety

Go to **ClassZone.com** to find information about weather safety. Find out the types of dangerous weather that may affect your region.

Observe and Think
What can you do ahead of time to be ready for severe weather?

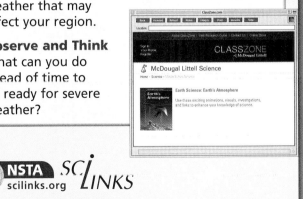

NSTA
scilinks.org
SCiLINKS

Severe Weather Code: MDL011

Getting Ready to Learn

◀ CONCEPT REVIEW

- Air temperature decreases as you rise in the troposphere.
- Temperature affects air density.
- Pressure differences make air move.
- Uneven heating of Earth's surface produces winds.
- Clouds form as air rises, expands, and cools.

◀ VOCABULARY REVIEW

altitude p. 10
convection p. 19
evaporation p. 56
condensation p. 56
relative humidity p. 58

CONTENT REVIEW
CLASSZONE.COM
Review concepts and vocabulary.

▶ TAKING NOTES

MAIN IDEA WEB

Write each new blue heading—a main idea—in a box. Then put notes with important terms and details into boxes around the main idea.

VOCABULARY STRATEGY

Draw a **word triangle** diagram for each new vocabulary term. In the bottom row write and define the term. In the middle row, use the term correctly in a sentence. At the top, draw a small picture to help you remember the term.

See the Note-Taking Handbook on pages R45–R51.

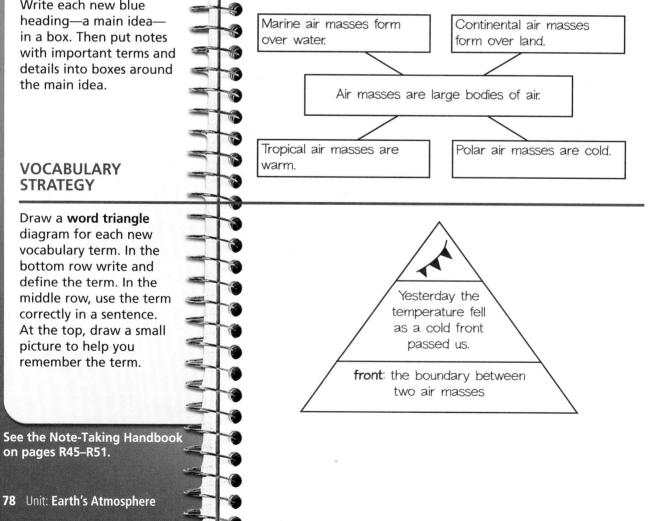

SCIENCE NOTEBOOK

Marine air masses form over water.

Continental air masses form over land.

Air masses are large bodies of air.

Tropical air masses are warm.

Polar air masses are cold.

Yesterday the temperature fell as a cold front passed us.

front: the boundary between two air masses

3.1

Weather changes as air masses move.

<table>
<tr><td>

◀ **BEFORE,** you learned

- Air pressure changes with location and altitude
- Water vapor in the atmosphere condenses when air rises

</td><td>

▶ **NOW,** you will learn

- What air masses are
- What happens when air masses meet
- How pressure systems affect the weather

</td></tr>
</table>

VOCABULARY

air mass p. 79
front p. 82
high-pressure
  system p. 84
low-pressure system p. 85

EXPLORE Air Masses

How does an air mass form?

PROCEDURE

① Put ice into one bowl and warm water into a second bowl. Leave the third bowl empty.

② Place each bowl in a different box and cover the box with plastic wrap. Wait a few minutes.

③ Put your hand into each box in turn.

WHAT DO YOU THINK?

- How would you describe the air in each box?
- Which box's air feels the most humid? Why?

MATERIALS

- 3 bowls
- ice
- warm water
- 3 shoeboxes
- plastic wrap

Air masses are large bodies of air.

MAIN IDEA WEB
Organize important terms and details about air masses.

You have probably experienced the effects of air masses—one day is hot and humid, and the next day is cool and pleasant. The weather changes when a new air mass moves into your area. An **air mass** is a large volume of air in which temperature and humidity are nearly the same in different locations at the same altitude. An air mass can cover many thousands of square kilometers.

An air mass forms when the air over a large region of Earth sits in one place for many days. The air gradually takes on the characteristics of the land or water below it. Where Earth's surface is cold, the air becomes cold. Where Earth's surface is wet, the air becomes moist. As an air mass moves, it brings its temperature and moisture to new locations.

CHECK YOUR READING Explain how the weather can change with the arrival of a new air mass. Your answer should include two ways that weather changes.

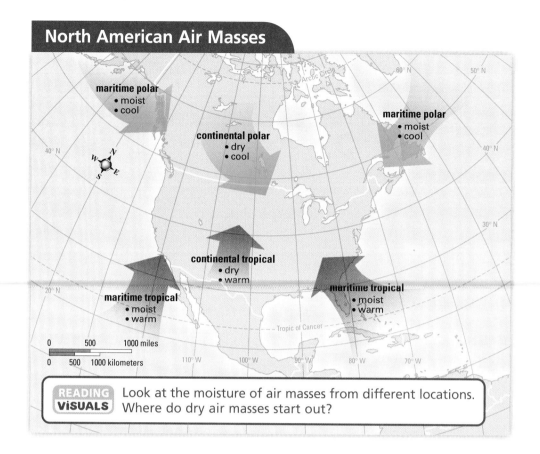

North American Air Masses

maritime polar
- moist
- cool

maritime polar
- moist
- cool

continental polar
- dry
- cool

continental tropical
- dry
- warm

maritime tropical
- moist
- warm

maritime tropical
- moist
- warm

0   500   1000 miles
0   500   1000 kilometers

READING ViSUALS Look at the moisture of air masses from different locations. Where do dry air masses start out?

Characteristics of an Air Mass

Some regions of Earth's surface, such as those shown in the map above, produce air masses again and again. The characteristics of an air mass depend on the region where it forms. A hot desert produces dry, hot air masses, while cool ocean waters produce moist, cool air masses. Scientists classify air masses into categories according to the characteristics of regions. Each category name is made of two words—one for moisture, one for temperature.

The first word of an air mass's category name tells whether the air mass formed over water or dry land. It describes the moisture of the air mass.

- **Continental** air masses form over land. Air becomes dry as it loses its moisture to the dry land below it.
- **Maritime** (MAR-ih-TYM) air masses form over water. Air becomes moist as it gains water vapor from the water below it.

The second word of a category name tells whether an air mass formed close to the equator. It describes the air mass's temperature.

- **Tropical** air masses form near the equator. Air becomes warm as it gains energy from the warm land or water.
- **Polar** air masses form far from the equator. Air becomes cool as it loses energy to the cold land or water.

READING TiP

The word *maritime* has the same root as the word *marine*. Both come from the Latin word *mare*, which means "sea."

The combination of words gives the characteristics of the air mass. A maritime tropical air mass is moist and warm, while a continental polar air mass is dry and cold.

CHECK YOUR READING What can you tell from each word of an air mass's name?

Movement of an Air Mass

Air masses can travel away from the regions where they form. They move with the global pattern of winds. In most of the United States, air masses generally move from west to east. They may move along with the jet stream in more complex and changing patterns.

When an air mass moves to a new region, it carries along its characteristic moisture and temperature. As the air moves over Earth's surface, the characteristics of the surface begin to change the air mass. For example, if a continental polar air mass moves over warm water, the air near the surface will become warmer and gain moisture. These changes begin where the air touches the surface. It may take days or weeks for the changes to spread upward through the entire air mass. An air mass that moves quickly may not change much. If it moves quickly enough, a continental polar air mass can move cold air from northern Canada all the way to the southern United States.

INVESTIGATE Air Masses

What happens when air masses collide?

PROCEDURE

1. Cut the cardboard to create a snug barrier that divides your beaker in half.

2. Mix about 5 mL of salt, 50 mL of water, and a drop of blue food coloring in one cup. This dense mixture represents a cold air mass.

3. Mix 50 mL of water with a drop of red food coloring in the other cup. This less-dense mixture represents a warm air mass.

4. Carefully pour the red water into one side of your divided beaker and the blue saltwater into the other side. As you look through the side of the beaker, quickly remove the barrier.

WHAT DO YOU THINK?

• What happened when the two liquids met?
• To what extent did the liquids mix together?

CHALLENGE How are the liquids like air masses?

SKILL FOCUS
Inferring

MATERIALS
• 500 mL beaker
• stiff cardboard
• scissors
• 2 cups
• small beaker for measuring
• salt
• water
• food coloring

TIME
25 minutes

Weather changes where air masses meet.

When a new air mass moves over your area, you can expect the weather to change. Perhaps you have heard a weather forecaster talk about fronts. A **front** is a boundary between air masses. The weather near a front can differ from the weather inside the rest of an air mass. As one air mass pushes another, some of the air at the boundary will be pushed upward. Clouds can form in this rising air. The weather often becomes cloudy or stormy as a front passes. Afterward, you experience the temperature and humidity of the air mass that has moved in.

MAIN IDEA WEB
Organize the notes you take about fronts.

Fronts and Weather

Different types of fronts produce different patterns of weather. When a cold, dense air mass pushes warmer air, it produces a cold front. When a warm air mass pushes colder air, it produces a warm front. These names tell you which way the temperature will change but not how much it will change. A cold front can turn a heat wave into normal summer weather or turn cold winter air into very cold weather.

 CHECK YOUR READING How would the weather change if a cold front moved into your area?

VISUALIZATION
CLASSZONE.COM

See how the air moves in warm fronts and cold fronts.

❶ **Cold fronts** can move into regions quickly. As you can see on page 83, a cold front is steeper than the other types of fronts. As a mass of cold, dense air moves forward, warmer air ahead of it is pushed upward. Water vapor in the warm air condenses as the air rises. Cold fronts often produce tall cumulonimbus clouds and precipitation. Brief, heavy storms are likely. After the storms, the air is cooler and often very clear.

❷ **Warm fronts** move more slowly than cold fronts. Warm air moves gradually up and over a mass of denser and colder air. Moisture in the warm air condenses all along the sloping front, producing cloud-covered skies. As a warm front approaches, you may first see high cirrus clouds, then high stratus clouds, then lower and lower stratus clouds. Often, a warm front brings many hours of steady rain or snow. After the front passes, the air is warmer.

❸ **Stationary fronts** occur when air masses first meet or when a cold or warm front stops moving. For a while, the boundary between the air masses stays in the same location—it stays stationary. The air in each air mass can still move sideways along the front or upward. The upward air motion may produce clouds that cover the sky, sometimes for days at a time. When the front starts moving, it becomes a warm front if the warm air advances and pushes the cold air. If the cold air moves forward instead, the front becomes a cold front.

Fronts and Weather

As fronts move across Earth's surface, they produce changes in the weather.

 **Cold Front**

Triangles show the direction that a cold front moves.

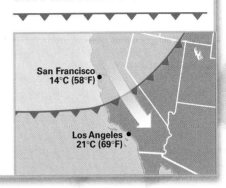

San Francisco
14°C (58°F)

Los Angeles
21°C (69°F)

A **cold front** forms when a cold air mass pushes a warm air mass and forces the warm air to rise. As the warm air rises, its moisture condenses and forms tall clouds.

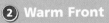 **Warm Front**

Semicircles show the direction that a warm front moves.

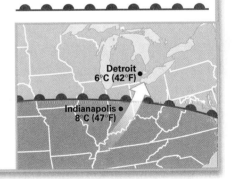

Detroit
6°C (42°F)

Indianapolis
8°C (47°F)

A **warm front** forms when a warm air mass pushes a cold air mass. The warm air rises slowly over the cold air and its moisture condenses into flat clouds.

③ **Stationary Front**

Alternating triangles and semicircles show a stationary front.

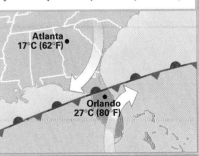

Atlanta
17°C (62°F)

Orlando
27°C (80°F)

A **stationary front** occurs when two air masses push against each other without moving. A stationary front becomes a warm or cold front when one air mass advances.

 PREDICT Which city will the cold front affect next?

High-Pressure Systems

You may have seen the letters H and L on a weather map. These letters mark high-pressure centers and low-pressure centers, often simply called highs and lows. Each center is the location of the highest or lowest pressure in a region. The pressure differences cause air to move in ways that may make a high or low become the center of a whole system of weather.

READING TiP

A *system* includes different parts that work together.

At a high-pressure center, air sinks slowly down. As the air nears the ground, it spreads out toward areas of lower pressure. In the Northern Hemisphere, the Coriolis effect makes the air turn clockwise as it moves outward. A **high-pressure system** is formed when air moves all the way around a high-pressure center. Most high-pressure systems are large and change slowly. When a high-pressure system stays in one location for a long time, an air mass may form. The air—and resulting air mass—can be warm or cold, moist or dry.

A high-pressure system generally brings clear skies and calm air or gentle breezes. This is because as air sinks to lower altitudes, it warms up a little bit. Water droplets evaporate, so clouds often disappear.

CHECK YOUR READING What type of weather do you expect in a high-pressure system?

Weather Systems in the Northern Hemisphere

High-pressure systems and low-pressure systems produce patterns of weather across Earth's surface.

A spiral of clouds often shows the location of a low-pressure system.

Air sinks at a high-pressure center and spreads out toward locations with low pressure. The spreading air moves slowly clockwise.

Air circles into a low-pressure center and moves upward. The motion is counterclockwise and can be quick.

READING VISUALS With your finger, trace the motion of air, starting above the high. Where have you seen similar patterns in earlier chapters?

Low-Pressure Systems

A small area of low pressure can also develop into a larger system. A **low-pressure system** is a large weather system that surrounds a center of low pressure. It begins as air moves around and inward toward the lowest pressure and then up to higher altitudes. The upward motion of the air lowers the air pressure further, and so the air moves faster. The pattern of motion strengthens into a low-pressure weather system. The rising air produces stormy weather. In the Northern Hemisphere, the air in a low-pressure system circles in a counterclockwise direction.

A low-pressure system can develop wherever there is a center of low pressure. One place this often happens is along a boundary between a warm air mass and a cold air mass. The diagram shows an example of this process.

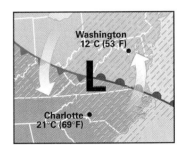

- Part of the boundary between the air masses moves south and becomes a cold front.

- Part of the boundary moves north and becomes a warm front.

- A center of low pressure forms where the ends of the two fronts meet.

The low-pressure center and fronts become parts of a whole system of weather. Rising air at the fronts and at the low can cause very stormy weather.

The diagram on page 84 shows how air moves between pressure centers. Air moves down, out, and around a high-pressure center. Then it swirls around and into a low-pressure center and moves upward. Highs and lows affect each other as they move across the surface. Large weather systems generally move with the pattern of global winds—west to east over most of North America. But, within a weather system, winds can blow in different directions.

3.1 Review

KEY CONCEPTS

1. What are the two characteristics of an air mass that you need to know in order to classify it?

2. What happens when a warmer air mass pushes a cooler air mass?

3. What type of weather system brings calm, clear weather?

CRITICAL THINKING

4. **Compare and Contrast** Explain how air moves differently in low- and high-pressure systems.

5. **Apply** If the weather becomes stormy for a short time and then becomes colder, which type of front has passed?

⬤ CHALLENGE

6. **Synthesize** You check a barometer and observe that the air pressure has been dropping all day. Is tonight's weather more likely to be calm or stormy?

MATH TUTORIAL
CLASSZONE.COM

Click on Math Tutorial for more help with rates as ratios.

Movement of a Front

Scientists measure the speeds of weather fronts to forecast weather conditions. The speed at which a front moves is an example of a rate. A rate can be written as a ratio. For example, the rate of a front that moves a distance of 500 kilometers in 1 day can be written as follows:

500 kilometers : 1 day

The map below shows the movement of a cold front over four consecutive days. Use the map scale to determine the distance that the front moves on each day.

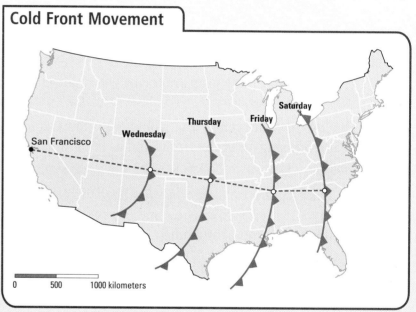

Cold Front Movement

Answer the following questions.

1. What was the front's rate of movement between Wednesday and Thursday? Express your answer as a ratio.

    ? : 1 day

2. What was the front's rate of movement between Friday and Saturday? Express your answer as a ratio.

3. What was the mean rate of the front's movement from Wednesday to Saturday? Remember, *mean* means "average." Express your answer as a ratio.

CHALLENGE Use the rate from Wednesday to Saturday to estimate the day on which the front must have moved through San Francisco.

KEY CONCEPT
Low-pressure systems can become storms.

BEFORE, you learned

- Moving air masses cause changes in weather
- A low-pressure system brings stormy weather

NOW, you will learn

- How hurricanes develop
- About the dangers of hurricanes
- About different types of winter storms

VOCABULARY

tropical storm p. 87
hurricane p. 87
storm surge p. 89
blizzard p. 90

EXPLORE Hurricanes

What things make hurricanes lose strength?

PROCEDURE

1. Crumple a piece of paper, then flatten it out. Crumple and flatten it out again.

2. Spin the top on the flattened paper. Count the seconds until it stops spinning.

3. Spin the top on a smooth surface. Count the seconds until it stops spinning.

WHAT DO YOU THINK?

How does the texture of the surface affect the rate at which the top loses energy?

MATERIALS
- sheet of paper
- top

Hurricanes form over warm ocean water.

MAIN IDEA WEB
Remember to make notes about hurricanes.

Near the equator, warm ocean water provides the energy that can turn a low-pressure center into a violent storm. As water evaporates from the ocean, energy moves from the ocean water into the air. This energy makes warm air rise faster. Tall clouds and strong winds develop. As winds blow across the water from different directions into the low, the Coriolis effect bends their paths into a spiral. The winds blow faster and faster around the low, which becomes the center of a storm system.

A **tropical storm** is a low-pressure system that starts near the equator and has winds that blow at 65 kilometers per hour (40 mi/h) or more. A **hurricane** (HUR ih KAYN) is a tropical low-pressure system with winds blowing at speeds of 120 kilometers per hour (74 mi/h) or more—strong enough to uproot trees. Hurricanes are called typhoons or cyclones when they form over the Indian Ocean or the western Pacific Ocean.

Formation of Hurricanes

VISUALIZATION
CLASSZONE.COM

Watch the progress of
a hurricane.

In the eastern United States, hurricanes most often strike between August and October. Energy from warm water is necessary for a low-pressure center to build into a tropical storm and then into a hurricane. The ocean water where these storms develop only gets warm enough—26°C (80°F) or more—near the end of summer.

Tropical storms and hurricanes generally move westward with the trade winds. Near land, however, they will often move north, south, or even back eastward. As long as a storm stays above warm water, it can grow bigger and more powerful. As soon as a hurricane moves over land or over cooler water, it loses its source of energy. The winds lose strength and the storm dies out. If a hurricane moves over land, the rough surface of the land reduces the winds even more.

The map below shows the progress of a storm. The tropical storm gained energy and became a hurricane as it moved westward. When the hurricane moved north, the storm lost energy and was called a tropical storm again as its winds slowed.

CHECK YOUR READING What is the source of a hurricane's energy?

Structure of a Hurricane

Saffir-Simpson Hurricane Scale

A hurricane does not stay at the same category of strength its entire life. The strength of each hurricane when it first hit land is recorded here.

Category	Wind Speed	Examples		Typical Damage
1	74–95 mph (119–153 km/h)	Irene Lili Gaston	1999 2002 2004	Minimal. Trees and unanchored mobile homes damaged. Some coastal flooding.
2	96–110 mph (154–177 km/h)	Isabel Frances	2003 2004	Moderate. Minor damage to buildings. Some trees blown down.
3	111–130 mph (178–209 km/h)	Jeanne Ivan Emily Rita	2004 2004 2005 2005	Extensive. Some structural damage to small buildings. Mobile homes destroyed.
4	131–155 mph (210–249 km/h)	Iris Charley Dennis Katrina	2001 2004 2005 2005	Extreme. Some roofs destroyed. Evacuations as far as 6 miles (10 km) inland. Storm surge 13–18 feet (4–5.5 m) above normal.
5	155+ mph (250+ km/h)	Camille Andrew	1969 1992	Catastrophic. Buildings destroyed. Evacuations as far as 10 miles (16 km) inland. Storm surge over 18 feet (5.5 m) above normal.

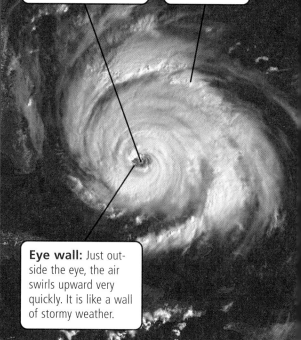

Eye: The small center of a hurricane is clear and calm because air is moving downward.

Bands of thunderstorms give the hurricane a spiral shape.

Eye wall: Just outside the eye, the air swirls upward very quickly. It is like a wall of stormy weather.

At the center of a hurricane is a small area of clear weather, 20–50 kilometers (10–30 mi) in diameter, called the eye. The storm's center is calm because air moves downward there. Just around the eye, the air moves very quickly around and upward, forming a tall ring of cumulonimbus clouds called the eye wall. This ring produces very heavy rains and tremendous winds. Farther from the center, bands of heavy clouds and rain spiral inward toward the eye.

Effects of Hurricanes

A hurricane can pound a coast with huge waves and sweep the land with strong winds and heavy rains. The storms cause damage and dangerous conditions in several ways. Hurricane winds can lift cars, uproot trees, and tear the roofs off buildings. Hurricanes may also produce tornadoes that cause even more damage. Heavy rains from hurricanes may make rivers overflow their banks and flood nearby areas. When a hurricane moves into a coastal area, it often pushes a huge mass of ocean water known as a **storm surge.** In a storm surge, the sea level rises several meters, backing up rivers and flooding the shore. A storm surge can be destructive and deadly. Large waves add to the destruction. A hurricane may affect an area for a few hours or a few days, but the damage may take weeks or even months to clean up.

⬤ **CHECK YOUR READING** What are the effects of hurricanes? Make a list for your answer.

The National Hurricane Center helps people know when to prepare for a hurricane. The center puts out a tropical-storm or hurricane watch when a storm is likely to strike within 36 hours. People may be evacuated, or moved away for safety, from areas where they may be in danger. As the danger gets closer—24 hours or less—the center issues a tropical-storm or hurricane warning. The warning stays in effect until the danger has passed.

⚠ **SAFETY TIPS**

HURRICANES

- Before a storm, prepare a plan to leave the area. Gather emergency supplies.
- Listen to weather reports for storm updates.
- Secure loose objects outside, and cover windows.
- If ordered to evacuate, leave immediately.
- During a storm, stay indoors and away from windows.
- After a storm, be aware of power lines, hanging branches, and flooded areas.

This photograph shows New Orleans, Louisiana, after it was hit by Hurricane Katrina in August 2005. The hurricane's storm surge flooded part of the city and also weakened several levees, or earthen dams. Most of the flooding happened after levees broke and allowed water from a nearby lake to pour Into the city.

Winter storms produce snow and ice.

Most severe winter storms in the United States are part of low-pressure systems. Unlike hurricanes, the systems that cause winter storms form when two air masses collide. A continental polar air mass that forms over snow-covered ground is especially cold, dry, and dense. It can force moist air to rise very quickly, producing a stormy low-pressure system.

The National Weather Service (NWS) alerts people to dangerous weather. The NWS issues a winter storm watch up to 48 hours before a storm is expected. A winter storm warning means that dangerous conditions are already present or will affect an area shortly.

Blizzards Strong winds can blow so much snow into the air at once that it becomes difficult to see and dangerous to travel. **Blizzards** are blinding snowstorms with winds of at least 56 kilometers per hour (35 mi/h) and low temperatures—usually below −7°C (20°F). Blizzards occur in many parts of the northern and central United States. Wind and snow can knock down trees and power lines. Without heat, buildings can become very cold, and water in pipes may freeze. Schools, hospitals, and businesses may have to close. Deep, heavy snow on top of a building may cause the roof to cave in.

Lake-Effect Snowstorms Some of the heaviest snows fall in the areas just east and south of the Great Lakes. Cold air from the northwest gains moisture and warmth as it passes over the Great Lakes. Over cold land, the air cools again and releases the moisture as snow. The lake effect can cover areas downwind of the Great Lakes with clouds and snow even when the rest of the region has clear weather.

VOCABULARY
Remember to add a word triangle diagram for *blizzard*.

INVESTIGATE Ice

Why put salt on icy roads?

PROCEDURE

1. Place one ice cube in each cup.
2. Sprinkle salt onto the top of one of the ice cubes and observe the cubes for several minutes.

WHAT DO YOU THINK?

- Which ice cube melted more?
- Why do people put salt on roads in winter?

CHALLENGE Why do people put sand or cinders on icy roads? Design an experiment to test your ideas.

SKILL FOCUS
Observing

MATERIALS
- 2 ice cubes
- 2 cups
- table salt

TIME
10 minutes

SAFETY TIPS

WINTER STORMS

- Before a storm, prepare emergency kits for home and car.

- Listen to weather reports for updates.

- If caught in a storm, find or make a shelter and try to stay dry.

- If you are in a car or truck, make sure the exhaust pipe is clear and open a window a little bit.

- Use a colored cloth, fire, or light to help rescuers find you.

- Exercise a little to keep warm and keep blood flowing to your fingers and toes.

- If at home, stay inside even if there is no heat or power. Wear layers of clothing.

Ice Storms When rain falls onto freezing-cold ground, conditions can become dangerous. The cold rain freezes as it touches the ground and other surfaces. This freezing rain covers everything with heavy, smooth ice. The ice-covered roads become slippery and dangerous. Drivers may find it hard to steer and to stop their cars. Branches or even whole trees may break from the weight of ice. Falling branches can block roads, tear down power and telephone lines, and cause other damage. Damage from ice storms can sometimes shut down entire cities.

CHECK YOUR READING What type of precipitation occurs in each type of winter storm?

3.2 Review

KEY CONCEPTS

1. Where and when do hurricanes form?

2. In what two ways can hurricanes cause floods?

3. List three of the possible dangers from winter storms.

CRITICAL THINKING

4. **Compare and Contrast** What are the differences between the eye and the eye wall of a hurricane?

5. **Compare** What do hurricanes and winter storms have in common?

CHALLENGE

6. **Apply** If the wind is blowing from the west and the conditions are right for lake-effect snow, will the snow fall to the north, south, east, or west of a lake? Drawing a diagram may help you work out an answer.

3.3 Vertical air motion can cause severe storms.

BEFORE, you learned	NOW, you will learn
• Fronts produce changes in weather • Rising moist air can produce clouds and precipitation	• How thunderstorms develop • About the effects of thunderstorms • About tornadoes and their effects

VOCABULARY

thunderstorm p. 92
tornado p. 95

EXPLORE Lightning

Does miniature lightning cause thunder?

PROCEDURE

1. Use a thumbtack to attach the eraser to the center of a piece of foil.

2. Rub the foam tray quickly back and forth several times on the wool. Set the tray down.

3. Using the eraser as a handle, pick up the foil and set it onto the tray. Slowly move your finger close to the foil.

WHAT DO YOU THINK?
What happened when you touched the foil?

MATERIALS
• thumbtack
• eraser
• aluminum foil
• plastic foam tray
• wool fabric

Thunderstorms form from rising moist air.

If you have ever shuffled your shoes on a carpet, you may have felt a small shock when you touched a doorknob. Electrical charges collected on your body and then jumped to the doorknob in a spark of electricity.

In a similar way, electrical charges build up near the tops and bottoms of clouds as pellets of ice move up and down through the clouds. Suddenly, a charge sparks from one part of a cloud to another or between a cloud and the ground. The spark of electricity, called lightning, causes a bright flash of light. The air around the lightning is briefly heated to a temperature hotter than the surface of the Sun. This fast heating produces a sharp wave of air that travels away from the lightning. When the wave reaches you, you hear it as a crack of thunder. A **thunderstorm** is a storm with lightning and thunder.

VOCABULARY
Put new terms into a word triangle diagram.

CHECK YOUR READING Is thunder a cause or an effect of lightning?

Formation of Thunderstorms

Thunderstorms get their energy from humid air. When warm, humid air near the ground moves vertically into cooler air above, the rising air, or updraft, can build a thunderstorm quickly.

❶ Rising humid air forms a cumulus cloud. The water vapor releases energy when it condenses into cloud droplets. This energy increases the air motion. The cloud continues building up into the tall cumulonimbus cloud of a thunderstorm.

❷ Ice particles form in the low temperatures near the top of the cloud. As the ice particles grow large, they begin to fall and pull cold air down with them. This strong downdraft brings heavy rain or hail—the most severe stage of a thunderstorm.

❸ The downdraft can spread out and block more warm air from moving upward into the cloud. The storm slows down and ends.

Thunderstorms can form at a cold front or within an air mass. At a cold front, air can be forced upward quickly. Within an air mass, uneven heating can produce convection and thunderstorms. In some regions, the conditions that produce thunderstorms occur almost daily during part of the year. In Florida, for example, the wet land and air warm up during a long summer day. Then, as you see in the diagram, cool sea breezes blow in from both coasts of the peninsula at once. The two sea breezes together push the warm, humid air over the land upward quickly. Thunderstorms form in the rising air.

In contrast, the summer air along the coast of California is usually too dry to produce thunderstorms. The air over the land heats up, and a sea breeze forms, but there is not enough moisture in the rising warm air to form clouds and precipitation.

sea breeze

FLORIDA

sea breeze

warm air

INVESTIGATE Updrafts

How do updrafts form?

PROCEDURE

1. Set up the cardboard, the cups, the container, and the cool water as shown in the photograph. Wait for the water to become still.

2. Use the eyedropper to place 2–3 drops of coloring at the bottom of the water.

3. Slide a cup of hot water (about 70°C) beneath the food coloring.

WHAT DO YOU THINK?

In what ways was the motion of the water like the air in a thunderstorm?

CHALLENGE How could you observe updrafts in air?

SKILL FOCUS
Inferring

MATERIALS
- 4 cardboard squares
- 5 foam cups
- clear container
- cool water
- food coloring
- eyedropper
- hot tap water

TIME
20 minutes

Effects of Thunderstorms

A thunderstorm may provide cool rain at the end of a hot, dry spell. The rain can provide water for crops and restore lakes and streams. However, thunderstorms are often dangerous.

Flash floods can be strong enough to wash away people, cars, and even houses. One thunderstorm can produce millions of liters of rain. If a thunderstorm dumps all its rain in one place, or if a series of thunderstorms dump rain onto the same area, the water can cover the ground or make rivers overflow their banks.

Winds from a thunderstorm can be very strong. They can blow in bursts that exceed 270 kilometers per hour (170 mi/hr). Thunderstorm winds once knocked down a stretch of forest in Canada that was about 16 kilometers (10 mi) wide and 80 kilometers (50 mi) long. Thunderstorms can also produce sudden, dangerous bursts of air that move downward and spread out.

Hail causes nearly $1 billion in damage to property and crops in the United States every year. Hail can wipe out entire fields of a valuable crop in a few minutes. Large hailstones can damage roofs and kill livestock.

Lightning can kill or seriously injure any person it hits. It can damage power lines and other equipment. Lightning can also spark dangerous forest fires.

CHECK YOUR READING In what ways are thunderstorms dangerous? Did any surprise you?

⚠ SAFETY TIPS

THUNDERSTORMS

- Stay alert when storms are predicted or dark, tall clouds are visible.

- If you hear thunder, seek shelter immediately and stay there for 30 minutes after the last thunder ends.

- Avoid bodies of water, lone trees, flagpoles, and metal objects.

- Stay away from the telephone, electrical appliances, and pipes.

- If flash floods are expected, move away from low ground.

- Do not try to cross flowing water, even if it looks shallow.

Tornadoes form in severe thunderstorms.

Under some conditions, the up-and-down air motion that produces tall clouds, lightning, and hail may produce a tornado. A **tornado** is a violently rotating column of air stretching from a cloud to the ground. A tornado moves along the ground in a winding path underneath the cloud. The column may even rise off the ground and then come down in a different place.

READING **TiP**

A spinning column of air is not called a tornado unless it touches the ground. If it touches water instead, it is called a waterspout.

You cannot see air moving. A tornado may become visible when water droplets appear below the cloud in the center of the rotating column. A tornado may lift dust and debris from the ground, so the bottom of the column becomes visible, as you see in the photographs below. Water droplets and debris may make a tornado look like an upright column or a twisted rope.

 **CHECK YOUR READING** What makes a tornado become visible?

More tornadoes occur in North America than anywhere else in the world. Warm, humid air masses move north from the Gulf of Mexico to the central plains of the United States. There, the warm air masses often meet cold, dense air and form thunderstorms. In the spring, the winds in this region often produce the conditions that form tornadoes. A thunderstorm may form a series of tornadoes or even a group of tornadoes all at once.

Tornado Formation

As a tornado forms, a funnel cloud seems to stretch down from the cloud above.

The bottom becomes visible as the tornado picks up dust from the ground.

The tornado moves along the ground before it dies out.

Effects of Tornadoes

The powerful winds of a tornado can cause damage as the bottom of the tornado moves along the ground. Tornado winds can also pick up and slam dirt and small objects into buildings or anything else in the tornado's path.

The most common tornadoes are small and last only a few minutes. Their winds may be strong enough to break branches off trees, damage chimneys, and tear highway billboards. A typical path along the ground may be 100 meters (300 ft) wide and 1.5 kilometers (1 mi) long.

Larger tornadoes are less common but have stronger winds and last longer. About 20 percent of tornadoes are strong enough to knock over large trees, lift cars off the ground, and tear the roofs off houses. Very few—about 1 percent of all tornadoes—are violent enough to lift or completely demolish sturdy buildings. These huge tornadoes may last more than two hours. You can find more details about tornadoes in the Appendix.

Paths of Tornadoes

A tornado moves along with its thunderstorm. It travels at the same pace and weaves a path that is impossible to predict. A tornado may appear suddenly and then disappear before anyone has time to report it. However, the conditions that form tornadoes may persist, so citizens' reports are still useful. The National Weather Service issues a tornado watch when the weather conditions might produce tornadoes. A tornado warning is issued when a tornado has been detected.

⚠ SAFETY TIPS

TORNADOES

- Listen for tornado warnings when severe weather is predicted.
- If you are in a car or mobile home, get out and go into a sturdy building or a ditch or depression.
- Go to the basement if possible.
- Avoid windows and open areas.
- Protect your head and neck.

3.3 Review

KEY CONCEPTS

1. What conditions produce thunderstorms?
2. How can rain from thunderstorms become dangerous?
3. How do tornadoes cause damage?

CRITICAL THINKING

4. **Compare** What do hail and tornadoes have in common? **Hint:** Think about how each forms.
5. **Synthesize** Which type of front is most likely to produce thunderstorms and tornadoes? Explain why.

⚠ CHALLENGE

6. **Compare and Contrast** If you saw the photograph above in a newspaper, what details would tell you that the damage was due to a tornado and not a hurricane?

What Type of Weather Buried This Truck?

This picture was taken soon after a weather event partly buried this truck in Britannia Beach, British Columbia.

▶ Observations and Inferences

One observer made this analysis.

a. The truck, the tree, and two fences in the background were partly buried by sand and stones.

b. No stones are visible inside the truck.

c. The rounded stones must have come from an ocean or river.

d. The tree near the truck has green leaves. The wind must have been too weak to tear off the leaves.

e. The area is near the Pacific Ocean. It is far from the equator. There is a very large island between the location and the ocean.

▶ Hypotheses

The observer made the following hypotheses.

a. A storm surge carried sand and stones from the Pacific Ocean. The material covered a large area. The truck floated, so it was not filled with material.

b. A tornado picked up the truck with other material. It dumped everything together, and the material partly buried the truck, fences, and tree.

c. Thunderstorms produced a flash flood that carried sand and stones from a riverbed to this area. The flood receded and left material that covered the area.

d. The truck was parked on a pile of snow during a blizzard. When the snow melted, the area under the truck collapsed and the truck sank into the ground.

BRITISH COLUMBIA

Britannia Beach

PACIFIC OCEAN

Vancouver Island

A waterway leads south and west from Britannia Beach to a bay, around an island, to the Pacific Ocean.

▶ Evaluate Each Hypothesis

Review each hypothesis and think about whether the observations support it. Some facts may rule out some hypotheses. Some facts may neither support nor weaken some hypotheses.

CHALLENGE How could you model one or more of the hypotheses with a toy truck, sand, and a basin of water?

3.4 Weather forecasters use advanced technologies.

BEFORE, you learned	NOW, you will learn
• Weather changes when air masses move • High-pressure systems bring fair weather • Fronts and low-pressure systems bring stormy weather	• How weather data are collected • How weather data are displayed • How meteorologists forecast the weather

VOCABULARY

meteorologist p. 98
isobar p. 101

EXPLORE Weather Maps

What does a weather map show?

PROCEDURE

(1) Look at the weather outside. Write down the conditions you observe.

(2) Use the map to check the weather conditions for your region.

WHAT DO YOU THINK?

• What symbols on the map do you recognize?
• How does the information on the weather map compare with the weather you observed outside?

MATERIALS

newspaper
weather map

Weather data come from many sources.

Looking at the weather outside in the morning can help you decide what to wear. Different things give you clues to the current weather. If you see plants swaying from side to side, you might infer that it is windy. If you see a gray sky and wet, shiny streets, you might decide to wear a raincoat.

You might also check a weather report to get more information. A weather report can show conditions in your area and also in the region around you. You can look for weather nearby that might move into your area during the day. More detailed predictions of how the weather will move and change may be included in a weather report by a meteorologist. A **meteorologist** (MEE-tee-uh-RAHL-uh-jihst) is a scientist who studies weather.

VOCABULARY
Make a word triangle for *meteorologist*.

CHECK YOUR READING   What information can a weather report show?

In order to predict the weather, meteorologists look at past and current conditions. They use many forms of technology to gather data. The illustration below shows how weather information is gathered. For example, radar stations and satellites use advanced technologies to gather data for large areas at a time.

Instruments within the atmosphere can make measurements of local weather conditions. Newer instruments can make measurements frequently and automatically and then report the results almost instantly. Instruments are placed in many ground stations on land and weather buoys at sea. Instruments can also be carried by balloons, ships, and planes. These instruments report a series of measurements along a path within the atmosphere.

RESOURCE CENTER
CLASSZONE.COM
Learn more about weather forecasting and your local weather.

Collection of Weather Data

Instruments that gather weather data use many technologies and can be found in many places.

Satellites orbit Earth above the atmosphere. Images can show cloud cover, warm and cool regions, and invisible water vapor.

Radar stations locate clouds and measure their heights. Doppler radar, a special type of equipment, can detect air motion and precipitation.

Airplanes and ships can carry instrument packages that make measurements wherever they go.

Weather balloons make important measurements of the air at different altitudes as they carry instruments high into the stratosphere.

Ground stations hold instruments that measure air pressure, temperature, dew point, precipitation, wind speed, wind direction, and cloud cover.

Weather buoys record the weather far from cities. They also measure conditions in the ocean that affect the atmosphere.

READING VISUALS Which two of these sources report conditions for wide areas?

Meteorologists use maps to display a lot of weather information at once.

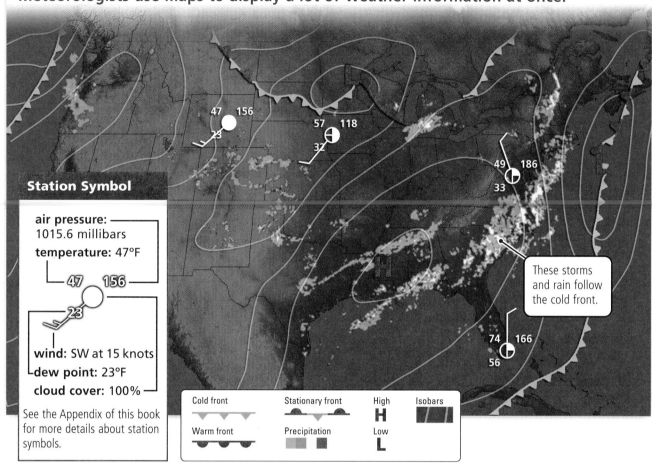

Station Symbol

air pressure:
1015.6 millibars

temperature: 47°F

47   156

23

wind: SW at 15 knots

dew point: 23°F

cloud cover: 100%

See the Appendix of this book for more details about station symbols.

These storms and rain follow the cold front.

Cold front

Warm front

Stationary front

Precipitation

High **H**

Low **L**

Isobars

Weather data can be displayed on maps.

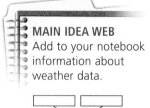

MAIN IDEA WEB
Add to your notebook information about weather data.

Automatic measurements from many sources constantly pour in to the National Oceanic and Atmospheric Administration. Scientists use computers to record and use the enormous amount of data gathered. One way to make the information easier to understand is to show it on maps. A single map can show many different types of data together to give a more complete picture of the weather. The map above combines information from ground stations with Doppler radar measurements of precipitation.

• Precipitation is shown as patches of blue, green, yellow, and red. The colors indicate the amounts of rain or other precipitation.

• Station symbols on the map show data from ground stations. Only a few stations are shown.

• Symbols showing fronts and pressure patterns are added to the map to make the overall weather patterns easier to see.

CHECK YOUR READING How is information from Doppler radar shown?

Computer programs are used to combine information from many ground stations. The resulting calculations give the highs, lows, and fronts that are marked on the map. The cold front near the East Coast has triangles to show that the front is moving eastward. This cold front produced the heavy rain that is visible in the Doppler radar data.

Air Pressure on Weather Maps

The map below shows conditions from the same date as the map on page 100. Thin lines represent air pressure. An **isobar** (EYE-suh-BAHR) is a line that connects places that have the same air pressure. Each isobar represents a different air pressure value. All the isobars together, combined with the symbols for highs and lows, show the patterns of air pressure that produce weather systems.

Each isobar is labeled with the air pressure for that whole line in units called millibars (MIHL-uh-BAHRZ). A lower number means a lower air pressure. As you read earlier, differences in pressure cause air to move. Meteorologists use isobars to understand air motion.

Sometimes air-pressure measurements are listed in inches of mercury. This unit comes from an old type of barometer that measures how high the air pressure pushes a column of mercury, a liquid metal. Computer-controlled instruments are used more often today, but the measurements may be converted to inches of mercury.

READING TiP

Iso- means "equal," and *bar* means "pressure."

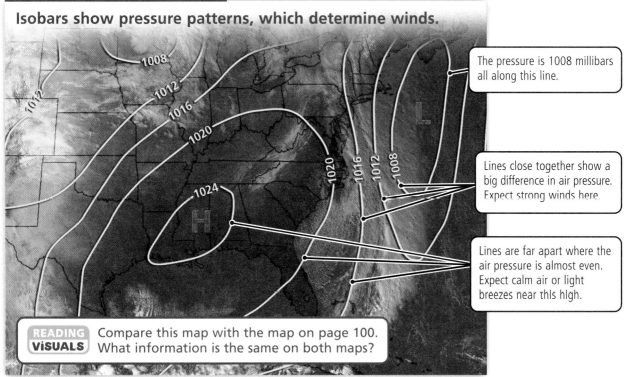

Understanding Isobars

Isobars show pressure patterns, which determine winds.

The pressure is 1008 millibars all along this line.

Lines close together show a big difference in air pressure. Expect strong winds here.

Lines are far apart where the air pressure is almost even. Expect calm air or light breezes near this high.

READING VISUALS Compare this map with the map on page 100. What information is the same on both maps?

Visible Light

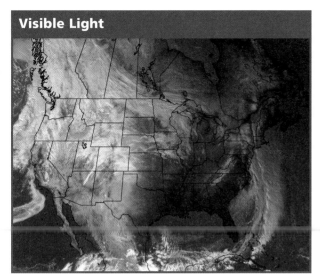

Infrared Radiation

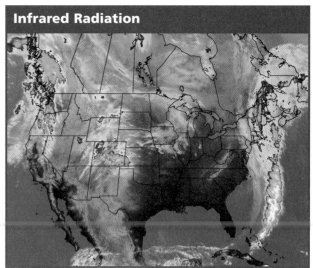

This visible-light satellite image shows clouds from above. The patches of white are clouds.

This infrared satellite image also shows clouds, but uses colors to show where there are tall clouds.

READING VISUALS Find a location on these maps and the map on page 100. What were the weather conditions?

Satellite Images and Special Maps

Satellites take different types of images from space. Some images record the visible light that reflects off clouds and Earth's surface. Clouds and snow-covered land look white in sunlight. Unfortunately, visible-light images do not show much at night.

Another type of image shows infrared radiation given off by the warm surface and cooler clouds. These infrared images can show cloud patterns even at night because objects with different temperatures show up differently. Air temperatures change with altitude, so infrared images also show which clouds are low and which are high or tall. You can see in the maps above how visible and infrared satellite images show similar clouds but different details. Outlines of the states have been added to make the images easier to understand.

Data from ground stations and other sources can be used to make other types of maps. The map at left shows the pattern of temperatures on the same date as the images above and the map on page 100. Other maps may show winds or amounts of pollution. A map can be made to show any type of measurement or weather prediction. Different types of maps are often used together to give a more complete picture of the current weather.

The colors on this map represent different ranges of temperature (°F).

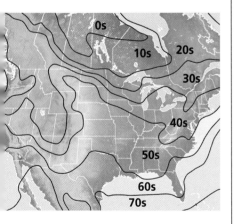

CHECK YOUR READING Why would a weather report show more than one map?

Forecasters use computer models to predict weather.

Instruments can only measure the current weather conditions. Most people want to know what the weather will be like in the future.

Forecasters can make some predictions from their own observations. If they see cirrus clouds above and high stratus clouds to the west, they might infer that a warm front is approaching. They would predict weather typical for a warm front—more clouds, then rain, and eventually warmer weather. If they also have information from other places, the forecasters might be able to tell where the warm front is already and how fast it is moving. They might be able to predict how soon it will arrive and even how warm the weather will be after the front passes.

Computers have become an important tool for forecasting weather. When weather stations send in data, computers can create maps right away. Computer models combine many types of data to forecast what might happen next. Different computer models give different types of forecasts. Scientists study the computer forecasts, then apply their knowledge and experience to make weather predictions.

Forecasting the weather is complicated. As a result, some forecasts are more dependable than others. The farther in advance a forecast is made, the more time there is for small differences between the predicted and the actual weather to add up. For this reason, short-range forecasts—up to three days in advance—are the most accurate. Forecasts of fast-changing weather, such as severe storms, are less accurate far in advance. It is best to watch for new predictions close to the time the storm is forecast.

Forecasters use maps and satellite images to communicate weather conditions and predictions.

3.4 Review

KEY CONCEPTS

1. List three of the sources of weather data.
2. What does a map with isobars show?
3. How do meteorologists use computers?

CRITICAL THINKING

4. **Draw Conclusions** Why do meteorologists not combine all their weather information into one map?
5. **Analyze** How is the information from radar and satellites different from the information from ground stations?

⬥ CHALLENGE

6. **Apply** Suppose you are planning an afternoon picnic a week in advance. Fair weather is forecast for that day, but a storm is expected that night. What will you do? Explain your reasoning.

CHAPTER INVESTIGATION

Design a Weather Center

OVERVIEW AND PURPOSE The accuracy of a weather forecast depends largely on the type and quality of the data that it is based on. In this lab, you will use what you have learned about weather to

- observe and measure weather conditions
- record and analyze the weather-related data

▶ Procedure

1. Survey the possible sources of weather data in and around your classroom. You can use a thermometer to record the outside air temperature. You can observe cloud types and the amount of cloud cover from a window or doorway. You can also observe precipitation and notice if it is heavy or light. If there is a flag in view, use it to find the wind direction and to estimate wind speed.

2. Assemble or make tools for your observations. You may want to make a reference chart with pictures of different cloud types or other information. Decide if you wish to use homemade weather instruments. You may have made a barometer, a psychrometer, and a rain gauge already. If not, see the instructions on pages 45, 64, and 67. You may also wish to do research to learn how to make or use other weather instruments.

3. Make an initial set of observations. Write down the date and time in your **Science Notebook.** Record the readings from the thermometer and other instruments.

MATERIALS
- thermometer
- magnetic compass
- other weather instruments
- graph paper

4 Decide how to record your observations of the clouds, the wind, and any precipitation. Organize your notes to make it easy for you to record later observations in a consistent way.

5 Create a chart with a row for each type of observation you are making. You might darken fractions of circles to record amounts of cloud cover, as in the station symbols on page 100. Make sure each row has a heading and enough room for numbers, words, or sketches. Include a row for notes that do not belong in the data rows.

6 Record your observations every day at the same time. Try to make the observations exactly the same way each time. If you have to redraw your chart, copy the information carefully.

▶ Observe and Analyze

1. **GRAPH** Graph the data you collected that represent measurable quantities. Use graphs that are appropriate to your data. Often a simple line graph will work. Choose an appropriate scale and interval based on the range of your data. Make the x-axis of each graph the same so that you can compare the different types of data easily.

2. **COMPARE AND CONTRAST** Look at your graphs for patterns in your data. Some aspects of weather change at the same time because they are related to each other. Did one type of change occur before a different type of change? If so, this pattern may help you predict weather.

▶ Conclude

1. **INTERPRET** Did a front pass through your area during the period you observed? What observations helped you answer this question?

2. **EVALUATE** Why was it necessary to observe at the same time each day?

3. **APPLY** If you predicted that each day's weather would be repeated the next day, how often would you be right?

▶ INVESTIGATE Further

CHALLENGE Locate a newspaper weather page for the period during which you were making your weather observations. How do the weather data reported for your area compare with your measurements? How do you account for any differences you notice in the data?

Design a Weather Center

Table 1. Daily Weather Chart

Date/time of observations			
Temperature (°C)			
Cloud types			
Cloud coverage	○	○	○
Precipitation (cm) and notes			
Wind direction			
Other notes			

Chapter Review

the **BIG** idea

The interaction of air masses causes changes in weather.

CONTENT REVIEW
CLASSZONE.COM

◀ KEY CONCEPTS SUMMARY

3.1 Weather changes as air masses move.

Air masses meet and produce **fronts,** which can bring lowered pressure and stormy weather. Fronts can be cold, warm, or stationary.

VOCABULARY
air mass p. 79
front p. 82
high-pressure system p. 84
low-pressure system p. 85

3.2 Low-pressure systems can become storms.

Hurricanes and winter storms develop from low-pressure systems.

Hurricanes form over warm ocean water.

VOCABULARY
tropical storm p. 87
hurricane p. 87
storm surge p. 89
blizzard p. 90

3.3 Vertical air motion can cause severe storms.

Rising moist air can produce **thunderstorms.** The up-and-down motion of air in a thunderstorm can produce a **tornado.**

VOCABULARY
thunderstorm p. 92
tornado p. 95

3.4 Weather forecasters use advanced technologies.

Weather information comes from many sources.

Meteorologists use weather data and computer models to forecast weather.

VOCABULARY
meteorologist p. 98
isobar p. 101

Reviewing Vocabulary

Describe each term below, using the related term as part of the description.

Term	Related Term	Description
EXAMPLE hurricane	low-pressure system	a low-pressure system in the tropics with winds at least 120 km/h
1. front	air mass	
2. low-pressure system	low-pressure center	
3. storm surge	hurricane	
4. tropical storm	low-pressure system	
5. air mass	humidity	
6. thunderstorm	convection	
7. tornado	thunderstorm	
8. blizzard	low-pressure system	

Reviewing Key Concepts

Multiple Choice *Choose the letter of the best answer.*

9. What qualities are nearly the same at different locations in a single air mass?
- **a.** temperature and pressure
- **b.** temperature and humidity
- **c.** air pressure and wind speed
- **d.** air pressure and humidity

10. Which is the name for an air mass that forms over the ocean near the equator?
- **a.** maritime tropical
- **b.** maritime polar
- **c.** continental tropical
- **d.** continental polar

11. A meteorologist is a scientist who
- **a.** predicts meteor showers
- **b.** studies maps
- **c.** studies the weather
- **d.** changes the weather

12. An isobar shows locations with the same
- **a.** temperature
- **b.** rainfall
- **c.** air pressure
- **d.** wind speed

13. Which is produced when a warm air mass pushes a colder air mass?
- **a.** a stationary front
- **b.** a cold front
- **c.** a warm front
- **d.** a thunderstorm

14. Which can be measured in inches of mercury?
- **a.** air pressure
- **b.** temperature
- **c.** hail
- **d.** lightning

15. Which source provides measurements for just one location?
- **a.** ground station
- **b.** radar station
- **c.** weather balloon
- **d.** satellite

16. Compared with warm fronts, cold fronts are
- **a.** faster moving
- **b.** less dense
- **c.** more cloudy
- **d.** less steep

17. Which statement is usually true of high-pressure systems in North America?
- **a.** They bring fair weather.
- **b.** They change quickly.
- **c.** The air in them is cold and dense.
- **d.** The air in them moves counterclockwise.

18. Thunderstorms often begin with the rising of
- **a.** cool, dry air
- **b.** cool, humid air
- **c.** warm, dry air
- **d.** warm, humid air

19. What is the relationship between lightning and thunder?
- **a.** They have separate causes.
- **b.** They have the same cause.
- **c.** Lightning causes thunder.
- **d.** Thunder causes lightning.

Short Answer *Write a short answer to each question.*

20. Why are hurricanes in the eastern United States more likely in autumn than in spring?

21. What causes lake-effect snow?

22. In what four ways can thunderstorms be dangerous?

Thinking Critically

Use this weather map to answer the next six questions. The numbers under each city name are the highest and the lowest temperature for the day in degrees Fahrenheit.

23. **INFER** Name and describe the air mass that has moved south to Omaha from Canada.

24. **IDENTIFY EFFECTS** How are two low-pressure systems affecting the weather near Boston?

25. **PREDICT** Explain whether Washington, D.C., or Orlando is more likely to have a big change in weather in the next two days.

26. **COMPARE AND CONTRAST** Explain the difference in temperature between Oklahoma City and Little Rock.

27. **PREDICT** How will the weather in Little Rock change in the next day or two?

28. **APPLY** Does this map indicate that it is hurricane season? Explain your reasoning.

29. **CONNECT** Describe today's weather and explain what fronts and pressure systems might be influencing it.

30. **COMPARE AND CONTRAST** Use a Venn diagram to compare images from visible light and infrared radiation.

PREDICT *For each set of conditions listed in the chart, write a weather prediction.*

Conditions	Prediction
31. A cold front is moving into an area that has warm, moist air.	
32. A warm front is moving into an area that has cold, dense air.	
33. A cool sea breeze is blowing inland, causing warm, humid air to rise.	
34. Air pressure is falling and the temperature is rising.	
35. Air pressure is increasing and the temperature is steady.	
36. A thunderstorm is developing spinning winds at its center.	
37. A low-pressure center is over the Atlantic Ocean where the water temperature is above 27°C (81°F).	
38. Cold air is pushing warm air where the air is 2°C (36°F) and the ground is -3°C (27°F).	

39. **COMPARE** How is the air motion in the eye of a hurricane similar to the air motion at a high-pressure center?

40. **EVALUATE** Which type of storm is most dangerous? Explain your reasoning.

the BIG idea

41. **APPLY** Look again at the photograph on pages 76–77. Now that you have finished the chapter, how would you change your response to the question on the photograph?

42. **SEQUENCE** Draw a storyboard with at least four sketches to show how cool, sunny weather might change into warm, rainy weather.

UNIT PROJECTS

Check your schedule for your unit project. How are you doing? Be sure that you have placed data or notes from your research in your project folder.

Analyzing a Map

Use this weather map to answer the questions below.

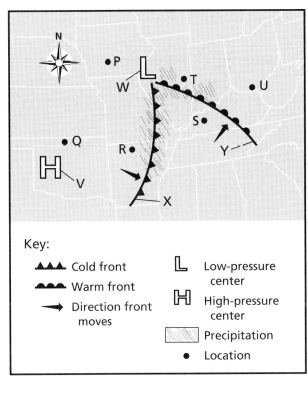

Key:

▲▲▲ Cold front

●●● Warm front

→ Direction front moves

L Low-pressure center

H High-pressure center

▨ Precipitation

● Location

1. Which letter labels a cold front?

  a. Q   **c.** X

  b. U   **d.** Y

2. Which word best describes the general movement of the fronts?

  a. to the north   **c.** clockwise

  b. to the east   **d.** counterclockwise

3. A warm front occurs where warm air moves into colder air. Which of these locations is probably warmest?

  a. R   **c.** T

  b. S   **d.** U

4. Temperatures usually change quickly near a front and more slowly away from a front. The temperature at Q is 10°C (50°F). The temperature at S is 20°C (68°F). Which is the best estimate for the temperature at R?

  a. 6°C (43°F)   **c.** 20°C (68°F)

  b. 11°C (52°F)   **d.** 24°C (75°F)

5. If the fronts continue to move as shown, which location will get warmer soon?

  a. Q   **c.** S

  b. R   **d.** T

6. Low pressure often brings stormy weather, and high pressure often brings fair weather. Which of these locations is most likely to have clear skies?

  a. Q   **c.** S

  b. R   **d.** U

Extended Response

Use the map above to answer the two questions below in detail. Include some of the terms shown in the word box. Underline each term you use in your answers.

cold front	humid	west
warm front	east	prevailing winds

7. Along which front on the weather map above would you expect to find cumulonimbus clouds? Explain why.

8. The weather system shown on the map above is in the continental United States. In which direction do you expect it to move? Explain why.

TIMELINES in Science

OBSERVING THE ATMOSPHERE

The atmosphere is always changing, and scientists are developing better ways to observe these changes. Accurate weather forecasts help people make everyday decisions, such as what kind of clothing to wear. Forecasts also allow us to plan for dangerous storms and other natural disasters. Scientists are now warning of long-term changes to the atmosphere that can affect the entire world. These predictions are possible because of the work of scientists and observers over hundreds of years.

The timeline shows some historical events in the study of Earth's air and weather. The boxes below the timeline show how technology has led to new knowledge about the atmosphere and show how that knowledge has been applied.

1686

Trade Winds Are Linked to Sun's Energy

Sailors have used trade winds for centuries to sail from Europe to the Americas. Now, Edmund Halley, a British astronomer, explains global winds in a new theory. He argues that trade winds blowing toward the equator replace air that rises due to solar heating.

EVENTS

| | 1640 | 1660 | 1680 |

APPLICATIONS AND TECHNOLOGY

TECHNOLOGY

Measuring Air Pressure

The mercury barometer was invented in 1643 to measure air pressure. Changes in outside air pressure cause the level of mercury to rise and fall in a tall glass tube. This remarkably accurate type of barometer was used for centuries. Now, most air-pressure measurements are taken with aneroid barometers, which are easier to use.

1804

Atmosphere Explorations Pass 7000 Meters

French chemist Joseph Louis Gay-Lussac rises to an altitude of 7016 meters in a balloon to study the atmosphere. His studies show that the atmosphere's composition remains the same up to that altitude.

1827

Atmospheric Greenhouse Warms Earth

French scientist Jean-Baptiste Fourier coins a new term, "greenhouse effect." He suggests that the atmosphere slows the movement of energy from Earth's surface out toward space. Fourier compares this effect to the way heat is trapped in a greenhouse.

1743

Franklin Tracks Storms

Benjamin Franklin tries to look at an eclipse of the Moon, but a storm blocks his view. Meanwhile, a friend in another city has a clear view during the eclipse, and soon afterward the storm arrives there. Franklin concludes that storms travel instead of forming and dying in the same place.

1740   **1760**   **1780**   **1800**   **1820**

APPLICATION

Telegraphing the Weather

The development of the telegraph in the 1800s was important for weather forecasting because it allowed observers to quickly send data to distant locations. In 1870, the U.S. government organized a system of weather observers who communicated by telegraph. This was the beginning of the National Weather Service, which at first focused on providing storm warnings for coastal regions. However, the weather reporting service was soon extended to cover the entire nation. The National Weather Service has become a crucial information agency.

1942
Pilots Find Jet Streams

Wartime pilots discover very fast winds called jet streams at high altitudes. Pilots find that the jet streams are like narrow rivers of air moving at speeds that average 180 kilometers per hour (110 mi/h).

1958
Greenhouse Gas Monitored

Carbon dioxide and other greenhouse gases are measured at Mauna Loa Observatory on the Big Island of Hawaii, 11,000 feet above sea level. Accurate measurements can be obtained from this location because it is far from cities and other human influences.

1918
Storm Fronts Explained

Norway's Jacob Bjerknes explains how large storm systems develop at the boundaries between masses of air. He calls the boundaries "fronts," comparing them to battlefronts between armies.

1900	1920	1940	1960

TECHNOLOGY

Picturing the Weather

Ground-based weather stations cannot collect data from high altitudes or from areas between stations. The development of weather technology helped fill the gaps. In the 1930s, weather balloons carried instruments to different altitudes. In 1953, the development of Doppler radar showed raindrop sizes and speeds. Scientists later began using Doppler radar to measure precipitation for a wide area all at once.

In 1960, weather satellites began to provide images of weather from space. Satellites can show hurricanes long before they hit the shore. Fifteen years later, scientists began to use instruments on satellites to detect radiation other than visible light. Infrared cameras showed clouds at night and made detailed measurements that improved forecasts.

1985
Hole Found in Ozone Layer

Using data from a ground-based instrument in Antarctica, scientists discover a large area where the protective layer of ozone is very thin. They call it the ozone hole. The discovery confirms earlier predictions that certain industrial chemicals can result in ozone destruction.

RESOURCE CENTER
CLASSZONE.COM

Learn more about current research on the atmosphere.

1980   **2000**

APPLICATION
Computer Modeling

Scientists use computers not only to collect data but also to make models of the atmosphere. Models show how the atmosphere changed in the past and how it may change in the future. As computers become faster and better, the models can be made more detailed and therefore more reliable.

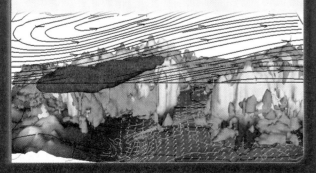

SPOTLIGHT on
WARREN WASHINGTON

Warren Washington is one of today's most distinguished atmospheric scientists. His career has spanned five decades. Throughout this time, he has been associated with the National Center for Atmospheric Research. He uses 3-d computer models to describe Earth's climate. His models consider temperature, moisture, and other geologic features. His work has led to a better understanding of the greenhouse effect and global climate change.

Dr. Washington has received many awards for his research on climate. President Bill Clinton appointed him to the National Science Board in 1995. He was elected chairman of the board in 2002 and served as chair until the end of his term in 2006.

ACTIVITIES
Reliving History

Ancient peoples made simple weather instruments, such as wind vanes. You can make a wind vane and then map the wind directions in your neighborhood.

Push a straight pin through the middle of a drinking straw and then into an eraser at the end of a pencil. Tape a square of cardboard vertically to one end of the straw. Put a small piece of clay on the other end so that the wind vane is balanced. The straw will turn so that the clay end of the straw points into the wind.

Use your wind vane and a magnetic compass to find the wind direction in several places in your neighborhood. Record the results on a copy of a map. Do you notice any patterns?

Writing About Science

Suppose scientists learn to control the weather. What factors have to be considered in choosing the weather? Write a conversation in which opposing viewpoints are debated.

Climate and Climate Change

the **BIG** idea

Climates are long-term weather patterns that may change over time.

Key Concepts

SECTION

4.1 Climate is a long-term weather pattern.
Learn about the main factors that affect climate and about seasons.

SECTION

4.2 Earth has a variety of climates.
Learn about different categories of climate.

SECTION

4.3 Climates can change suddenly or slowly.
Learn about climate changes caused by natural events and human activity.

Internet Preview

CLASSZONE.COM

Chapter 4 online resources: Content Review, Simulation, four Resource Centers, Math Tutorial, Test Practice

What evidence of different types of climate can you see in this photo?

EXPLORE (the **BIG** idea)

Why Are Climates Different?

Look at a newspaper weather map. Find some cities that usually have very different weather from the weather in your area.

Observe and Think
Where are those cities located on the map? Are they north or south of your location? What geographical differences might help make the weather in those cities different from the weather in your area?

How Do Microclimates Form?

Go outside with a thermometer and take temperature readings in four different places. Repeat your observations at a later time of day.

Observe and Think
What temperature readings did you observe? Did the readings stay the same later in the day?

Internet Activity: El Niño

Go to **ClassZone.com** to find out information about El Niño.

Observe and Think
How does El Niño affect temperature and precipitation patterns in your region?

NSTA
scilinks.org
SCI**LINKS**
What Is Climate? **Code: MDL012**

Getting Ready to Learn

◀ CONCEPT REVIEW

- Earth's atmosphere supports life.
- In a system that consists of many parts, the parts usually influence one another.
- Human activities are increasing greenhouse gases.

◀ VOCABULARY REVIEW

altitude p. 10

greenhouse gas p. 24

weather p. 47

precipitation p. 57

CONTENT REVIEW
CLASSZONE.COM
Review concepts and vocabulary.

▶ TAKING NOTES

MAIN IDEA AND DETAIL NOTES

Make a two-column chart. Write the main ideas, such as those in the blue headings, in the column on the left. Write details about each of those main ideas in the column on the right.

CHOOSE YOUR OWN STRATEGY

Take notes about new vocabulary terms, using one or more of the strategies from earlier chapters—**frame game, description wheel,** or **word triangle.** Feel free to mix and match the strategies, or use an entirely different vocabulary strategy.

See the Note-Taking Handbook on pages R45–R51.

SCIENCE NOTEBOOK

MAIN IDEAS	DETAIL NOTES
1. Latitude affects climate.	1. Places close to the equator are usually warmer than places close to the poles.
	1. Latitude has the same effect in both hemispheres.
2. Altitude affects climate.	2. Temperature decreases with altitude.
	2. Altitude can overcome the effect of latitude on temperature.

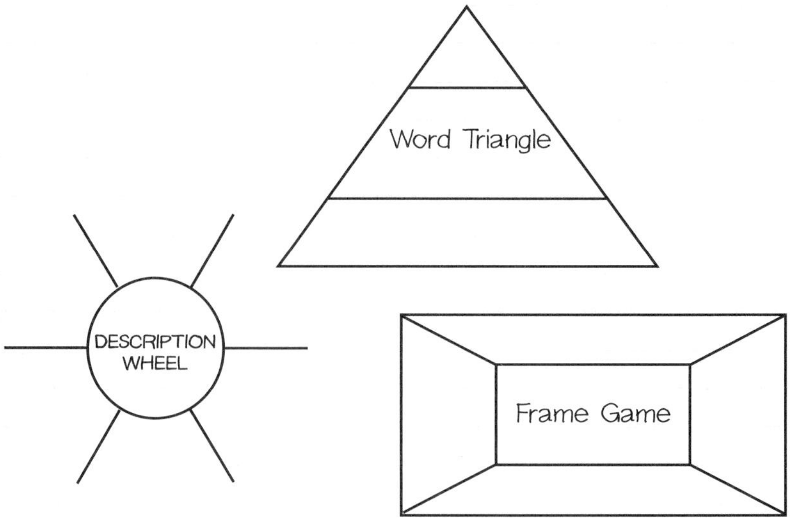

Word Triangle

DESCRIPTION WHEEL

Frame Game

4.1 Climate is a long-term weather pattern.

BEFORE, you learned

- The Sun's energy heats Earth's surface unevenly
- The atmosphere's temperature changes with altitude
- Oceans affect wind flow

NOW, you will learn

- How climate is related to weather
- What factors affect climate
- About seasonal patterns of temperature and precipitation

VOCABULARY

climate p. 117
latitude p. 118
marine climate p. 120
continental climate p. 120
ocean current p. 121
season p. 122

EXPLORE Solar Energy

How does the angle of light affect heating?

PROCEDURE

1. Tape a black square over the bulb of each thermometer. Then tape the thermometers to the cardboard tube as shown.

2. Place the arrangement on a sunny windowsill or under a lamp. One square should directly face the light. Record the temperatures.

3. Wait 10 minutes. Record the temperature changes.

WHAT DO YOU THINK?

- How did the temperature readings change?
- How did the angle of light affect the amount of heat absorbed?

MATERIALS

- tape
- 2 black paper squares
- 2 thermometers
- 1 cardboard tube from a paper towel roll
- sunny windowsill or lamp

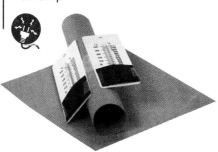

Geography affects climate.

VOCABULARY
You could use a frame game diagram to take notes about the term *climate*.

You can check your current local weather simply by looking out a window. Weather conditions may not last very long; they can change daily or even hourly. In contrast, the climate of your area changes over much longer periods of time. **Climate** is the characteristic weather conditions in a place over a long period. Climate influences the kind of clothes you own, the design of your home, and even the sports you play.

All parts of weather make up climate, including wind, humidity, and sunshine. However, meteorologists usually focus on patterns of temperature and precipitation when they classify climates. Four key geographical factors affect temperature and precipitation: latitude, altitude, distance from large bodies of water, and ocean currents.

Latitude and Temperature

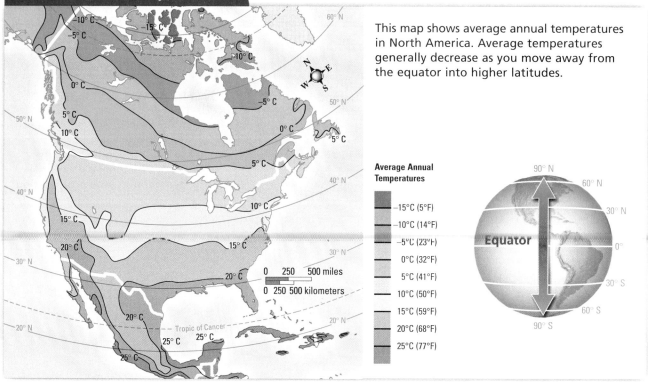

This map shows average annual temperatures in North America. Average temperatures generally decrease as you move away from the equator into higher latitudes.

Average Annual Temperatures

	−15°C (5°F)
	−10°C (14°F)
	−5°C (23°F)
	0°C (32°F)
	5°C (41°F)
	10°C (50°F)
	15°C (59°F)
	20°C (68°F)
	25°C (77°F)

Latitude

READING TIP

Notice on the globe in the illustration that latitude numbers get higher as you move away from the equator.

One factor that affects temperature is latitude. **Latitude** is the distance in degrees north or south of the equator, which is 0°. Each degree equals 1/360 of the distance around the world.

As you read in Chapter 2, the Sun heats Earth's curved surface unevenly. Sunlight strikes Earth's surface directly near the equator. Near the poles, sunlight strikes the surface at a lower angle, so it is more spread out. In addition, the polar regions receive little or no solar energy during winter.

Because of this pattern of uneven heating, average annual temperatures generally decrease as you move closer to the poles. For example, Belém, Brazil, which is almost on the equator, has an average temperature of about 26°C (79°F). Qaanaaq, Greenland, located close to the North Pole, has an average temperature of only −11°C (12°F).

Latitude has the same effect on temperature in both hemispheres. Suppose one city is located at 45° N and another city is located at 45° S. The first city is in the Northern Hemisphere, and the second is in the Southern Hemisphere. However, they are both nearly 5000 kilometers (3100 mi) from the equator, so they would receive about the same amount of sunlight over a year.

CHECK YOUR READING What is the connection between latitude and temperature?

Altitude

Altitude, the height above sea level, is another geographical factor that affects temperature. If you rode a cable car up a mountain, the temperature would decrease by about 6.5°C (11.7°F) for every kilometer you rose in altitude. Why does it get colder as you move higher up? The troposphere is mainly warmed from below by Earth's surface. As convection lifts the warmed air to higher altitudes, the air expands and cools.

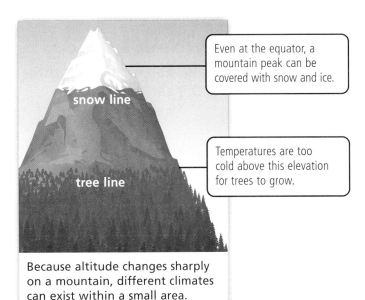

snow line

tree line

Even at the equator, a mountain peak can be covered with snow and ice.

Temperatures are too cold above this elevation for trees to grow.

Because altitude changes sharply on a mountain, different climates can exist within a small area.

Altitude increases can overcome the effect of lower latitudes on temperature. The temperature at the peak of a tall mountain is low regardless of the mountain's latitude. One example is Mount Stanley, near the border of Uganda and the Democratic Republic of the Congo in central Africa. Although it lies just a short distance from the equator, Mount Stanley has ice sheets and a permanent covering of snow. Notice in the illustration how one mountain can have several types of climates.

SIMULATION
CLASSZONE.COM

Explore the effects of latitude and altitude.

INVESTIGATE Heating and Cooling Rates

How quickly do soil and water heat and cool?

PROCEDURE

1. Mark a line 3 centimeters from the top of each cup. Fill one cup to the line with water and the other with soil. Place a thermometer into the contents of each cup. Wait 2 minutes. Record the temperature in each cup.

2. Place the cups side by side in bright sunlight or under a lamp. Wait 10 minutes. Record the temperature in each cup.

3. Move the cups into a shaded area to cool. Wait 10 minutes. Record the temperature in each cup.

WHAT DO YOU THINK?

- Which heats up faster, soil or water?
- Which cools faster?
- How might the heating and cooling rates of inland areas compare with those of coastal areas?

CHALLENGE Will adding gravel to the soil change your results? Repeat the activity to test your prediction.

SKILL FOCUS
Comparing

MATERIALS
- 2 cups
- ruler
- soil
- water at room temperature
- 2 thermometers
- sunlight or lamp

TIME
25 minutes

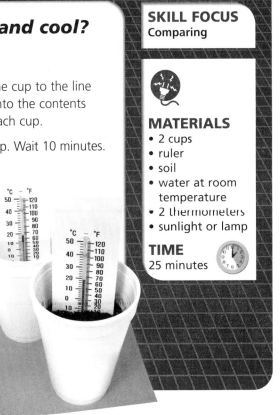

How Oceans Affect Climate

Regions near oceans have milder temperatures than inland regions at the same latitudes.

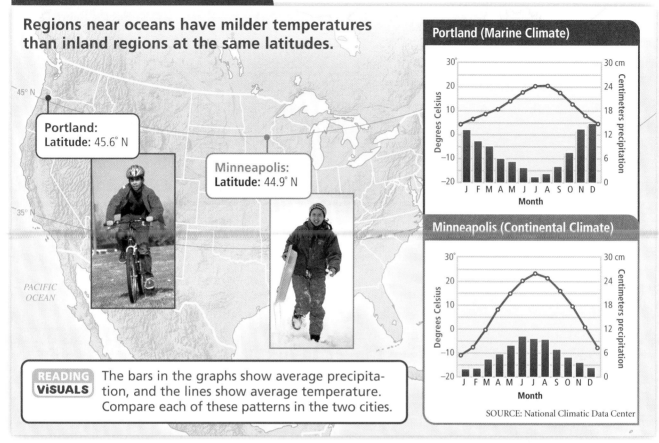

Portland:
Latitude: 45.6° N

Minneapolis:
Latitude: 44.9° N

45° N

35° N

PACIFIC
OCEAN

Portland (Marine Climate)

Degrees Celsius / Centimeters precipitation / Month

Minneapolis (Continental Climate)

Degrees Celsius / Centimeters precipitation / Month

SOURCE: National Climatic Data Center

READING VISUALS The bars in the graphs show average precipitation, and the lines show average temperature. Compare each of these patterns in the two cities.

Large Bodies of Water

Land heats up and cools off faster than water. Because oceans and large lakes slow down heating and cooling of the air, coastal regions tend to have milder temperatures than areas far inland. Large bodies of water also affect precipitation. Climates influenced by these factors are called marine and continental climates.

- **Marine climates** occur near the ocean, usually along the west coasts of continents. Temperatures do not drop very far at night. Summers and winters are mild. Many marine climates receive steady precipitation because winds blowing off the ocean bring moisture to the atmosphere. Large lakes can have a similar effect on the climates near their shores.

- **Continental climates** occur in the interior of continents. Weather patterns vary in the different types of continental climates. However, most have large differences between daytime and nighttime temperatures because they lack the influence of nearby oceans. For the same reason, winter months are usually much colder than summer months.

CHECK YOUR READING How are marine climates different from continental climates?

Ocean Currents

Ocean currents are streams of water that flow through oceans in regular patterns. They influence climates by transferring energy from one part of an ocean to another. In general, warm-water currents carry warmth from the tropics to higher latitudes, where they help keep coastal regions warm. Cold-water currents have the opposite effect. They cool coastal regions by carrying cold water from polar regions toward the equator.

The illustration below shows the paths of ocean currents in the North Atlantic. Find the Gulf Stream on the illustration. The Gulf Stream is a major warm-water current. As the waters that feed the Gulf Stream pass near the Caribbean Sea and the Gulf of Mexico, the concentrated solar rays that strike there warm its water. Water flowing in the Gulf Stream can be 6°C to 10°C (11–18°F) warmer than the surrounding water. The Gulf Stream warms the winds that blow over it. In turn, those winds warm coastal regions.

Like altitude, ocean currents can overcome the effects of latitude. For example, London, England, has an average annual temperature of nearly 11°C (52°F). Natashquan, a town in eastern Canada at about the same latitude and altitude, has an average annual temperature of only 1°C (34°F). London's milder climate is the result of an ocean current carrying warm water to Europe's west coast.

Ocean Currents

Ocean currents can cause two places at the same latitude to have different climates.

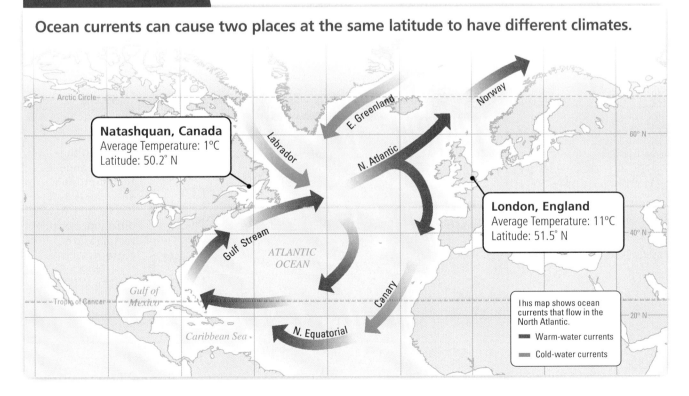

Natashquan, Canada
Average Temperature: 1°C
Latitude: 50.2° N

London, England
Average Temperature: 11°C
Latitude: 51.5° N

This map shows ocean currents that flow in the North Atlantic.

■ Warm-water currents
■ Cold-water currents

Seasonal changes are part of climate.

What marks the change of seasons where you live? In the Midwest and New England, there are four distinct seasons. Mild spring and autumn months come between hotter summers and colder winters. In Florida and other southern states, the seasonal changes are much less extreme. **Seasons** are periods of the year associated with specific weather conditions, such as cold temperatures or frequent rain. These periods are part of the overall pattern that makes up a climate.

Temperature Patterns

MAIN IDEA AND DETAILS
Record in your notes the important details about seasonal changes.

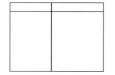

Seasons occur because the amounts of energy that the Northern Hemisphere and the Southern Hemisphere receive from the Sun change over the course of a year. Winter begins in the Northern Hemisphere around December 21, when the daytime is shortest. Summer begins around June 21, when the daytime is longest. Spring begins around March 21, and autumn begins around September 22. On the first day of spring and of autumn, day and night are equal in length. There are 12 hours of daylight and 12 hours of darkness.

CHECK YOUR READING Which seasons have the longest and the shortest periods of daytime?

Temperature patterns are an important feature of climate. The graph below shows the average monthly temperatures in Half Moon Bay, California, and Bloomington, Indiana. Each city has an average annual temperature of about 12°C (54°F). However, Bloomington has hot summers and cold winters, while Half Moon Bay has mild weather all year. Although their average annual temperatures are the same, they have different climates.

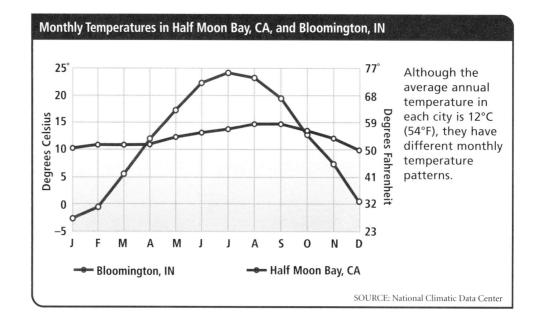

Monthly Temperatures in Half Moon Bay, CA, and Bloomington, IN

Although the average annual temperature in each city is 12°C (54°F), they have different monthly temperature patterns.

— Bloomington, IN   — Half Moon Bay, CA

SOURCE: National Climatic Data Center

Dry Season

Wet Season

INDIA

These photos show the same rice fields in India at different times of the year.

Precipitation Patterns

Like temperature patterns, seasonal patterns of precipitation vary among different climates. For example, Connecticut's precipitation is distributed fairly evenly throughout the year. In contrast, nearly half of Montana's precipitation falls during May, June, and July. Many tropical regions have wet and dry seasons. These regions stay warm all year long, but certain months are much rainier than other months.

The seasonal pattern of precipitation can determine the types of plants that grow in a region and the length of the growing season. Although Montana is a fairly dry state, much of its precipitation falls during the growing season. This pattern allows the state to be a major grain producer.

4.1 Review

KEY CONCEPTS

1. Explain the difference between climate and weather.

2. Make a chart showing how latitude, altitude, large bodies of water, and ocean currents affect climate.

3. How does the length of daytime change with each season?

CRITICAL THINKING

4. **Predict** How would a region's climate change if a cold-water ocean current stopped flowing past it?

5. **Identify Cause** What geographical factors might cause a region to have a narrow temperature range and mild weather all year?

● CHALLENGE

6. **Infer** Suggest specific climate characteristics that might make the owners of a vacation resort decide to advertise the average annual temperature rather than provide temperature averages for each month or season.

Climate and Architecture

When architects design houses, office towers, and other buildings, they think about how the climate will affect the structures and the people who will use them. For example, when planning a house for a cold climate, an architect will consider ways to keep warm air inside. He or she might call for energy-efficient glass in the windows, thick insulation in walls, and an extra set of inside doors to close off entryways.

Snow

Snow is very heavy. Because of snow's weight, architects usually design slanted roofs on houses built in snowy climates. The sharper the slant, the easier snow slides off. This church was built in Norway around 1150.

Heat

In the 1960s, Houston wanted to get a major league baseball team. City officials asked architects to design a stadium suitable for Houston's hot, rainy climate. They created the first domed, air-conditioned ballpark, the Astrodome.

Floods

Intense rains and high winds combine to make floods common in many places. To protect themselves, some people who live on the shores of large rivers, lakes, and oceans build their homes on stilts. This home is in the Northern Territory of Australia. It was designed by the architect Glenn Murcutt and completed in 1994.

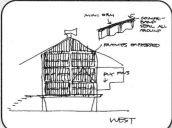

EXPLORE

1. **ANALYZING** Bring to class photos of buildings located in various climate regions. Discuss whether the architecture reflects the influence of the climate.

2. **CHALLENGE** Use building blocks to make a model of a house for a warm climate in which the wind usually blows from the west. Place doors, windows, and walls to get the best flow of air through the house. To check the airflow, dust your model with a light powder. Blow lightly and note how much powder moves.

4.2 Earth has a variety of climates.

BEFORE, you learned

- The main factors that affect climate are latitude, altitude, distance from large bodies of water, and ocean currents
- Seasonal changes in temperature and precipitation are part of climate

NOW, you will learn

- How scientists classify climates
- About the characteristics of different climate zones
- How natural features and human activity affect climate

VOCABULARY

climate zone p. 125
microclimate p. 128
urban heat island p. 128
rain shadow p. 129

THINK ABOUT

What does ground cover reveal about climate?

For trees and bushes to grow, they must have enough precipitation and at least a few months of mild temperatures each year. Lichens and some small plants can grow in harsher climates. The photograph shows typical ground cover along Greenland's rocky coast. What does the ground cover tell you about Greenland's long-term weather patterns?

Scientists have identified six major climate zones.

Classification systems can help you see patterns. For example, communities are often classified as cities, towns, and villages. This classification system organizes communities on the basis of size. Two cities in different parts of a country might have more in common than a village and a nearby city.

To show patterns in climate data, scientists have developed systems for classifying climates. A **climate zone** is one of the major divisions in a system for classifying the climates of different regions based on characteristics they have in common. The most widely used system groups climates by temperature and precipitation. The six major climate zones of this classification system are (1) humid tropical, (2) dry, (3) moist mid-latitude with mild winters, (4) moist mid-latitude with severe winters, (5) polar, and (6) highland.

RESOURCE CENTER
CLASSZONE.COM

Find out more about climate zones.

The chart on page 127 summarizes information about the different climate zones. Each climate zone has a specific set of characteristics. For example, humid tropical climates are hot and rainy. Many areas close to the equator have this type of climate.

Notice that most of the climate zones are further divided into subclimates. When scientists identify a subclimate, they choose one characteristic that makes it different from other subclimates within the same climate zone. For example, the humid tropical climate zone includes tropical wet climates and tropical wet and dry climates. The difference between them is that tropical wet climates have abundant rainfall every month, while tropical wet and dry climates have a few months of dry weather.

The climate map below shows that many regions scattered throughout the world have similar climates. When you use the map, keep in mind that climates do not change suddenly at the borders of the colored areas. Instead, each climate gradually blends into neighboring ones.

READING TiP

The colors on the map below correspond to the colors in the chart on page 127. As you read descriptions on the chart, look back to the map to find examples.

World Climates

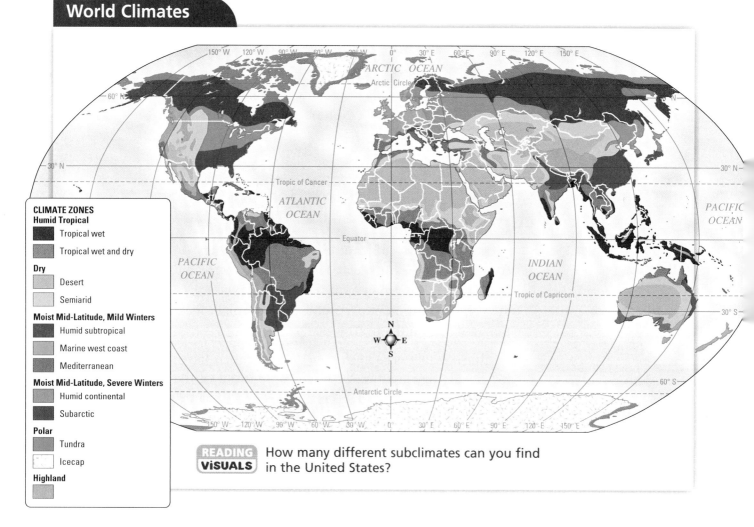

CLIMATE ZONES
Humid Tropical
- Tropical wet
- Tropical wet and dry

Dry
- Desert
- Semiarid

Moist Mid-Latitude, Mild Winters
- Humid subtropical
- Marine west coast
- Mediterranean

Moist Mid-Latitude, Severe Winters
- Humid continental
- Subarctic

Polar
- Tundra
- Icecap

Highland

READING VISUALS How many different subclimates can you find in the United States?

Climate Classification

Climate Zone	Subclimate	Description
Humid tropical	**Tropical wet** Example: Amazon rain forest in South America	Temperatures remain high throughout the year. Rising hot, humid air causes heavy cloud cover and abundant rainfall, with no dry season. Annual rainfall usually is more than 2.5 meters (8 ft).
	Tropical wet and dry Example: Miami, Florida	Like tropical wet climates, these climates are hot and rainy, but they have a dry season in winter.
Dry	**Desert** Example: Phoenix, Arizona	Precipitation is infrequent and scanty—usually less than 20 centimeters (8 in.) per year. Deserts include the hottest places on Earth, but they can be cool, especially at night. In most deserts high daytime temperatures lead to rapid evaporation, which increases the dryness.
	Semiarid Example: Denver, Colorado	These regions are found next to deserts. They have wider temperature ranges than deserts and are not as dry. Most of the Great Plains region in North America is semiarid.
Moist mid-latitude with mild winters	**Humid subtropical** Example: Charlotte, North Carolina	Summers are hot and muggy. Winters are usually mild. Precipitation is fairly even throughout the year.
	Marine west coast Example: Seattle, Washington	These regions have mild temperatures year-round and steady precipitation. Low clouds and fog are common.
	Mediterranean Example: San Francisco, California	Dry summers and mild, wet winters are typical of these regions. Some coastal areas have cool summers and frequent fog.
Moist mid-latitude with severe winters	**Humid continental** Example: Des Moines, Iowa	These regions have hot summers and cold winters. Precipitation is fairly even throughout the year. Snow covers the ground for 1 to 4 months in winter.
	Subarctic Example: Fairbanks, Alaska	Temperatures usually stay below freezing for 6 to 8 months each year. Summers are brief and cool. The amount of precipitation is low, but snow remains on the ground for long periods because of the cold.
Polar	**Tundra** Example: Barrow, Alaska	The average temperature of the warmest month is below 10°C (50°F). A deep layer of soil is frozen year-round. During summer a shallow layer at the surface thaws out and turns muddy.
	Icecap Example: Antarctica	The surface is permanently covered with ice and snow. Temperatures rarely rise above freezing, even in summer.
Highland	**Highland** Example: Rocky Mountains	Because temperature drops as altitude increases, mountain regions can contain many climates. Tall mountains may have a year-round covering of ice and snow at their peaks.

Tropical wet

Desert

Marine west coast

Humid continental

Tundra

Natural features and human activity can affect local climates.

The climate map on page 126 shows three subclimates in Madagascar, a large island off the east coast of Africa. But if you went to Madagascar, you would probably notice a greater variety of climates. A meadow might be warmer than a nearby wooded area, and a city block might be warmer than a meadow.

READING TIP

You can use word parts to help you recall the meaning of climate terms. The prefix *sub-* can indicate a part of a larger unit. The prefix *micro-* means "very small."

The climates of smaller areas within a subclimate are called **microclimates.** The area of a microclimate can be as large as a river valley or smaller than a garden. Forests, beaches, lakes, valleys, hills, and mountains are some of the features that influence local climates. For example, sea breezes often make beaches cooler than nearby inland areas on warm afternoons.

Shade from the tree produces a cooler microclimate where snow takes longer to melt.

Urban Heat Islands

Humans create artificial surfaces that can also affect local climates. Cities are usually warmer than surrounding rural areas. The warmer body of air over a city is called an **urban heat island.** At certain times the air temperature may be as much as 12°C (22°F) higher in a large city than in the nearby countryside. The following factors contribute to this effect:

- During the day, buildings and streets absorb more solar energy than do grass, trees, and soil. These artificial surfaces release the additional stored energy at night, which warms the air over a city.

- Evaporation of moisture helps cool areas. Because artificial surfaces absorb less water than most natural surfaces, there is less cooling from evaporation in cities than in rural areas.

- Cities use a lot of energy for cooling, transportation, and other activities. The use of energy releases heat into the atmosphere.

CHECK YOUR READING How do cities influence local temperature?

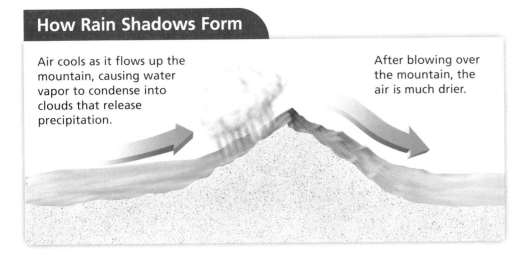

How Rain Shadows Form

Air cools as it flows up the mountain, causing water vapor to condense into clouds that release precipitation.

After blowing over the mountain, the air is much drier.

Rain Shadows

Mountains have a strong effect on climate in places where steady winds blow inland from oceans. The illustration above shows how mountains can affect precipitation:

- Air is forced to rise as it flows over a mountain.
- As the air rises and cools, it condenses into clouds. Areas near the side of a mountain that faces wind may get heavy precipitation.
- After passing over the mountain, the air is much drier because it has lost moisture through condensation and precipitation.

The dry area on the downwind side of a mountain where this process occurs is called a **rain shadow.** Mountains do not affect only local climates. Many dry climate zones that extend over large regions are found in the rain shadows of mountain ranges.

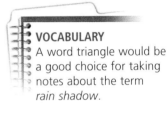

VOCABULARY
A word triangle would be a good choice for taking notes about the term *rain shadow.*

4.2 Review

KEY CONCEPTS

1. What two weather characteristics do meteorologists usually focus on when they determine climate zones?

2. Why do highland climate zones contain more than one climate?

3. How do mountains affect precipitation patterns?

CRITICAL THINKING

4. **Compare and Contrast** How are tundra and icecap subclimates similar? How are they different?

5. **Infer** In which climates would you expect to find the most vacation resorts? Explain.

⬥ CHALLENGE

6. **Apply** What is the subclimate of the region where you live? What microclimates exist in your local area?

CHAPTER INVESTIGATION

Microclimates

OVERVIEW AND PURPOSE Microclimates are local variations within a region's climate. Natural and artificial features such as beaches, hills, wooded areas, buildings, and pavement can cause such variations. Even trees planted around a house or parking lot may influence the climate of that small area. In this lab, you will use what you have learned about weather and climate to

- measure weather factors, such as air temperature, in two different microclimates
- discover how natural and artificial features affect local climate

MATERIALS

- 2 thermometers
- 2 other weather instruments of the same kind

▶ Problem

How do natural and artificial features affect the climate of a small area?

▶ Hypothesize

Write a hypothesis to explain how you expect the microclimates of two nearby locations to be affected by the different natural and artificial features in those areas. Your hypothesis should take the form of an "If . . . , then . . . , because . . ." statement. You should complete steps 1–3 of the procedure before writing your hypothesis.

▶ Procedure

1. Work in a group of four students. You will use a thermometer to record air temperature. Choose another weather instrument that you have made or that is available to you. You might use a psychrometer to measure relative humidity, a barometer to measure air pressure, or an anemometer to measure wind speed.

2. Make data tables similar to the ones in the sample notebook page. The label in the second row of each table should identify what you will measure with the instrument you chose in step 1.

3. Go outside the school with your teacher, taking your instruments and notebook. Choose two locations near the school with different features for your group to study. For example, you might choose a grassy area and a paved area, or one area with trees and another area without trees.

4. Divide your group into two pairs. Each pair of students should have one thermometer and the other instrument you have chosen. You and your partner will study one location. The other pair will study the second location.

5. Decide ahead of time how you will control for variables. For example, both pairs might take measurements at a set height above the ground.

6. Draw pictures of the location you are studying in your notebook. Write a description of the natural and artificial features in this area.

7. Set up the instruments in your location. Record the air temperature. Take follow-up readings five and ten minutes later. Take a reading with the other weather instrument each time you take a temperature reading.

8. Record data gathered by the other two members of your group in your data table. Calculate the average temperature for each location. Then calculate the average reading for the other weather factor that you measured.

▶ Observe and Analyze   Write It Up

1. **IDENTIFY VARIABLES AND CONSTANTS** Identify the variables and constants in the investigation. List these factors in your **Science Notebook.**

2. **COMPARE AND CONTRAST** Which average measurements in the two locations were the same? What differences did your investigations reveal? For example, was one area cooler or less windy than the other?

▶ Conclude   Write It Up

1. **INFER** Answer the question posed in the problem.

2. **INTERPRET** Compare your results with your hypothesis. Did the results support your hypothesis? Did the natural and artificial features have the effects you expected?

3. **EVALUATE** What were the limitations of your instruments? What other sources of error could have affected the results?

4. **APPLY** How could you apply the results of your investigation to help you make land-scaping or building decisions? For example, what could you do to make a picnic area more comfortable?

▶ INVESTIGATE Further

CHALLENGE Return to the locations you investigated at the same time of day on three consecutive days. Take readings with the same weather instruments that you used before. Are these new readings consistent with the patterns you observed on the first day? If not, how would you alter your earlier conclusions?

Microclimates

Problem How do natural and artificial features affect the climate of a small area?

Hypothesize

Observe and Analyze

Table 1. Weather Factors Within Microclimates

Time (min)	Location 1		Location 2	
	Temp (°C)	Wind Speed	Temp (°C)	Wind Speed
0				
5				
10				

Conclude

4.3 Climates can change suddenly or slowly.

BEFORE, you learned

- Earth absorbs and reflects solar energy
- Greenhouse gases help keep Earth warm
- Human activities are contributing to global warming

NOW, you will learn

- How climates can cool when particles block sunlight
- About climate changes that repeat over time
- How climates may change because of global warming

VOCABULARY

ice age p. 135
El Niño p. 136

THINK ABOUT

How do particles affect light?

If you shine a light through foggy air, you may notice that the beam of light is dimmer than usual. The droplets, or liquid particles, that make up fog block some of the light from reaching objects in the beam's path. Which natural events can suddenly add many particles to the atmosphere?

Climates cool when particles block sunlight.

Our atmosphere contains many particulates—tiny solid and liquid particles mixed in with air. Particulates block some of the Sun's energy, preventing it from reaching Earth's surface. Occasionally a natural event will suddenly release enormous amounts of particulates. Such an event may cause a temporary change in climates around the world.

Large volcanic eruptions can send huge clouds of gas and dust into the stratosphere. When these clouds enter the stratosphere, they spread out and drift around the world. Volcanoes affect global climate mainly by releasing sulfur dioxide gas. The gas combines with water to form sulfuric acid droplets, which block sunlight. Because Earth absorbs less solar energy, average global temperatures may decrease for up to several years.

CHECK YOUR READING How can a sudden release of particles affect climate?

In 1991, Mount Pinatubo erupted in the Philippines. The eruption, one of the largest of the last century, affected climates for about two years. During the summer of 1992, parts of North America were more than 3°C (5.4°F) cooler than usual. Over that entire year, global temperatures dropped by 0.5°C (0.9°F).

The impact of rocky objects from space can also release particles into the atmosphere. Earth is often hit by space objects. Most are too small to have much of an effect. However, objects 3 kilometers (2 mi) in diameter strike Earth about once every million years. These powerful collisions can suddenly change climates.

When a large space object strikes Earth, it explodes and leaves behind a crater, or pit, in the surface. The explosion throws dust into the atmosphere. The largest impacts may have raised so much dust that temperatures around the world dropped sharply for months. They may also have caused changes in the atmosphere by setting off forest fires. A space object that hit Earth 65 million years ago blasted out a crater about 200 kilometers (120 mi) in diameter in what is now Mexico. Many scientists think that climate changes following this impact led to the extinction of the dinosaurs and other species.

The eruption of Mount Pinatubo in 1991 affected temperatures around the world for about two years.

INVESTIGATE Climate Change

How does blocking sunlight affect temperature?

PROCEDURE

1. Tape the tissue paper to a window frame to cover one window. If you cannot cover the whole window, adjust the blinds or shade so that sunlight enters that window only through the tissue paper. Leave a second window on the same side of the room uncovered.

2. Adjust the shade or blinds of the uncovered window so that sunlight enters the room through equal areas of both windows. Place a thermometer in front of each window. Record the temperature for each window.

3. Wait 15 minutes. Record the temperature for each window.

WHAT DO YOU THINK?

• How did blocking one window with the tissue paper affect the temperature?

• What do you think caused this result?

CHALLENGE How would adding a second layer of tissue paper to the covered window affect the results? Add the second layer and repeat the activity to test your prediction.

SKILL FOCUS
Measuring

MATERIALS
• white tissue paper
• tape
• 2 thermometers

TIME
20 minutes

Climates change as continents move.

Climates can change suddenly for brief periods after a volcanic eruption. In contrast, the movement of continents causes steady climate changes over many millions of years. The maps below show two stages of this movement in the distant past.

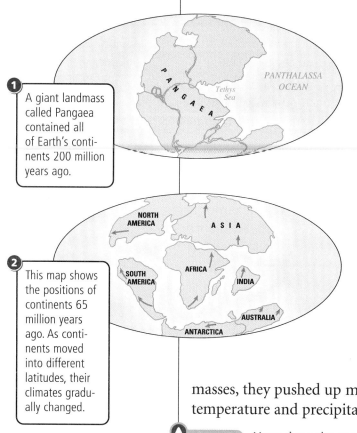

1 A giant landmass called Pangaea contained all of Earth's continents 200 million years ago.

2 This map shows the positions of continents 65 million years ago. As continents moved into different latitudes, their climates gradually changed.

1 Earth's continents were once joined together in a gigantic landmass called Pangaea (pan-JEE-uh). This giant landmass began to break up about 200 million years ago.

2 By 65 million years ago, the continents had moved closer to their present positions. As the continents moved, their climates gradually changed in different ways. Some continents cooled as they moved toward higher latitudes. Other continents grew warmer as they moved toward the equator.

The movement of continents had other effects on climate. As they drifted apart, the continents changed the paths of ocean currents that help warm coastal regions. When landmasses collided with other landmasses, they pushed up mountain ranges. Mountains influence temperature and precipitation patterns by altering the paths of winds.

 CHECK YOUR READING How does the movement of continents change climate? Find three examples in the text above.

Some climate changes repeat over time.

In most climates, a cooler period regularly follows a warmer period each year. Some climate changes also occur in cycles. Ice ages and El Niño are two kinds of climate change that repeat over time.

Ice Ages

RESOURCE CENTER
CLASSZONE.COM

Learn more about climate change.

For much of Earth's history, the poles were free of ice because Earth was warmer than it is today. However, there have been about seven major periods of global cooling that lasted millions of years. Temperatures became low enough for ice to form year-round at the poles. The most recent of these periods began 2 million years ago and is still continuing.

How Ice Expands in an Ice Age

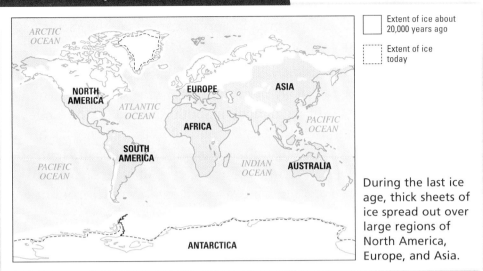

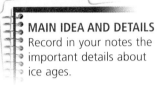

Extent of ice about 20,000 years ago

Extent of ice today

During the last ice age, thick sheets of ice spread out over large regions of North America, Europe, and Asia.

During major periods of global cooling, there are times when polar ice expands. **Ice ages** are periods in which huge sheets of ice spread out beyond the polar regions. The map above shows how far the ice sheets reached in the last ice age, which ended between 14,000 and 10,000 years ago. These sheets were several kilometers thick and covered nearly a third of Earth's land area.

Ice ages usually last tens of thousands of years. They are separated by warmer periods in which ice sheets shrink back toward the poles. We are living in one of these warmer periods. Average global temperatures are now 5°C to 10°C (9–18°F) higher than they were during the last ice age. Only Greenland and Antarctica have large ice sheets today.

Various sources of evidence show that ice ages occurred. Scientists study polar ice and the ocean floor to estimate past changes in temperature. Geological features that formed during ice ages, such as scratches on rocks, can reveal the movement of ice sheets. Some of the evidence also provides clues about what causes ice ages. Most scientists think that there are two main causes:

- Ice ages are closely linked to changes in how Earth moves around the Sun. These changes may have caused ice sheets to grow by altering the temperature patterns of the seasons.

- As you learned in Chapter 1, carbon dioxide is a greenhouse gas. Levels of carbon dioxide in the atmosphere dropped during ice ages. Lower carbon dioxide levels may have caused global cooling by weakening the greenhouse effect.

Other factors probably play a role in the development of ice ages. Scientists are still trying to understand how different factors work in combination to cause global cooling.

MAIN IDEA AND DETAILS
Record in your notes the important details about ice ages.

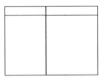

El Niño

The oceans are closely connected to climate. **El Niño** (ehl NEEN-yoh) is a disturbance of wind patterns and ocean currents in the Pacific Ocean. It usually occurs every 3 to 7 years and lasts for 12 to 18 months.

El Niño causes temporary climate changes in many parts of the world. It can cause unusually dry conditions in the western Pacific region and unusually heavy rainfall in South America. In the United States, El Niño tends to bring heavier rainfall to the Southeast. During winter, storms may be stronger than usual in California, and temperatures are often milder in some northern states. All of these unusual conditions follow changes in wind strength and ocean temperatures.

1 **Normal Year** Strong trade winds normally push warm water toward the western Pacific, where an area of low pressure develops. The rising warm air condenses into clouds that release heavy rain. Cooler water flows near the west coast of South America.

2 **El Niño Year** Weak trade winds allow warm water to flow back toward the central and eastern Pacific. The clouds and heavy rain also shift eastward, toward South America. The effects of El Niño vary, depending on how much warming occurs in the eastern Pacific.

READING TiP

In the diagrams, color is used to show ocean temperature. **Red** means warmer water. **Blue** means cooler water.

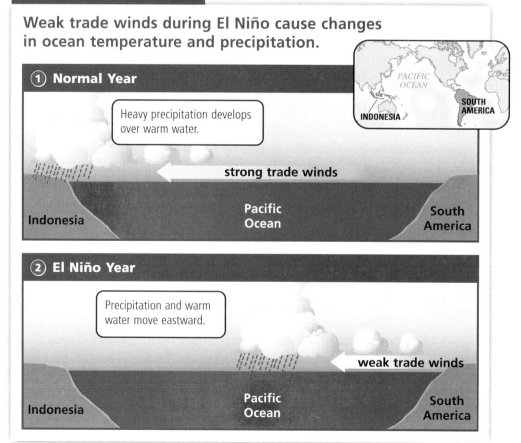

How El Niño Forms

Weak trade winds during El Niño cause changes in ocean temperature and precipitation.

PACIFIC OCEAN
SOUTH AMERICA
INDONESIA

1 **Normal Year**

Heavy precipitation develops over warm water.

strong trade winds

Indonesia   Pacific Ocean   South America

2 **El Niño Year**

Precipitation and warm water move eastward.

weak trade winds

Indonesia   Pacific Ocean   South America

1983

2002

This ice sheet on a mountain in Peru has shrunk 820 meters (2690 ft) in 19 years.

Human activities are changing climate.

Most climate experts predict that by 2100, there will be a rise in global temperature of 1.4°C to 5.8°C (2.5–10.4°F). As you read in Chapter 1, human activities release greenhouse gases. Higher levels of greenhouse gases in the atmosphere cause global warming. Earth hasn't warmed so rapidly at any time in at least the last 10,000 years. Even a small temperature increase could have a great impact on climate.

REMINDER

Remember that greenhouse gases are gases that absorb infrared energy.

Predictions of Climate Change

Although scientists expect all land areas to warm up by 2100, the rate of warming will be uneven. The greatest warming is expected to occur in the high latitudes of the Northern Hemisphere. The increase in Greenland's temperature, for example, may be two or three times the global average. Higher temperatures have recently started to melt the ice sheet that covers much of Greenland. Ice is also melting in the Arctic Ocean and on mountains in many parts of the world.

The effects of global warming on precipitation will also vary. Scientists predict an overall increase in precipitation, because more water will evaporate from Earth's warmer surface. Precipitation will tend to fall more heavily in short periods of time, which will increase flooding. However, some areas where water is already scarce may get even less precipitation. Lower precipitation in those areas will make droughts more frequent and severe.

CHECK YOUR READING Summarize how global warming is expected to affect temperature and precipitation.

Impact of Global Warming

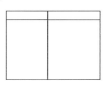

MAIN IDEA AND DETAILS
Record in your notes the important details about the impact of global warming.

Global warming affects many of Earth's systems. Because these systems work together in complex ways, it is difficult to predict the full impact of global warming. Most climate scientists predict that global warming will probably cause the following changes.

Sea Levels As temperatures warm, the oceans will expand. They will also gain additional water from melting ice. Scientists expect the average sea level to rise 9 to 88 centimeters (4–35 in.) over the next century. Higher sea levels will damage coastal regions and increase flooding. These problems could be severe in small island nations.

Wildlife Global warming will endanger many plant and animal species by altering natural habitats. Some species will die out or move to cooler areas. Other species, such as warm-water fishes, will benefit from an expansion of their habitats.

RESOURCE CENTER
CLASSZONE.COM
Find out more about the effects of global warming.

Agriculture Changes in temperature and precipitation can affect crops and livestock. If Earth warms more than a few degrees Celsius, most of the world's agriculture will be harmed. More moderate warming will help agriculture in some regions by lengthening the growing season. However, even moderate warming will harm agriculture in other regions.

Human Health Warmer temperatures could increase heat-related deaths and deaths from some diseases, such as malaria, especially in areas near the equator. On the other hand, deaths caused by extreme cold could decrease at higher latitudes.

Some scientists predict more dangerous changes beyond 2100 if humans continue to add greenhouse gases to the atmosphere at current levels. However, the harmful effects of global warming can be limited if we reduce emissions of greenhouse gases.

4.3 Review

KEY CONCEPTS

1. How can volcanic eruptions and impacts of large objects from space change climate?

2. What changes in climate occur during an ice age?

3. Give two examples of ways in which global warming will probably affect life on Earth.

CRITICAL THINKING

4. **Connect** What is the connection between latitude, the movement of continents, and climate change?

5. **Compare and Contrast** Compare and contrast the effects of El Niño and ice ages on climate.

⬥ CHALLENGE

6. **Infer** Discuss why some countries might be more reluctant than others to take steps to reduce levels of greenhouse gases.

MATH in SCIENCE

MATH TUTORIAL
CLASSZONE.COM
Click on Math Tutorial for more help with interpreting line graphs.

Carbon Dioxide Levels

Since the 1950s, carbon dioxide levels have been measured in air samples collected at the Mauna Loa Observatory in Hawaii. The graphs below show the carbon dioxide data plotted in two different ways. In the graph on the left, the scale showing carbon dioxide levels starts at 0 parts per million (ppm) and goes up to 400 ppm. The graph on the right offers a close-up view of the same data. The scale on the right-hand graph is broken to focus on the values from 310 ppm to 380 ppm.

Amount of Carbon Dioxide in the Air

SOURCE: Scripps Institution of Oceanography (SIO)

[Left graph: Carbon Dioxide (parts per million) on y-axis from 0 to 400; Year on x-axis from 1955 to 2005]

Amount of Carbon Dioxide in the Air

SOURCE: Scripps Institution of Oceanography (SIO)

[Right graph: Carbon Dioxide (parts per million) on y-axis from 310 to 380 (broken scale); Year on x-axis from 1955 to 2005]

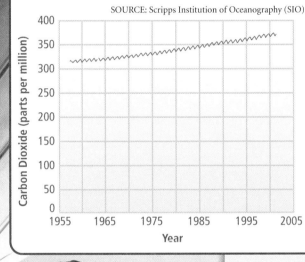

Use the graphs to answer the following questions.

1. What was the carbon dioxide level at the beginning of 1995?

2. The data show a 17 percent increase in the carbon dioxide level in the air from 1958 through 2001. Which graph shows this increase more clearly? Why?

3. In both graphs, the line that shows carbon dioxide levels is jagged, because carbon dioxide levels rise and fall regularly as the seasons change. In some years, the seasonal rise and fall is greater than in other years. Which graph emphasizes these variations more? Why?

CHALLENGE The carbon dioxide level in the air starts falling in May or June each year and continues to fall through October. What do you think causes this change to occur?

the **BIG** idea

Climates are long-term weather patterns that may change over time.

◀ KEY CONCEPTS SUMMARY

4.1 **Climate is a long-term weather pattern.**

The main factors that influence climate are

- latitude
- altitude
- distance from large bodies of water
- ocean currents

Seasonal changes are also part of climate patterns.

Temperatures usually decrease as latitude increases.

VOCABULARY
climate p. 117
latitude p. 118
marine climate p. 120
continental climate p. 120
ocean current p. 121
season p. 122

4.2 **Earth has a variety of climates.**

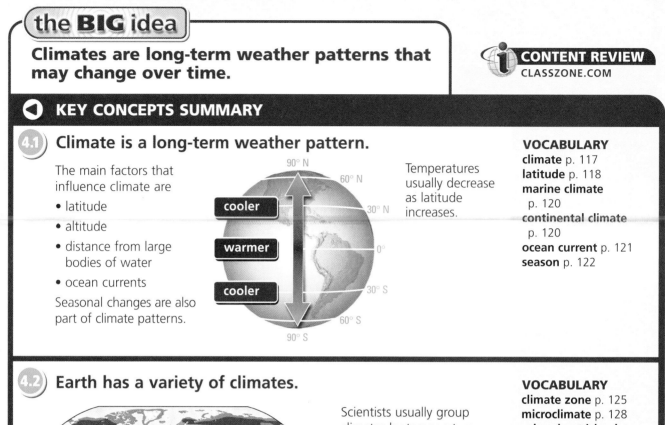

Each color on the map shows a different subclimate.

Scientists usually group climates by temperature and precipitation. There are six major climate zones. Climate zones can be divided into subclimates. Microclimates are smaller areas within subclimates.

VOCABULARY
climate zone p. 125
microclimate p. 128
urban heat island p. 128
rain shadow p. 129

4.3 **Climates can change suddenly or slowly.**

Natural events, such as eruptions of volcanoes, can change climate. Human activities that release greenhouse gases are also changing climate.

VOCABULARY
ice age p. 135
El Niño p. 136

Reviewing Vocabulary

Make a magnet word diagram for each of the vocabulary terms listed below. Write the term in the magnet. Write other terms or ideas related to it on the lines around the magnet.

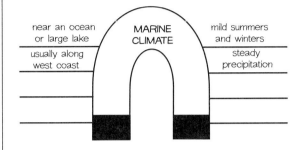

near an ocean or large lake

usually along west coast

MARINE CLIMATE

mild summers and winters

steady precipitation

1. continental climate
2. ocean current
3. microclimate
4. urban heat island
5. rain shadow
6. ice age

Reviewing Key Concepts

Multiple Choice *Choose the letter of the best answer.*

7. Compared with weather patterns, climate patterns are more
   a. severe
   b. long-term
   c. local
   d. unusual

8. Climates are usually classified by
   a. plant cover and animal life
   b. altitude and latitude
   c. bodies of water and ocean currents
   d. temperature and precipitation

9. Which latitude receives the least amount of solar energy?
   a. 30° N
   b. 0°
   c. 30° S
   d. 90° S

10. What is El Niño?
    a. a change in wind patterns and ocean currents
    b. an increase in carbon dioxide levels
    c. a decrease in global temperature
    d. a change in solar energy

11. Which effect is a likely result of global warming?
    a. fewer droughts
    b. lower sea levels
    c. more flooding
    d. more cold-related deaths

12. Volcanoes can cool the climate by
    a. increasing wind speeds
    b. using up Earth's energy
    c. releasing gas and particles
    d. raising air pressure

13. A large coastal city probably has cooler summers than a city at the same latitude that is
    a. on a mountain
    b. much smaller
    c. near a volcano
    d. far inland

14. Which carries warmth from the tropics toward the polar regions?
    a. urban heat islands
    b. warm-water currents
    c. cold-water currents
    d. trade winds

15. Several different climates can exist within a small area in
    a. marine climates
    b. continental climates
    c. polar climates
    d. highland climates

16. Day and night are equal in length on the first day of
    a. spring
    b. summer
    c. winter
    d. El Niño

Short Answer *Write a short answer to each question.*

17. How can changes caused by the movement of continents affect climate?

18. Identify the two main causes of ice ages.

19. Describe how a space object might have helped kill off the dinosaurs.

20. How is the climate of a city usually different from the climate of a nearby rural area?

Thinking Critically

Use the climate graphs to answer the next four questions.

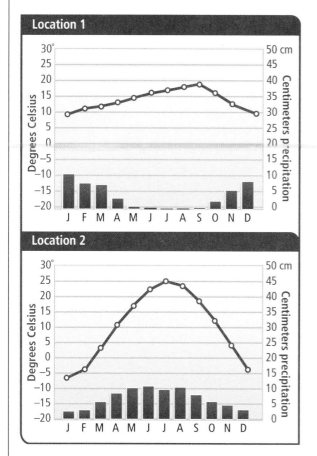

Location 1

Location 2

21. **COMPARE AND CONTRAST** Compare and contrast the seasonal precipitation patterns shown in the graphs.

22. **COMPARE AND CONTRAST** Contrast the seasonal temperature patterns shown in the graphs.

23. **HYPOTHESIZE** Which of the four main geographical factors that affect climate is the most likely cause of the difference in temperature patterns in the two locations? Explain.

24. **SYNTHESIZE** Suppose you want to plant a crop that requires a long growing season. Which location would you choose? Why?

25. **IDENTIFY EFFECTS** Describe the possible effect on the microclimate of a city if people planted grass lawns on the roofs of buildings.

26. **SYNTHESIZE** Would you expect to find a greater variety of climates on a tall mountain at 10° N or at 65° N? Explain.

27. **APPLY** In the evening after a hot summer day, the temperature at a beach stays higher longer than it does farther inland. Explain why this happens.

28. **APPLY** Both Kathmandu, Nepal, and Fuzhou, China, are located at about 25° N. Kathmandu is far inland and high in the mountains. Fuzhou is a seaport. How would you expect their climates to differ?

29. **PREDICT** What might be the impact of global warming in the area where you live?

the BIG idea

30. **APPLY** Look again at the photograph on pages 114–115. Now that you have finished the chapter, how would you change your response to the question on the photograph?

31. **EVALUATE** Describe a place that has what you consider to be a perfect climate. Explain how the following geographical factors affect the climate of that place:
    - latitude
    - altitude
    - distance from large bodies of water
    - ocean currents

UNIT PROJECTS

Evaluate all the data, results, and information in your project folder. Prepare to present your project.

Standardized Test Practice

For practice on your
state test, go to . . .
TEST PRACTICE
CLASSZONE.COM

Analyzing Data

*The following tables show the average temperatures in four cities and the temperature characteristics
of four climate zones. Use the information in the tables to answer the questions below.*

City	Avg. Temperature in Coldest Month	Avg. Temperature in Warmest Month
Miami, Florida	20°C	29°C
Minneapolis, Minnesota	–11°C	23°C
Little Rock, Arkansas	4°C	28°C
Barrow, Alaska	–26°C	4°C

Climate Zone	Characteristics
Polar	Average temperature of warmest month is below 10°C.
Moist mid-latitude with severe winters	Average temperature of coldest month is below –2°C.
Moist mid-latitude with mild winters	Average temperature of coldest month is between –2°C and 18°C.
Humid tropical	Average temperature of every month is greater than 18°C.

1. What is the average temperature in Miami in the coldest month?

a. –11°C   **c.** 20°C

b. 4°C   **d.** 29°C

2. What is the average temperature in Little Rock in the warmest month?

a. 4°C   **c.** 28°C

b. 23°C   **d.** 29°C

3. Which city has a moist mid-latitude climate with mild winters?

a. Miami   **c.** Little Rock

b. Minneapolis   **d.** Barrow

4. Which city has a humid tropical climate?

a. Miami   **c.** Little Rock

b. Minneapolis   **d.** Barrow

5. Which city has a moist mid-latitude climate with severe winters?

a. Miami   **c.** Little Rock

b. Minneapolis   **d.** Barrow

6. In which climate zone would Little Rock be if its average temperature in the coldest month were 10° colder?

a. polar

b. moist mid-latitude with severe winters

c. moist mid-latitude with mild winters

d. humid tropical

Extended Response

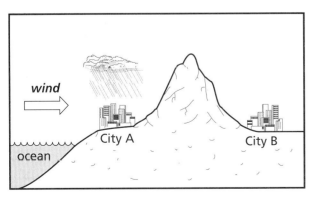

Use information in the diagram to answer the two questions below in detail.

7. City A receives 165 centimeters of rain each year. Explain why its climate is so moist. Use the words *wind, evaporate, condense,* and *precipitation* in your answer.

8. City B receives an average of 22 centimeters of rain each year. Explain why city B is much drier than city A. Use the term *rain shadow* in your answer.

Today's Scientist at Work

Name: J. Marshall Shepherd	
Degree: PhD, Meteorology, Florida State University	
Profession: Research Meteorologist, Associate Professor of Geography	
Location: Metropolitan Atlanta, Georgia	

Photo courtesy of Marshall Shepherd

Dr. Marshall Shepherd has been interested in weather since he made his own weather data-collecting instruments for a school science project. Although the instruments he uses today are much larger and much more powerful, they give him some of the same information.

In his work, Dr. Shepherd tries to understand weather events, such as hurricanes and thunderstorms, and relate them to current weather and climate change. Recently, he led a team that used space-based radar to measure rainfall over urban areas. The measurements confirmed that the areas downwind of major cities experience more rainfall in summer than other areas in the same region. The large number of buildings and paved roads retain heat. The excess heat changes the way air circulates, and this causes the formation of rain clouds. For this work, Dr. Shepherd was honored at the White House.

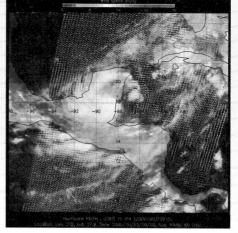

This image of a hurricane was taken with the Tropical Rainfall Measuring Mission (TRMM) satellite. Data from TRMM allowed Dr. Shepherd and other scientists to study how hurricanes form, grow, and diminish.

NASA Goddard Space Flight Center

Dr. Shepherd might say that one of his most rewarding jobs is explaining weather phenomena to the public. It's a job he loves. He even has written a children's book about weather. If Dr. Shepherd looks familiar to you, it may be because you've seen him on television. During the hurricane seasons of 2004 and 2005, he made over 50 media appearances to explain what was occurring in the affected regions.

Student Resource Handbooks

Making Observations

An **observation** is an act of noting and recording an event, character-istic, behavior, or anything else detected with an instrument or with the senses.

Observations allow you to make informed hypotheses and to gather data for experiments. Careful observations often lead to ideas for new experiments. There are two categories of observations:

- **Quantitative observations** can be expressed in numbers and include records of time, temperature, mass, distance, and volume.

- **Qualitative observations** include descriptions of sights, sounds, smells, and textures.

EXAMPLE

A student dissolved 30 grams of Epsom salts in water, poured the solution into a dish, and let the dish sit out uncovered overnight. The next day, she made the following observations of the Epsom salt crystals that grew in the dish.

Table 1. Observations of Epsom Salt Crystals

To determine the mass, the student found the mass of the dish before and after growing the crystals and then used subtraction to find the difference.

The student measured several crystals and calculated the mean length. (To learn how to calculate the mean of a data set, see page R36.)

Quantitative Observations	Qualitative Observations
• mass = 30 g	• Crystals are clear.
• mean crystal length = 0.5 cm	• Crystals are long, thin, and rectangular.
• longest crystal length = 2 cm	• White crust has formed around edge of dish.

Photographs or sketches are useful for recording qualitative observations.

Epsom salt crystals

MORE ABOUT OBSERVING

- Make quantitative observations whenever possible. That way, others will know exactly what you observed and be able to compare their results with yours.

- It is always a good idea to make qualitative observations too. You never know when you might observe something unexpected.

Predicting and Hypothesizing

A **prediction** is an expectation of what will be observed or what will happen. A **hypothesis** is a tentative explanation for an observation or scientific problem that can be tested by further investigation.

EXAMPLE

Suppose you have made two paper airplanes and you wonder why one of them tends to glide farther than the other one.

1. Start by asking a question.

2. Make an educated guess. After examination, you notice that the wings of the airplane that flies farther are slightly larger than the wings of the other airplane.

3. Write a prediction based upon your educated guess, in the form of an "If . . . , then . . ." statement. Write the independent variable after the word *if,* and the dependent variable after the word *then.*

4. To make a hypothesis, explain why you think what you predicted will occur. Write the explanation after the word *because.*

1. Why does one of the paper airplanes glide farther than the other?

2. The size of an airplane's wings may affect how far the airplane will glide.

3. Prediction: If I make a paper airplane with larger wings, then the airplane will glide farther.

To read about independent and dependent variables, see page R30.

4. Hypothesis: If I make a paper airplane with larger wings, then the airplane will glide farther, because the additional surface area of the wing will produce more lift.

Notice that the part of the hypothesis after *because* adds an explanation of why the airplane will glide farther.

MORE ABOUT HYPOTHESES

- The results of an experiment cannot prove that a hypothesis is correct. Rather, the results either support or do not support the hypothesis.

- Valuable information is gained even when your hypothesis is not supported by your results. For example, it would be an important discovery to find that wing size is not related to how far an airplane glides.

- In science, a hypothesis is supported only after many scientists have conducted many experiments and produced consistent results.

Inferring

An **inference** is a logical conclusion drawn from the available evidence and prior knowledge. Inferences are often made from observations.

EXAMPLE

A student observing a set of acorns noticed something unexpected about one of them. He noticed a white, soft-bodied insect eating its way out of the acorn.

The student recorded these observations.

Observations

- There is a hole in the acorn, about 0.5 cm in diameter, where the insect crawled out.
- There is a second hole, which is about the size of a pinhole, on the other side of the acorn.
- The inside of the acorn is hollow.

Here are some inferences that can be made on the basis of the observations.

Inferences

- The insect formed from the material inside the acorn, grew to its present size, and ate its way out of the acorn.
- The insect crawled through the smaller hole, ate the inside of the acorn, grew to its present size, and ate its way out of the acorn.
- An egg was laid in the acorn through the smaller hole. The egg hatched into a larva that ate the inside of the acorn, grew to its present size, and ate its way out of the acorn.

When you make inferences, be sure to look at all of the evidence available and combine it with what you already know.

MORE ABOUT INFERENCES

Inferences depend both on observations and on the knowledge of the people making the inferences. Ancient people who did not know that organisms are produced only by similar organisms might have made an inference like the first one. A student today might look at the same observations and make the second inference. A third student might have knowledge about this particular insect and know that it is never small enough to fit through the smaller hole, leading her to the third inference.

Identifying Cause and Effect

In a **cause-and-effect relationship,** one event or characteristic is the result of another. Usually an effect follows its cause in time.

There are many examples of cause-and-effect relationships in everyday life.

Cause	Effect
Turn off a light.	Room gets dark.
Drop a glass.	Glass breaks.
Blow a whistle.	Sound is heard.

Scientists must be careful not to infer a cause-and-effect relationship just because one event happens after another event. When one event occurs after another, you cannot infer a cause-and-effect relationship on the basis of that information alone. You also cannot conclude that one event caused another if there are alternative ways to explain the second event. A scientist must demonstrate through experimentation or continued observation that an event was truly caused by another event.

EXAMPLE

Make an Observation

Suppose you have a few plants growing outside. When the weather starts getting colder, you bring one of the plants indoors. You notice that the plant you brought indoors is growing faster than the others are growing. You cannot conclude from your observation that the change in temperature was the cause of the increased plant growth, because there are alternative explanations for the observation. Some possible explanations are given below.

- The humidity indoors caused the plant to grow faster.

- The level of sunlight indoors caused the plant to grow faster.

- The indoor plant's being noticed more often and watered more often than the outdoor plants caused it to grow faster.

- The plant that was brought indoors was healthier than the other plants to begin with.

To determine which of these factors, if any, caused the indoor plant to grow faster than the outdoor plants, you would need to design and conduct an experiment.

See pages R28–R35 for information about designing experiments.

Recognizing Bias

Television, newspapers, and the Internet are full of experts claiming to have scientific evidence to back up their claims. How do you know whether the claims are really backed up by good science?

Bias is a slanted point of view, or personal prejudice. The goal of scientists is to be as objective as possible and to base their findings on facts instead of opinions. However, bias often affects the conclusions of researchers, and it is important to learn to recognize bias.

When scientific results are reported, you should consider the source of the information as well as the information itself. It is important to critically analyze the information that you see and read.

SOURCES OF BIAS

There are several ways in which a report of scientific information may be biased. Here are some questions that you can ask yourself:

1. **Who is sponsoring the research?**

   Sometimes, the results of an investigation are biased because an organization paying for the research is looking for a specific answer. This type of bias can affect how data are gathered and interpreted.

2. **Is the research sample large enough?**

   Sometimes research does not include enough data. The larger the sample size, the more likely that the results are accurate, assuming a truly random sample.

3. **In a survey, who is answering the questions?**

   The results of a survey or poll can be biased. The people taking part in the survey may have been specifically chosen because of how they would answer. They may have the same ideas or lifestyles. A survey or poll should make use of a random sample of people.

4. **Are the people who take part in a survey biased?**

   People who take part in surveys sometimes try to answer the questions the way they think the researcher wants them to answer. Also, in surveys or polls that ask for personal information, people may be unwilling to answer questions truthfully.

SCIENTIFIC BIAS

It is also important to realize that scientists have their own biases because of the types of research they do and because of their scientific viewpoints. Two scientists may look at the same set of data and come to completely different conclusions because of these biases. However, such disagreements are not necessarily bad. In fact, a critical analysis of disagreements is often responsible for moving science forward.

Identifying Faulty Reasoning

Faulty reasoning is wrong or incorrect thinking. It leads to mistakes and to wrong conclusions. Scientists are careful not to draw unreasonable conclusions from experimental data. Without such caution, the results of scientific investigations may be misleading.

EXAMPLE

Scientists try to make generalizations based on their data to explain as much about nature as possible. If only a small sample of data is looked at, however, a conclusion may be faulty. Suppose a scientist has studied the effects of the El Niño and La Niña weather patterns on flood damage in California from 1989 to 1995. The scientist organized the data in the bar graph below.

The scientist drew the following conclusions:

1. The La Niña weather pattern has no effect on flooding in California.

2. When neither weather pattern occurs, there is almost no flood damage.

3. A weak or moderate El Niño produces a small or moderate amount of flooding.

4. A strong El Niño produces a lot of flooding.

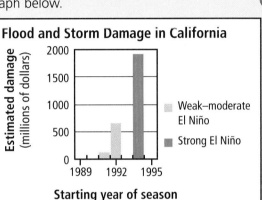

SOURCE: *Governor's Office of Emergency Services, California*

For the six-year period of the scientist's investigation, these conclusions may seem to be reasonable. However, a six-year study of weather patterns may be too small of a sample for the conclusions to be supported. Consider the following graph, which shows information that was gathered from 1949 to 1997.

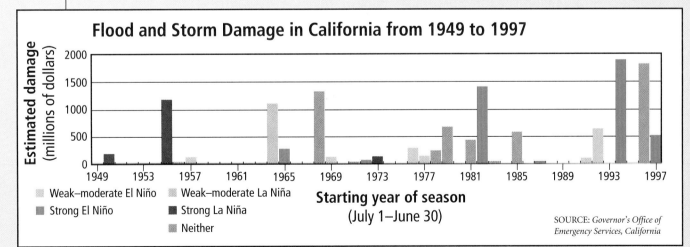

SOURCE: *Governor's Office of Emergency Services, California*

The only one of the conclusions that all of this information supports is number 3: a weak or moderate El Niño produces a small or moderate amount of flooding. By collecting more data, scientists can be more certain of their conclusions and can avoid faulty reasoning.

Analyzing Statements

To **analyze** a statement is to examine its parts carefully. Scientific findings are often reported through media such as television or the Internet. A report that is made public often focuses on only a small part of research. As a result, it is important to question the sources of information.

Evaluate Media Claims

To **evaluate** a statement is to judge it on the basis of criteria you've established. Sometimes evaluating means deciding whether a statement is true.

Reports of scientific research and findings in the media may be misleading or incomplete. When you are exposed to this information, you should ask yourself some questions so that you can make informed judgments about the information.

1. **Does the information come from a credible source?**

   Suppose you learn about a new product and it is stated that scientific evidence proves that the product works. A report from a respected news source may be more believable than an advertisement paid for by the product's manufacturer.

2. **How much evidence supports the claim?**

   Often, it may seem that there is new evidence every day of something in the world that either causes or cures an illness. However, information that is the result of several years of work by several different scientists is more credible than an advertisement that does not even cite the subjects of the experiment.

3. **How much information is being presented?**

   Science cannot solve all questions, and scientific experiments often have flaws. A report that discusses problems in a scientific study may be more believable than a report that addresses only positive experimental findings.

4. **Is scientific evidence being presented by a specific source?**

   Sometimes scientific findings are reported by people who are called experts or leaders in a scientific field. But if their names are not given or their scientific credentials are not reported, their statements may be less credible than those of recognized experts.

Differentiate Between Fact and Opinion

Sometimes information is presented as a fact when it may be an opinion. When scientific conclusions are reported, it is important to recognize whether they are based on solid evidence. Again, you may find it helpful to ask yourself some questions.

1. **What is the difference between a fact and an opinion?**

   A **fact** is a piece of information that can be strictly defined and proved true. An **opinion** is a statement that expresses a belief, value, or feeling. An opinion cannot be proved true or false. For example, a person's age is a fact, but if someone is asked how old they feel, it is impossible to prove the person's answer to be true or false.

2. **Can opinions be measured?**

   Yes, opinions can be measured. In fact, surveys often ask for people's opinions on a topic. But there is no way to know whether or not an opinion is the truth.

HOW TO DIFFERENTIATE FACT FROM OPINION

Human Activities and the Environment

Unfortunately, human use of fossil fuels is one of the most significant developments of the past few centuries. Humans rely on fossil fuels, a non-renewable energy resource, for more than 90 percent of their energy needs.

This careless misuse of our planet's resources has resulted in pollution, global warming, and the destruction of fragile ecosystems. For example, oil pipelines carry more than one million barrels of oil each day across tundra regions. Transporting oil across such areas can only result in oil spills that poison the land for decades.

Opinions
Notice words or phrases that express beliefs or feelings. The words *unfortunately* and *careless* show that opinions are being expressed.

Opinion
Look for statements that speculate about events. These statements are opinions, because they cannot be proved.

Facts
Statements that contain statistics tend to be facts. Writers often use facts to support their opinions.

Lab Handbook

Safety Rules

Before you work in the laboratory, read these safety rules twice. Ask your teacher to explain any rules that you do not completely understand. Refer to these rules later on if you have questions about safety in the science classroom.

Directions

- Read all directions and make sure that you understand them before starting an investigation or lab activity. If you do not understand how to do a procedure or how to use a piece of equipment, ask your teacher.
- Do not begin any investigation or touch any equipment until your teacher has told you to start.
- Never experiment on your own. If you want to try a procedure that the directions do not call for, ask your teacher for permission first.
- If you are hurt or injured in any way, tell your teacher immediately.

Dress Code

goggles

apron

gloves

- Wear goggles when
  — using glassware, sharp objects, or chemicals
  — heating an object
  — working with anything that can easily fly up into the air and hurt someone's eye
- Tie back long hair or hair that hangs in front of your eyes.
- Remove any article of clothing—such as a loose sweater or a scarf—that hangs down and may touch a flame, chemical, or piece of equipment.
- Observe all safety icons calling for the wearing of eye protection, gloves, and aprons.

Heating and Fire Safety

fire safety

heating safety

- Keep your work area neat, clean, and free of extra materials.
- Never reach over a flame or heat source.
- Point objects being heated away from you and others.
- Never heat a substance or an object in a closed container.
- Never touch an object that has been heated. If you are unsure whether something is hot, treat it as though it is. Use oven mitts, clamps, tongs, or a test-tube holder.
- Know where the fire extinguisher and fire blanket are kept in your classroom.
- Do not throw hot substances into the trash. Wait for them to cool or use the container your teacher puts out for disposal.

Electrical Safety

electrical
safety

- Never use lamps or other electrical equipment with frayed cords.
- Make sure no cord is lying on the floor where someone can trip over it.
- Do not let a cord hang over the side of a counter or table so that the equipment can easily be pulled or knocked to the floor.
- Never let cords hang into sinks or other places where water can be found.
- Never try to fix electrical problems. Inform your teacher of any problems immediately.
- Unplug an electrical cord by pulling on the plug, not the cord.

Chemical Safety

chemical
safety

poison

fumes

- If you spill a chemical or get one on your skin or in your eyes, tell your teacher right away.
- Never touch, taste, or sniff any chemicals in the lab. If you need to determine odor, waft. Wafting consists of holding the chemical in its container 15 centimeters (6 in.) away from your nose, and using your fingers to bring fumes from the container to your nose.
- Keep lids on all chemicals you are not using.
- Never put unused chemicals back into the original containers. Throw away extra chemicals where your teacher tells you to.
- Pour chemicals over a sink or your work area, not over the floor.
- If you get a chemical in your eye, use the eyewash right away.
- Always wash your hands after handling chemicals, plants, or soil.

Wafting

Glassware and Sharp-Object Safety

sharp
objects

- If you break glassware, tell your teacher right away.
- Do not use broken or chipped glassware. Give these to your teacher.
- Use knives and other cutting instruments carefully. Always wear eye protection and cut away from you.

Animal Safety

- Never hurt an animal.
- Touch animals only when necessary. Follow your teacher's instructions for handling animals.
- Always wash your hands after working with animals.

Cleanup

disposal

- Follow your teacher's instructions for throwing away or putting away supplies.
- Clean your work area and pick up anything that has dropped to the floor.
- Wash your hands.

Using Lab Equipment

Different experiments require different types of equipment. But even though experiments differ, the ways in which the equipment is used are the same.

Beakers

- Use beakers for holding and pouring liquids.
- Do not use a beaker to measure the volume of a liquid. Use a graduated cylinder instead. (See page R16.)
- Use a beaker that holds about twice as much liquid as you need. For example, if you need 100 milliliters of water, you should use a 200- or 250-milliliter beaker.

Test Tubes

- Use test tubes to hold small amounts of substances.
- Do not use a test tube to measure the volume of a liquid.
- Use a test tube when heating a substance over a flame. Aim the mouth of the tube away from yourself and other people.
- Liquids easily spill or splash from test tubes, so it is important to use only small amounts of liquids.

Test-Tube Holder

- Use a test-tube holder when heating a substance in a test tube.
- Use a test-tube holder if the substance in a test tube is dangerous to touch.
- Make sure the test-tube holder tightly grips the test tube so that the test tube will not slide out of the holder.
- Make sure that the test-tube holder is above the surface of the substance in the test tube so that you can observe the substance.

Test-Tube Rack

- Use a test-tube rack to organize test tubes before, during, and after an experiment.

- Use a test-tube rack to keep test tubes upright so that they do not fall over and spill their contents.

- Use a test-tube rack that is the correct size for the test tubes that you are using. If the rack is too small, a test tube may become stuck. If the rack is too large, a test tube may lean over, and some of its contents may spill or splash.

Forceps

- Use forceps when you need to pick up or hold a very small object that should not be touched with your hands.

- Do not use forceps to hold anything over a flame, because forceps are not long enough to keep your hand safely away from the flame. Plastic forceps will melt, and metal forceps will conduct heat and burn your hand.

Hot Plate

- Use a hot plate when a substance needs to be kept warmer than room temperature for a long period of time.

- Use a hot plate instead of a Bunsen burner or a candle when you need to carefully control temperature.

- Do not use a hot plate when a substance needs to be burned in an experiment.

- Always use "hot hands" safety mitts or oven mitts when handling anything that has been heated on a hot plate.

Microscope

Scientists use microscopes to see very small objects that cannot easily be seen with the eye alone. A microscope magnifies the image of an object so that small details may be observed. A microscope that you may use can magnify an object 400 times—the object will appear 400 times larger than its actual size.

Body The body separates the lens in the eyepiece from the objective lenses below.

Nosepiece The nosepiece holds the objective lenses above the stage and rotates so that all lenses may be used.

High-Power Objective Lens This is the largest lens on the nosepiece. It magnifies an image approximately 40 times.

Stage The stage supports the object being viewed.

Diaphragm The diaphragm is used to adjust the amount of light passing through the slide and into an objective lens.

Mirror or Light Source Some microscopes use light that is reflected through the stage by a mirror. Other microscopes have their own light sources.

Eyepiece Objects are viewed through the eyepiece. The eyepiece contains a lens that commonly magnifies an image 10 times.

Coarse Adjustment This knob is used to focus the image of an object when it is viewed through the low-power lens.

Fine Adjustment This knob is used to focus the image of an object when it is viewed through the high-power lens.

Low-Power Objective Lens This is the smallest lens on the nosepiece. It magnifies an image approximately 10 times.

Arm The arm supports the body above the stage. Always carry a microscope by the arm and base.

Stage Clip The stage clip holds a slide in place on the stage.

Base The base supports the microscope.

VIEWING AN OBJECT

1. Use the coarse adjustment knob to raise the body tube.
2. Adjust the diaphragm so that you can see a bright circle of light through the eyepiece.
3. Place the object or slide on the stage. Be sure that it is centered over the hole in the stage.
4. Turn the nosepiece to click the low-power lens into place.
5. Using the coarse adjustment knob, slowly lower the lens and focus on the specimen being viewed. Be sure not to touch the slide or object with the lens.
6. When switching from the low-power lens to the high-power lens, first raise the body tube with the coarse adjustment knob so that the high-power lens will not hit the slide.
7. Turn the nosepiece to click the high-power lens into place.
8. Use the fine adjustment knob to focus on the specimen being viewed. Again, be sure not to touch the slide or object with the lens.

MAKING A SLIDE, OR WET MOUNT

1 Place the specimen in the center of a clean slide.

2 Place a drop of water on the specimen.

3 Place a cover slip on the slide. Put one edge of the cover slip into the drop of water and slowly lower it over the specimen.

4 Remove any air bubbles from under the cover slip by gently tapping the cover slip.

5 Dry any excess water before placing the slide on the microscope stage for viewing.

Spring Scale (Force Meter)

- Use a spring scale to measure a force pulling on the scale.
- Use a spring scale to measure the force of gravity exerted on an object by Earth.
- To measure a force accurately, a spring scale must be zeroed before it is used. The scale is zeroed when no weight is attached and the indicator is positioned at zero.
- Do not attach a weight that is either too heavy or too light to a spring scale. A weight that is too heavy could break the scale or exert too great a force for the scale to measure. A weight that is too light may not exert enough force to be measured accurately.

Graduated Cylinder

- Use a graduated cylinder to measure the volume of a liquid.
- Be sure that the graduated cylinder is on a flat surface so that your measurement will be accurate.
- When reading the scale on a graduated cylinder, be sure to have your eyes at the level of the surface of the liquid.
- The surface of the liquid will be curved in the graduated cylinder. Read the volume of the liquid at the bottom of the curve, or meniscus (muh-NIHS-kuhs).
- You can use a graduated cylinder to find the volume of a solid object by measuring the increase in a liquid's level after you add the object to the cylinder.

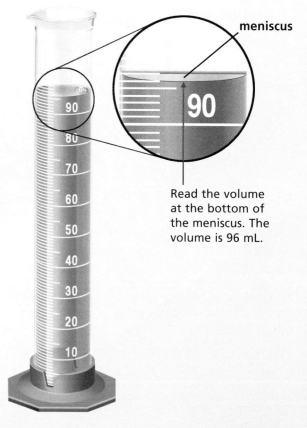

meniscus

Read the volume at the bottom of the meniscus. The volume is 96 mL.

Metric Rulers

- Use metric rulers or meter sticks to measure objects' lengths.

- Do not measure an object from the end of a metric ruler or meter stick, because the end is often imperfect. Instead, measure from the 1-centimeter mark, but remember to subtract a centimeter from the apparent measurement.

- Estimate any lengths that extend between marked units. For example, if a meter stick shows centimeters but not millimeters, you can estimate the length that an object extends between centimeter marks to measure it to the nearest millimeter.

- **Controlling Variables** If you are taking repeated measurements, always measure from the same point each time. For example, if you're measuring how high two different balls bounce when dropped from the same height, measure both bounces at the same point on the balls—either the top or the bottom. Do not measure at the top of one ball and the bottom of the other.

EXAMPLE

How to Measure a Leaf

1. Lay a ruler flat on top of the leaf so that the 1-centimeter mark lines up with one end. Make sure the ruler and the leaf do not move between the time you line them up and the time you take the measurement.

2. Look straight down on the ruler so that you can see exactly how the marks line up with the other end of the leaf.

3. Estimate the length by which the leaf extends beyond a marking. For example, the leaf below extends about halfway between the 4.2-centimeter and 4.3-centimeter marks, so the apparent measurement is about 4.25 centimeters.

4. Remember to subtract 1 centimeter from your apparent measurement, since you started at the 1-centimeter mark on the ruler and not at the end. The leaf is about 3.25 centimeters long (4.25 cm – 1 cm = 3.25 cm).

Triple-Beam Balance

This balance has a pan and three beams with sliding masses, called riders. At one end of the beams is a pointer that indicates whether the mass on the pan is equal to the masses shown on the beams.

1. Make sure the balance is zeroed before measuring the mass of an object. The balance is zeroed if the pointer is at zero when nothing is on the pan and the riders are at their zero points. Use the adjustment knob at the base of the balance to zero it.

2. Place the object to be measured on the pan.

3. Move the riders one notch at a time away from the pan. Begin with the largest rider. If moving the largest rider one notch brings the pointer below zero, begin measuring the mass of the object with the next smaller rider.

4. Change the positions of the riders until they balance the mass on the pan and the pointer is at zero. Then add the readings from the three beams to determine the mass of the object.

300 g	position of largest rider
90 g	position of middle rider
+ 3 g	position of smallest rider
393 g	mass of beaker

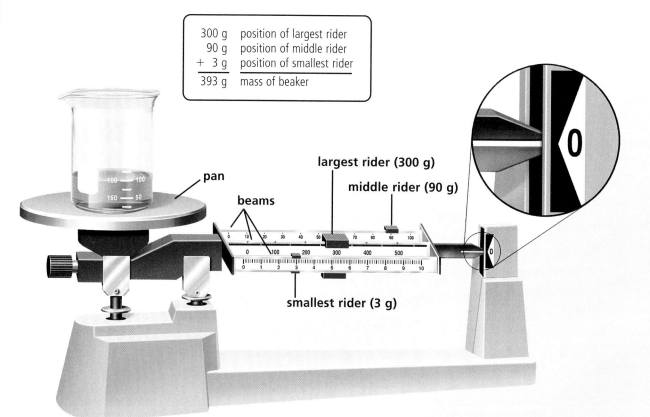

Double-Pan Balance

This type of balance has two pans. Between the pans is a pointer that indicates whether the masses on the pans are equal.

1. Make sure the balance is zeroed before measuring the mass of an object. The balance is zeroed if the pointer is at zero when there is nothing on either of the pans. Many double-pan balances have sliding knobs that can be used to zero them.

2. Place the object to be measured on one of the pans.

3. Begin adding standard masses to the other pan. Begin with the largest standard mass. If this adds too much mass to the balance, begin measuring the mass of the object with the next smaller standard mass.

4. Add standard masses until the masses on both pans are balanced and the pointer is at zero. Then add the standard masses together to determine the mass of the object being measured.

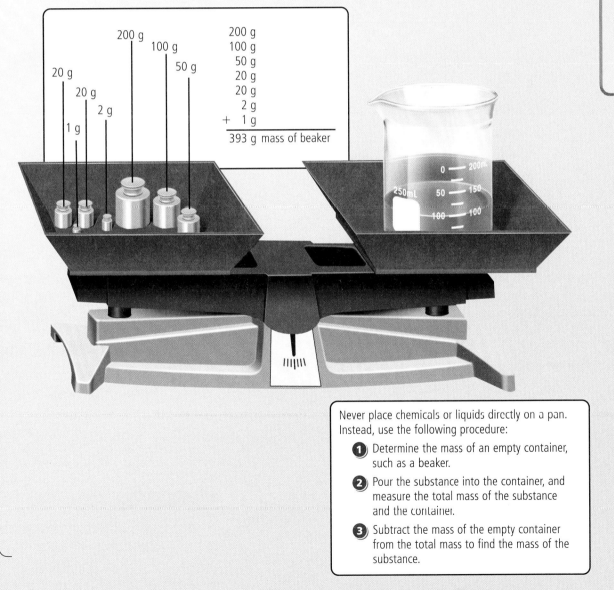

	200 g
	100 g
	50 g
	20 g
	20 g
	2 g
+	1 g

393 g mass of beaker

Never place chemicals or liquids directly on a pan. Instead, use the following procedure:

1. Determine the mass of an empty container, such as a beaker.

2. Pour the substance into the container, and measure the total mass of the substance and the container.

3. Subtract the mass of the empty container from the total mass to find the mass of the substance.

The Metric System and SI Units

Scientists use International System (SI) units for measurements of distance, volume, mass, and temperature. The International System is based on multiples of ten and the metric system of measurement.

Basic SI Units		
Property	Name	Symbol
length	meter	m
volume	liter	L
mass	kilogram	kg
temperature	kelvin	K

SI Prefixes		
Prefix	Symbol	Multiple of 10
kilo-	k	1000
hecto-	h	100
deca-	da	10
deci-	d	0.1 $\left(\frac{1}{10}\right)$
centi-	c	0.01 $\left(\frac{1}{100}\right)$
milli-	m	0.001 $\left(\frac{1}{1000}\right)$

Changing Metric Units

You can change from one unit to another in the metric system by multiplying or dividing by a power of 10.

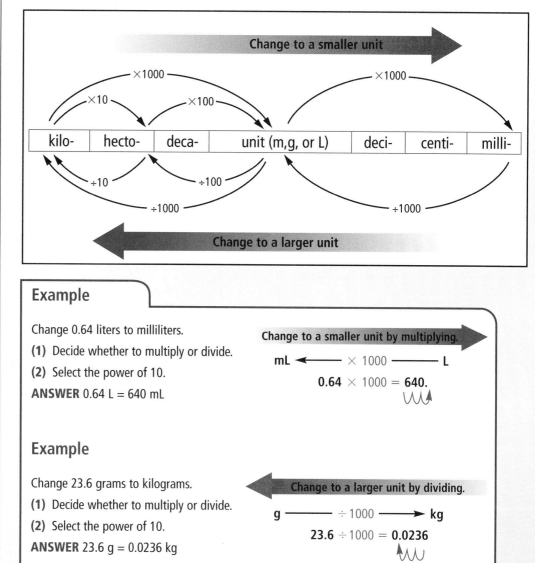

Example

Change 0.64 liters to milliliters.

(1) Decide whether to multiply or divide.
(2) Select the power of 10.
ANSWER 0.64 L = 640 mL

Change to a smaller unit by multiplying.

mL ◄——— × 1000 ——— L
0.64 × 1000 = **640.**

Example

Change 23.6 grams to kilograms.

(1) Decide whether to multiply or divide.
(2) Select the power of 10.
ANSWER 23.6 g = 0.0236 kg

Change to a larger unit by dividing.

g ——— ÷ 1000 ——► kg
23.6 ÷ 1000 = **0.0236**

Temperature Conversions

Even though the kelvin is the SI base unit of temperature, the degree Celsius will be the unit you use most often in your science studies. The formulas below show the relationships between temperatures in degrees Fahrenheit (°F), degrees Celsius (°C), and kelvins (K).

$$°C = \frac{5}{9}(°F - 32)$$

$$°F = \frac{9}{5}°C + 32$$

$$K = °C + 273$$

See page R42 for help with using formulas.

Examples of Temperature Conversions		
Condition	**Degrees Celsius**	**Degrees Fahrenheit**
Freezing point of water	0	32
Cool day	10	50
Mild day	20	68
Warm day	30	86
Normal body temperature	37	98.6
Very hot day	40	104
Boiling point of water	100	212

Converting Between SI and U.S. Customary Units

Use the chart below when you need to convert between SI units and U.S. customary units.

SI Unit	From SI to U.S. Customary			From U.S. Customary to SI		
Length	**When you know**	**multiply by**	**to find**	**When you know**	**multiply by**	**to find**
kilometer (km) = 1000 m	kilometers	0.62	miles	miles	1.61	kilometers
meter (m) = 100 cm	meters	3.28	feet	feet	0.3048	meters
centimeter (cm) = 10 mm	centimeters	0.39	inches	inches	2.54	centimeters
millimeter (mm) = 0.1 cm	millimeters	0.04	inches	inches	25.4	millimeters
Area	**When you know**	**multiply by**	**to find**	**When you know**	**multiply by**	**to find**
square kilometer (km²)	square kilometers	0.39	square miles	square miles	2.59	square kilometers
square meter (m²)	square meters	1.2	square yards	square yards	0.84	square meters
square centimeter (cm²)	square centimeters	0.155	square inches	square inches	6.45	square centimeters
Volume	**When you know**	**multiply by**	**to find**	**When you know**	**multiply by**	**to find**
liter (L) = 1000 mL	liters	1.06	quarts	quarts	0.95	liters
	liters	0.26	gallons	gallons	3.79	liters
	liters	4.23	cups	cups	0.24	liters
	liters	2.12	pints	pints	0.47	liters
milliliter (mL) = 0.001 L	milliliters	0.20	teaspoons	teaspoons	4.93	milliliters
	milliliters	0.07	tablespoons	tablespoons	14.79	milliliters
	milliliters	0.03	fluid ounces	fluid ounces	29.57	milliliters
Mass	**When you know**	**multiply by**	**to find**	**When you know**	**multiply by**	**to find**
kilogram (kg) = 1000 g	kilograms	2.2	pounds	pounds	0.45	kilograms
gram (g) = 1000 mg	grams	0.035	ounces	ounces	28.35	grams

Precision and Accuracy

When you do an experiment, it is important that your methods, observations, and data be both precise and accurate.

low precision

precision, but not accuracy

precision and accuracy

LAB HANDBOOK

Precision

In science, **precision** is the exactness and consistency of measurements. For example, measurements made with a ruler that has both centimeter and millimeter markings would be more precise than measurements made with a ruler that has only centimeter markings. Another indicator of precision is the care taken to make sure that methods and observations are as exact and consistent as possible. Every time a particular experiment is done, the same procedure should be used. Precision is necessary because experiments are repeated several times and if the procedure changes, the results will change.

EXAMPLE

Suppose you are measuring temperatures over a two-week period. Your precision will be greater if you measure each temperature at the same place, at the same time of day, and with the same thermometer than if you change any of these factors from one day to the next.

Accuracy

In science, it is possible to be precise but not accurate. **Accuracy** depends on the difference between a measurement and an actual value. The smaller the difference, the more accurate the measurement.

EXAMPLE

Suppose you look at a stream and estimate that it is about 1 meter wide at a particular place. You decide to check your estimate by measuring the stream with a meter stick, and you determine that the stream is 1.32 meters wide. However, because it is hard to measure the width of a stream with a meter stick, it turns out that you didn't do a very good job. The stream is actually 1.14 meters wide. Therefore, even though your estimate was less precise than your measurement, your estimate was actually more accurate.

Making Data Tables and Graphs

Data tables and graphs are useful tools for both recording and communicating scientific data.

Making Data Tables

You can use a **data table** to organize and record the measurements that you make. Some examples of information that might be recorded in data tables are frequencies, times, and amounts.

EXAMPLE

Suppose you are investigating photosynthesis in two elodea plants. One sits in direct sunlight, and the other sits in a dimly lit room. You measure the rate of photosynthesis by counting the number of bubbles in the jar every ten minutes.

1. Title and number your data table.
2. Decide how you will organize the table into columns and rows.
3. Any units, such as seconds or degrees, should be included in column headings, not in the individual cells.

Table 1. Number of Bubbles from Elodea

Time (min)	Sunlight	Dim Light
0	0	0
10	15	5
20	25	8
30	32	7
40	41	10
50	47	9
60	42	9

> Always number and title data tables.

The data in the table above could also be organized in a different way.

Table 1. Number of Bubbles from Elodea

Light Condition	Time (min)						
	0	10	20	30	40	50	60
Sunlight	0	15	25	32	41	47	42
Dim light	0	5	8	7	10	9	9

> Put units in column heading.

Making Line Graphs

You can use a **line graph** to show a relationship between variables. Line graphs are particularly useful for showing changes in variables over time.

EXAMPLE

Suppose you are interested in graphing temperature data that you collected over the course of a day.

Table 1. Outside Temperature During the Day on March 7

	Time of Day						
	7:00 A.M.	9:00 A.M.	11:00 A.M.	1:00 P.M.	3:00 P.M.	5:00 P.M.	7:00 P.M.
Temp (°C)	8	9	11	14	12	10	6

1. Use the vertical axis of your line graph for the variable that you are measuring—temperature.

2. Choose scales for both the horizontal axis and the vertical axis of the graph. You should have two points more than you need on the vertical axis, and the horizontal axis should be long enough for all of the data points to fit.

3. Draw and label each axis.

4. Graph each value. First find the appropriate point on the scale of the horizontal axis. Imagine a line that rises vertically from that place on the scale. Then find the corresponding value on the vertical axis, and imagine a line that moves horizontally from that value. The point where these two imaginary lines intersect is where the value should be plotted.

5. Connect the points with straight lines.

Be sure to add a number and a title to your graph.

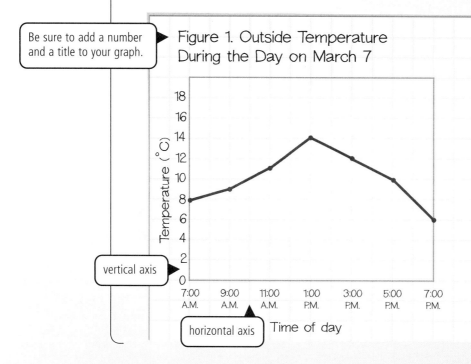

Figure 1. Outside Temperature During the Day on March 7

vertical axis

horizontal axis — Time of day

Making Circle Graphs

You can use a **circle graph,** sometimes called a pie chart, to represent data as parts of a circle. Circle graphs are used only when the data can be expressed as percentages of a whole. The entire circle shown in a circle graph is equal to 100 percent of the data.

EXAMPLE

Suppose you identified the species of each mature tree growing in a small wooded area. You organized your data in a table, but you also want to show the data in a circle graph.

1. To begin, find the total number of mature trees.

   $56 + 34 + 22 + 10 + 28 = 150$

2. To find the degree measure for each sector of the circle, write a fraction comparing the number of each tree species with the total number of trees. Then multiply the fraction by 360°.

   Oak: $\frac{56}{150} \times 360° = 134.4°$

3. Draw a circle. Use a protractor to draw the angle for each sector of the graph.

4. Color and label each sector of the graph.

5. Give the graph a number and title.

Table 1. Tree Species in Wooded Area

Species	Number of Specimens
Oak	56
Maple	34
Birch	22
Willow	10
Pine	28

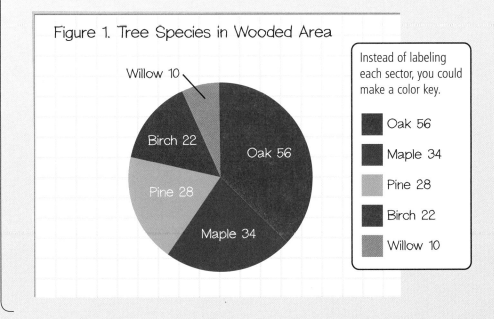

Figure 1. Tree Species in Wooded Area

Willow 10
Birch 22
Pine 28
Oak 56
Maple 34

Instead of labeling each sector, you could make a color key.

■ Oak 56
■ Maple 34
■ Pine 28
■ Birch 22
■ Willow 10

Bar Graph

A **bar graph** is a type of graph in which the lengths of the bars are used to represent and compare data. A numerical scale is used to determine the lengths of the bars.

EXAMPLE

To determine the effect of water on seed sprouting, three cups were filled with sand, and ten seeds were planted in each. Different amounts of water were added to each cup over a three-day period.

Table 1. Effect of Water on Seed Sprouting

Daily Amount of Water (mL)	Number of Seeds That Sprouted After 3 Days in Sand
0	1
10	4
20	8

1. Choose a numerical scale. The greatest value is 8, so the end of the scale should have a value greater than 8, such as 10. Use equal increments along the scale, such as increments of 2.

2. Draw and label the axes. Mark intervals on the vertical axis according to the scale you chose.

3. Draw a bar for each data value. Use the scale to decide how long to make each bar.

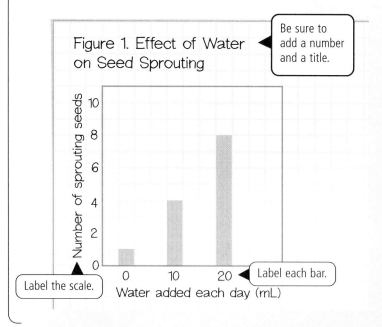

Figure 1. Effect of Water on Seed Sprouting

Be sure to add a number and a title.

Label the scale.

Label each bar.

Double Bar Graph

A **double bar graph** is a bar graph that shows two sets of data. The two bars for each measurement are drawn next to each other.

EXAMPLE

The seed-sprouting experiment was done using both sand and potting soil. The data for sand and potting soil can be plotted on one graph.

1. Draw one set of bars, using the data for sand, as shown below.

2. Draw bars for the potting-soil data next to the bars for the sand data. Shade them a different color. Add a key.

Table 2. Effect of Water and Soil on Seed Sprouting

Daily Amount of Water (mL)	Number of Seeds That Sprouted After 3 Days in Sand	Number of Seeds That Sprouted After 3 Days in Potting Soil
0	1	2
10	4	5
20	8	9

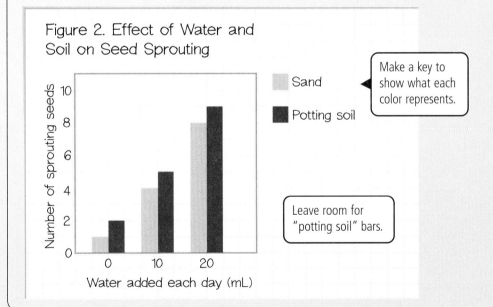

Figure 2. Effect of Water and Soil on Seed Sprouting

Make a key to show what each color represents.

Leave room for "potting soil" bars.

Designing an Experiment

Use this section when designing or conducting an experiment.

Determining a Purpose

You can find a purpose for an experiment by doing research, by examining the results of a previous experiment, or by observing the world around you. An **experiment** is an organized procedure to study something under controlled conditions.

Don't forget to learn as much as possible about your topic before you begin.

1. Write the purpose of your experiment as a question or problem that you want to investigate.

2. Write down research questions and begin searching for information that will help you design an experiment. Consult the library, the Internet, and other people as you conduct your research.

EXAMPLE

Middle school students observed an odor near the lake by their school. They also noticed that the water on the side of the lake near the school was greener than the water on the other side of the lake. The students did some research to learn more about their observations. They discovered that the odor and green color in the lake

came from algae. They also discovered that a new fertilizer was being used on a field nearby. The students inferred that the use of the fertilizer might be related to the presence of the algae and designed a controlled experiment to find out whether they were right.

> **Problem**
> How does fertilizer affect the presence of algae in a lake?
>
> **Research Questions**
> - Have other experiments been done on this problem? If so, what did those experiments show?
> - What kind of fertilizer is used on the field? How much?
> - How do algae grow?
> - How do people measure algae?
> - Can fertilizer and algae be used safely in a lab? How?

Research
As you research, you may find a topic that is more interesting to you than your original topic, or learn that a procedure you wanted to use is not practical or safe. It is OK to change your purpose as you research.

Writing a Hypothesis

A **hypothesis** is a tentative explanation for an observation or scientific problem that can be tested by further investigation. You can write your hypothesis in the form of an "If . . . , then . . . , because . . ." statement.

Hypothesis

If the amount of fertilizer in lake water is increased, then the amount of algae will also increase, because fertilizers provide nutrients that algae need to grow.

Hypotheses
For help with hypotheses, refer to page R3.

Determining Materials

Make a list of all the materials you will need to do your experiment. Be specific, especially if someone else is helping you obtain the materials. Try to think of everything you will need.

Materials
- 1 large jar or container
- 4 identical smaller containers
- rubber gloves that also cover the arms
- sample of fertilizer-and-water solution
- eyedropper
- clear plastic wrap
- scissors
- masking tape
- marker
- ruler

Determining Variables and Constants

EXPERIMENTAL GROUP AND CONTROL GROUP

An experiment to determine how two factors are related always has two groups—a control group and an experimental group.

1. Design an experimental group. Include as many trials as possible in the experimental group in order to obtain reliable results.

2. Design a control group that is the same as the experimental group in every way possible, except for the factor you wish to test.

Experimental Group: two containers of lake water with one drop of fertilizer solution added to each

Control Group: two containers of lake water with no fertilizer solution added

> Go back to your materials list and make sure you have enough items listed to cover both your experimental group and your control group.

VARIABLES AND CONSTANTS

Identify the variables and constants in your experiment. In a controlled experiment, a **variable** is any factor that can change. **Constants** are all of the factors that are the same in both the experimental group and the control group.

1. Read your hypothesis. The **independent variable** is the factor that you wish to test and that is manipulated or changed so that it can be tested. The independent variable is expressed in your hypothesis after the word *if*. Identify the independent variable in your laboratory report.

2. The **dependent variable** is the factor that you measure to gather results. It is expressed in your hypothesis after the word *then*. Identify the dependent variable in your laboratory report.

> **Hypothesis**
> If the amount of fertilizer in lake water is increased, then the amount of algae will also increase, because fertilizers provide nutrients that algae need to grow.

Table 1. Variables and Constants in Algae Experiment

Independent Variable	Dependent Variable	Constants
Amount of fertilizer in lake water	Amount of algae that grow	• Where the lake water is obtained • Type of container used • Light and temperature conditions where water will be stored

> Set up your experiment so that you will test only one variable.

MEASURING THE DEPENDENT VARIABLE

Before starting your experiment, you need to define how you will measure the dependent variable. An **operational definition** is a description of the one particular way in which you will measure the dependent variable.

Your operational definition is important for several reasons. First, in any experiment there are several ways in which a dependent variable can be measured. Second, the procedure of the experiment depends on how you decide to measure the dependent variable. Third, your operational definition makes it possible for other people to evaluate and build on your experiment.

EXAMPLE 1

An operational definition of a dependent variable can be qualitative. That is, your measurement of the dependent variable can simply be an observation of whether a change occurs as a result of a change in the independent variable. This type of operational definition can be thought of as a "yes or no" measurement.

Table 2. Qualitative Operational Definition of Algae Growth

Independent Variable	Dependent Variable	Operational Definition
Amount of fertilizer in lake water	Amount of algae that grow	Algae grow in lake water

A qualitative measurement of a dependent variable is often easy to make and record. However, this type of information does not provide a great deal of detail in your experimental results.

EXAMPLE 2

An operational definition of a dependent variable can be quantitative. That is, your measurement of the dependent variable can be a number that shows how much change occurs as a result of a change in the independent variable.

Table 3. Quantitative Operational Definition of Algae Growth

Independent Variable	Dependent Variable	Operational Definition
Amount of fertilizer in lake water	Amount of algae that grow	Diameter of largest algal growth (in mm)

A quantitative measurement of a dependent variable can be more difficult to make and analyze than a qualitative measurement. However, this type of data provides much more information about your experiment and is often more useful.

Writing a Procedure

Write each step of your procedure. Start each step with a verb, or action word, and keep the steps short. Your procedure should be clear enough for someone else to use as instructions for repeating your experiment.

If necessary, go back to your materials list and add any materials that you left out.

Controlling Variables
The same amount of fertilizer solution must be added to two of the four containers.

Controlling Variables
All four containers must receive the same amount of light.

Procedure

1. Put on your gloves. Use the large container to obtain a sample of lake water.

2. Divide the sample of lake water equally among the four smaller containers.

3. Use the eyedropper to add one drop of fertilizer solution to two of the containers.

4. Use the masking tape and the marker to label the containers with your initials, the date, and the identifiers "Jar 1 with Fertilizer," "Jar 2 with Fertilizer," "Jar 1 without Fertilizer," and "Jar 2 without Fertilizer."

5. Cover the containers with clear plastic wrap. Use the scissors to punch ten holes in each of the covers.

6. Place all four containers on a window ledge. Make sure that they all receive the same amount of light.

7. Observe the containers every day for one week.

8. Use the ruler to measure the diameter of the largest clump of algae in each container, and record your measurements daily.

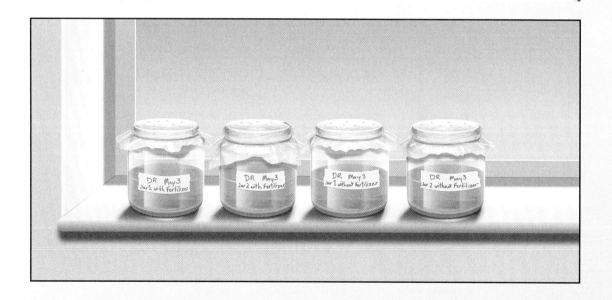

Recording Observations

Once you have obtained all of your materials and your procedure has been approved, you can begin making experimental observations. Gather both quantitative and qualitative data. If something goes wrong during your procedure, make sure you record that too.

Observations
For help with making qualitative and quantitative observations, refer to page R2.

For more examples of data tables, see page R23.

Table 4. Fertilizer and Algae Growth

Date and Time	Experimental Group		Control Group		Observations
	Jar 1 with Fertilizer (diameter of algae in mm)	Jar 2 with Fertilizer (diameter of algae in mm)	Jar 1 without Fertilizer (diameter of algae in mm)	Jar 2 without Fertilizer (diameter of algae in mm)	
5/3 4:00 P.M.	0	0	0	0	condensation in all containers
5/4 4:00 P.M.	0	3	0	0	tiny green blobs in jar 2 with fertilizer
5/5 4:15 P.M.	4	5	0	3	green blobs in jars 1 and 2 with fertilizer and jar 2 without fertilizer
5/6 4:00 P.M.	5	6	0	4	water light green in jar 2 with fertilizer
5/7 4:00 P.M.	8	10	0	6	water light green in jars 1 and 2 with fertilizer and in jar 2 without fertilizer
5/8 3:30 P.M.	10	18	0	6	cover off jar 2 with fertilizer
5/9 3:30 P.M.	14	23	0	8	drew sketches of each container

Notice that on the sixth day, the observer found that the cover was off one of the containers. It is important to record observations of unintended factors because they might affect the results of the experiment.

Use technology, such as a microscope, to help you make observations when possible.

Drawings of Samples Viewed Under Microscope on 5/9 at 100x

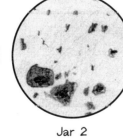

Jar 1 with Fertilizer   Jar 2 with Fertilizer

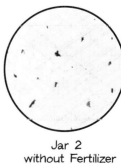

Jar 1 without Fertilizer   Jar 2 without Fertilizer

Summarizing Results

To summarize your data, look at all of your observations together. Look for meaningful ways to present your observations. For example, you might average your data or make a graph to look for patterns. When possible, use spreadsheet software to help you analyze and present your data. The two graphs below show the same data.

EXAMPLE 1

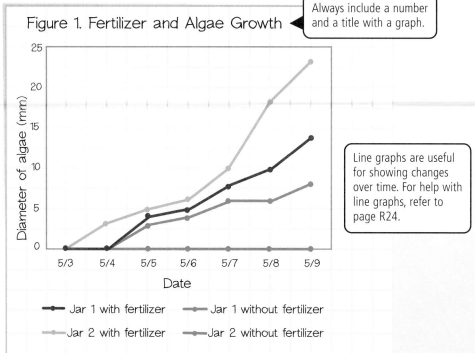

Figure 1. Fertilizer and Algae Growth

Always include a number and a title with a graph.

Line graphs are useful for showing changes over time. For help with line graphs, refer to page R24.

EXAMPLE 2

Bar graphs are useful for comparing different data sets. This bar graph has four bars for each day. Another way to present the data would be to calculate averages for the tests and the controls, and to show one test bar and one control bar for each day.

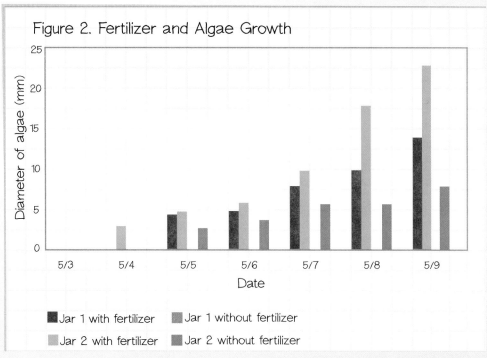

Figure 2. Fertilizer and Algae Growth

LAB HANDBOOK

Drawing Conclusions

RESULTS AND INFERENCES

To draw conclusions from your experiment, first write your results. Then compare your results with your hypothesis. Do your results support your hypothesis? Be careful not to make inferences about factors that you did not test.

For help with making inferences, see page R4.

Results and Inferences

The results of my experiment show that more algae grew in lake water to which fertilizer had been added than in lake water to which no fertilizer had been added. My hypothesis was supported. I infer that it is possible that the growth of algae in the lake was caused by the fertilizer used on the field.

Notice that you cannot conclude from this experiment that the presence of algae in the lake was due only to the fertilizer.

QUESTIONS FOR FURTHER RESEARCH

Write a list of questions for further research and investigation. Your ideas may lead you to new experiments and discoveries.

Questions for Further Research

- What is the connection between the amount of fertilizer and algae growth?
- How do different brands of fertilizer affect algae growth?
- How would algae growth in the lake be affected if no fertilizer were used on the field?
- How do algae affect the lake and the other life in and around it?
- How does fertilizer affect the lake and the life in and around it?
- If fertilizer is getting into the lake, how is it getting there?

Math Handbook

Describing a Set of Data

Means, medians, modes, and ranges are important math tools for describing data sets such as the following widths of fossilized clamshells.

13 mm   25 mm   14 mm   21 mm   16 mm   23 mm   14 mm

Mean

The **mean** of a data set is the sum of the values divided by the number of values.

> **Example**
>
> To find the mean of the clamshell data, add the values and then divide the sum by the number of values.
>
> $$\frac{13 \text{ mm} + 25 \text{ mm} + 14 \text{ mm} + 21 \text{ mm} + 16 \text{ mm} + 23 \text{ mm} + 14 \text{ mm}}{7} = \frac{126 \text{ mm}}{7} = 18 \text{ mm}$$
>
> **ANSWER** The mean is 18 mm.

Median

The **median** of a data set is the middle value when the values are written in numerical order. If a data set has an even number of values, the median is the mean of the two middle values.

> **Example**
>
> To find the median of the clamshell data, arrange the values in order from least to greatest. The median is the middle value.
>
> 13 mm   14 mm   14 mm   16 mm   21 mm   23 mm   25 mm
>
> **ANSWER** The median is 16 mm.

Mode

The **mode** of a data set is the value that occurs most often.

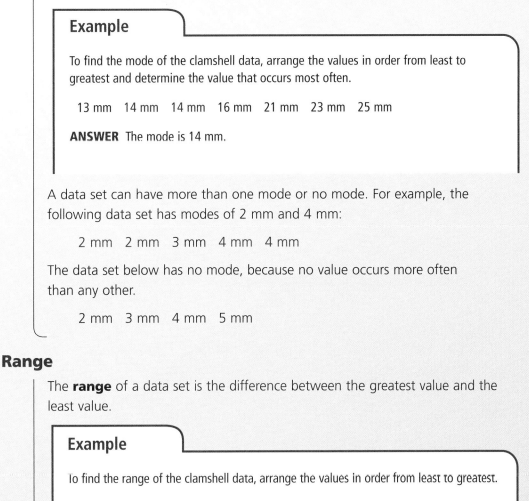

Example

To find the mode of the clamshell data, arrange the values in order from least to greatest and determine the value that occurs most often.

13 mm   14 mm   14 mm   16 mm   21 mm   23 mm   25 mm

ANSWER The mode is 14 mm.

A data set can have more than one mode or no mode. For example, the following data set has modes of 2 mm and 4 mm:

2 mm   2 mm   3 mm   4 mm   4 mm

The data set below has no mode, because no value occurs more often than any other.

2 mm   3 mm   4 mm   5 mm

Range

The **range** of a data set is the difference between the greatest value and the least value.

Example

To find the range of the clamshell data, arrange the values in order from least to greatest.

13 mm   14 mm   14 mm   16 mm   21 mm   23 mm   25 mm

Subtract the least value from the greatest value.

13 mm is the least value.
25 mm is the greatest value.

25 mm − 13 mm = 12 mm

ANSWER The range is 12 mm.

Using Ratios, Rates, and Proportions

You can use ratios and rates to compare values in data sets. You can use proportions to find unknown values.

Ratios

A **ratio** uses division to compare two values. The ratio of a value a to a nonzero value b can be written as $\frac{a}{b}$.

Example

The height of one plant is 8 centimeters. The height of another plant is 6 centimeters. To find the ratio of the height of the first plant to the height of the second plant, write a fraction and simplify it.

$$\frac{8 \text{ cm}}{6 \text{ cm}} = \frac{4 \times \overset{1}{\cancel{2}}}{3 \times \underset{1}{\cancel{2}}} = \frac{4}{3}$$

ANSWER The ratio of the plant heights is $\frac{4}{3}$.

You can also write the ratio $\frac{a}{b}$ as "a to b" or as $a:b$. For example, you can write the ratio of the plant heights as "4 to 3" or as $4:3$.

Rates

A **rate** is a ratio of two values expressed in different units. A unit rate is a rate with a denominator of 1 unit.

Example

A plant grew 6 centimeters in 2 days. The plant's rate of growth was $\frac{6 \text{ cm}}{2 \text{ days}}$. To describe the plant's growth in centimeters per day, write a unit rate.

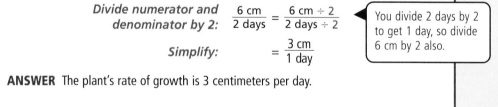

Divide numerator and denominator by 2: $\quad \frac{6 \text{ cm}}{2 \text{ days}} = \frac{6 \text{ cm} \div 2}{2 \text{ days} \div 2}$ ◀ You divide 2 days by 2 to get 1 day, so divide 6 cm by 2 also.

Simplify: $\quad = \frac{3 \text{ cm}}{1 \text{ day}}$

ANSWER The plant's rate of growth is 3 centimeters per day.

MATH HANDBOOK

Proportions

A **proportion** is an equation stating that two ratios are equivalent. To solve for an unknown value in a proportion, you can use cross products.

Example

If a plant grew 6 centimeters in 2 days, how many centimeters would it grow in 3 days (if its rate of growth is constant)?

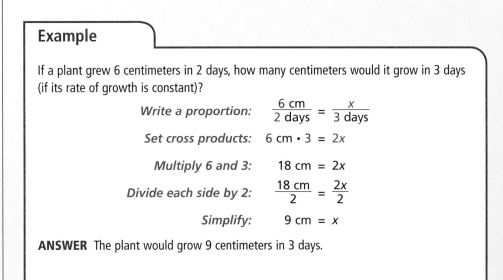

Write a proportion: $\dfrac{6 \text{ cm}}{2 \text{ days}} = \dfrac{x}{3 \text{ days}}$

Set cross products: $6 \text{ cm} \cdot 3 = 2x$

Multiply 6 and 3: $18 \text{ cm} = 2x$

Divide each side by 2: $\dfrac{18 \text{ cm}}{2} = \dfrac{2x}{2}$

Simplify: $9 \text{ cm} = x$

ANSWER The plant would grow 9 centimeters in 3 days.

Using Decimals, Fractions, and Percents

Decimals, fractions, and percentages are all ways of recording and representing data.

Decimals

A **decimal** is a number that is written in the base-ten place value system, in which a decimal point separates the ones and tenths digits. The values of each place is ten times that of the place to its right.

Example

A caterpillar traveled from point *A* to point *C* along the path shown.

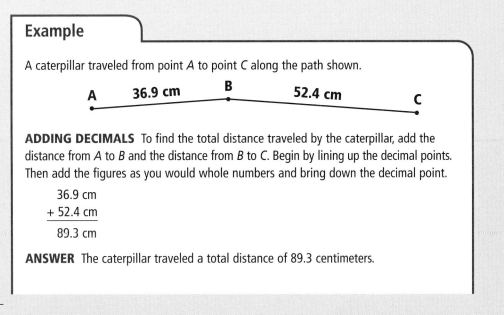

A   36.9 cm   B   52.4 cm   C

ADDING DECIMALS To find the total distance traveled by the caterpillar, add the distance from *A* to *B* and the distance from *B* to *C*. Begin by lining up the decimal points. Then add the figures as you would whole numbers and bring down the decimal point.

```
   36.9 cm
 + 52.4 cm
   89.3 cm
```

ANSWER The caterpillar traveled a total distance of 89.3 centimeters.

Example continued

SUBTRACTING DECIMALS To find how much farther the caterpillar traveled on the second leg of the journey, subtract the distance from *A* to *B* from the distance from *B* to *C*.

$$\begin{array}{r} 52.4 \text{ cm} \\ -\ 36.9 \text{ cm} \\ \hline 15.5 \text{ cm} \end{array}$$

ANSWER The caterpillar traveled 15.5 centimeters farther on the second leg of the journey.

Example

A caterpillar is traveling from point *D* to point *F* along the path shown. The caterpillar travels at a speed of 9.6 centimeters per minute.

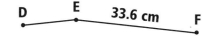

MULTIPLYING DECIMALS You can multiply decimals as you would whole numbers. The number of decimal places in the product is equal to the sum of the number of decimal places in the factors.

For instance, suppose it takes the caterpillar 1.5 minutes to go from *D* to *E*. To find the distance from *D* to *E*, multiply the caterpillar's speed by the time it took.

Align as shown.

$$\begin{array}{rll} 9.6 & 1 & \text{decimal place} \\ \times\ 1.5 & +\ 1 & \text{decimal place} \\ \hline 480 & & \\ 96 & & \\ \hline 14.40 & 2 & \text{decimal places} \end{array}$$

ANSWER The distance from *D* to *E* is 14.4 centimeters.

DIVIDING DECIMALS When you divide by a decimal, move the decimal points the same number of places in the divisor and the dividend to make the divisor a whole number.

For instance, to find the time it will take the caterpillar to travel from *E* to *F*, divide the distance from *E* to *F* by the caterpillar's speed.

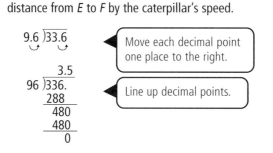

Move each decimal point one place to the right.

Line up decimal points.

ANSWER The caterpillar will travel from *E* to *F* in 3.5 minutes.

Fractions

A **fraction** is a number in the form $\frac{a}{b}$, where b is not equal to 0. A fraction is in **simplest form** if its numerator and denominator have a greatest common factor (GCF) of 1. To simplify a fraction, divide its numerator and denominator by their GCF.

Example

A caterpillar is 40 millimeters long. The head of the caterpillar is 6 millimeters long. To compare the length of the caterpillar's head with the caterpillar's total length, you can write and simplify a fraction that expresses the ratio of the two lengths.

Write the ratio of the two lengths: $\dfrac{\text{Length of head}}{\text{Total length}} = \dfrac{6 \text{ mm}}{40 \text{ mm}}$

Write numerator and denominator as products of numbers and the GCF: $= \dfrac{3 \times 2}{20 \times 2}$

Divide numerator and denominator by the GCF: $= \dfrac{3 \times \overset{1}{2}}{20 \times \underset{1}{2}}$

Simplify: $= \dfrac{3}{20}$

ANSWER In simplest form, the ratio of the lengths is $\dfrac{3}{20}$.

Percents

A **percent** is a ratio that compares a number to 100. The word *percent* means "per hundred" or "out of 100." The symbol for *percent* is %.

For instance, suppose 43 out of 100 caterpillars are female. You can represent this ratio as a percent, a decimal, or a fraction.

Percent	Decimal	Fraction
43%	0.43	$\dfrac{43}{100}$

Example

In the preceding example, the ratio of the length of the caterpillar's head to the caterpillar's total length is $\dfrac{3}{20}$. To write this ratio as a percent, write an equivalent fraction that has a denominator of 100.

Multiply numerator and denominator by 5: $\dfrac{3}{20} = \dfrac{3 \times 5}{20 \times 5}$

$= \dfrac{15}{100}$

Write as a percent: $= 15\%$

ANSWER The caterpillar's head represents 15 percent of its total length.

Using Formulas

A **formula** is an equation that shows the general relationship between two or more quantities.

In science, a formula often has a word form and a symbolic form. The formula below expresses Ohm's law.

Word Form

$$\text{Current} = \frac{\text{voltage}}{\text{resistance}}$$

Symbolic Form

$$I = \frac{V}{R}$$

> The term *variable* is also used in science to refer to a factor that can change during an experiment.

In this formula, I, V, and R are variables. A mathematical **variable** is a symbol or letter that is used to represent one or more numbers.

Example

Suppose that you measure a voltage of 1.5 volts and a resistance of 15 ohms. You can use the formula for Ohm's law to find the current in amperes.

Write the formula for Ohm's law: $\quad I = \dfrac{V}{R}$

Substitute 1.5 volts for V and 15 ohms for R: $\quad I = \dfrac{1.5 \text{ volts}}{15 \text{ ohms}}$

Simplify: $\quad I = 0.1$ amp

ANSWER The current is 0.1 ampere.

If you know the values of all variables but one in a formula, you can solve for the value of the unknown variable. For instance, Ohm's law can be used to find a voltage if you know the current and the resistance.

Example

Suppose that you know that a current is 0.2 amperes and the resistance is 18 ohms. Use the formula for Ohm's law to find the voltage in volts.

Write the formula for Ohm's law: $\qquad\qquad\qquad I = \dfrac{V}{R}$

Substitute 0.2 amp for I and 18 ohms for R: $\qquad 0.2 \text{ amp} = \dfrac{V}{18 \text{ ohms}}$

Multiply both sides by 18 ohms: $\quad 0.2 \text{ amp} \cdot 18 \text{ ohms} = V$

Simplify: $\qquad\qquad\qquad\qquad 3.6 \text{ volts} = V$

ANSWER The voltage is 3.6 volts.

Finding Areas

The area of a figure is the amount of surface the figure covers.

Area is measured in square units, such as square meters (m^2) or square centimeters (cm^2). Formulas for the areas of three common geometric figures are shown below.

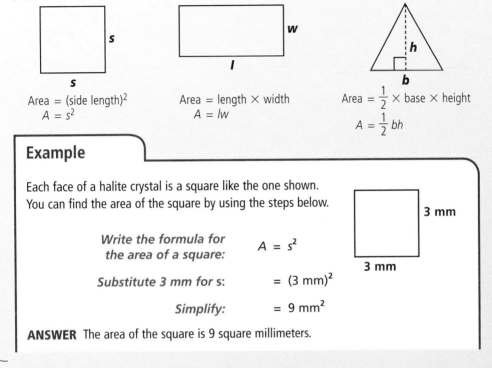

Area = (side length)^2
$A = s^2$

Area = length × width
$A = lw$

Area = $\frac{1}{2}$ × base × height
$A = \frac{1}{2} bh$

Example

Each face of a halite crystal is a square like the one shown. You can find the area of the square by using the steps below.

Write the formula for the area of a square:	$A = s^2$
Substitute 3 mm for s:	$= (3 \text{ mm})^2$
Simplify:	$= 9 \text{ mm}^2$

ANSWER The area of the square is 9 square millimeters.

Finding Volumes

The volume of a solid is the amount of space contained by the solid.

Volume is measured in cubic units, such as cubic meters (m^3) or cubic centimeters (cm^3). The volume of a rectangular prism is given by the formula shown below.

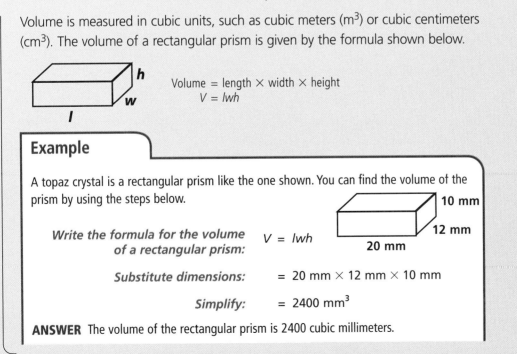

Volume = length × width × height
$V = lwh$

Example

A topaz crystal is a rectangular prism like the one shown. You can find the volume of the prism by using the steps below.

Write the formula for the volume of a rectangular prism:	$V = lwh$
Substitute dimensions:	$= 20 \text{ mm} \times 12 \text{ mm} \times 10 \text{ mm}$
Simplify:	$= 2400 \text{ mm}^3$

ANSWER The volume of the rectangular prism is 2400 cubic millimeters.

Using Significant Figures

The **significant figures** in a decimal are the digits that are warranted by the accuracy of a measuring device.

When you perform a calculation with measurements, the number of significant figures to include in the result depends in part on the number of significant figures in the measurements. When you multiply or divide measurements, your answer should have only as many significant figures as the measurement with the fewest significant figures.

Example

Using a balance and a graduated cylinder filled with water, you determined that a marble has a mass of 8.0 grams and a volume of 3.5 cubic centimeters. To calculate the density of the marble, divide the mass by the volume.

Write the formula for density: $\text{Density} = \dfrac{\text{mass}}{\text{Volume}}$

Substitute measurements: $= \dfrac{8.0 \text{ g}}{3.5 \text{ cm}^3}$

Use a calculator to divide: $\approx 2.285714286 \text{ g/cm}^3$

ANSWER Because the mass and the volume have two significant figures each, give the density to two significant figures. The marble has a density of 2.3 grams per cubic centimeter.

Using Scientific Notation

Scientific notation is a shorthand way to write very large or very small numbers. For example, 73,500,000,000,000,000,000,000 kg is the mass of the Moon. In scientific notation, it is 7.35×10^{22} kg.

Example

You can convert from standard form to scientific notation.

Standard Form	Scientific Notation
720,000 5 decimal places left	7.2×10^5 Exponent is 5.
0.000291 4 decimal places right	2.91×10^{-4} Exponent is −4.

You can convert from scientific notation to standard form.

Scientific Notation	Standard Form
4.63×10^7 Exponent is 7.	46,300,000 7 decimal places right
1.08×10^{-6} Exponent is −6.	0.00000108 6 decimal places left

Note-Taking Handbook

Note-Taking Strategies

Taking notes as you read helps you understand the information. The notes you take can also be used as a study guide for later review. This handbook presents several ways to organize your notes.

Content Frame

1. Make a chart in which each column represents a category.
2. Give each column a heading.
3. Write details under the headings.

NAME	GROUP	CHARACTERISTICS	DRAWING
snail	mollusks	mantle, shell	
ant	arthropods	six legs, exoskeleton	
earthworm	segmented worms	segmented body, circulatory and digestive systems	
heartworm	roundworms	digestive system	
sea star	echinoderms	spiny skin, tube feet	
jellyfish	cnidarians	stinging cells	

categories

details

Combination Notes

1. For each new idea or concept, write an informal outline of the information.
2. Make a sketch to illustrate the concept, and label it.

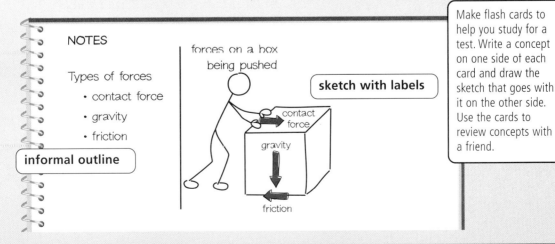

NOTES

Types of forces
- contact force
- gravity
- friction

informal outline

forces on a box being pushed

sketch with labels

contact force

gravity

friction

Make flash cards to help you study for a test. Write a concept on one side of each card and draw the sketch that goes with it on the other side. Use the cards to review concepts with a friend.

Main Idea and Detail Notes

1. In the left-hand column of a two-column chart, list main ideas. The blue headings express main ideas throughout this textbook.

2. In the right-hand column, write details that expand on each main idea.

You can shorten the headings in your chart. Be sure to use the most important words.

When studying for tests, cover up the detail notes column with a sheet of paper. Then use each main idea to form a question—such as "How does latitude affect climate?" Answer the question, and then uncover the detail notes column to check your answer.

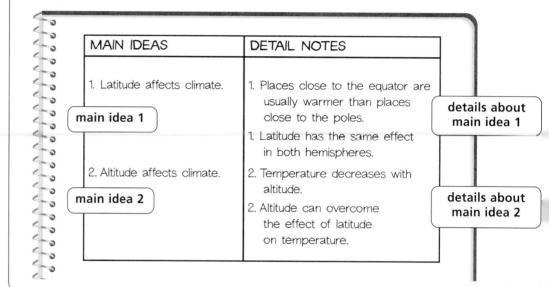

Main Idea Web

1. Write a main idea in a box.

2. Add boxes around it with related vocabulary terms and important details.

You can find definitions near highlighted terms.

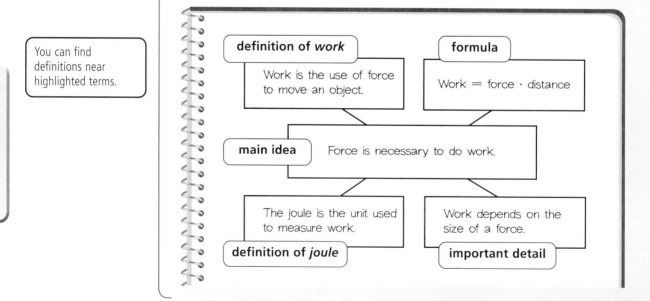

NOTE-TAKING HANDBOOK

Mind Map

1. Write a main idea in the center.

2. Add details that relate to one another and to the main idea.

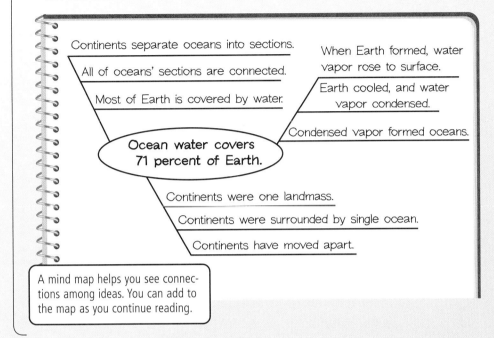

Continents separate oceans into sections.

All of oceans' sections are connected.

Most of Earth is covered by water.

When Earth formed, water vapor rose to surface.

Earth cooled, and water vapor condensed.

Condensed vapor formed oceans.

Ocean water covers 71 percent of Earth.

Continents were one landmass.

Continents were surrounded by single ocean.

Continents have moved apart.

A mind map helps you see connections among ideas. You can add to the map as you continue reading.

Supporting Main Ideas

1. Write a main idea in a box.

2. Add boxes underneath with information—such as reasons, explanations, and examples—that supports the main idea.

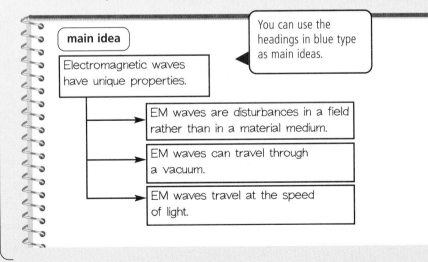

main idea

Electromagnetic waves have unique properties.

You can use the headings in blue type as main ideas.

EM waves are disturbances in a field rather than in a material medium.

EM waves can travel through a vacuum.

EM waves travel at the speed of light.

Outline

1. Copy the chapter title and headings from the book in the form of an outline.

2. Add notes that summarize in your own words what you read.

Cell Processes

1st key idea

I. Cells capture and release energy.

1st subpoint of I

   A. All cells need energy.

2nd subpoint of I

   B. Some cells capture light energy.

1st detail about B

      1. Process of photosynthesis

2nd detail about B

      2. Chloroplasts (site of photosynthesis)

      3. Carbon dioxide and water as raw materials

      4. Glucose and oxygen as products

   C. All cells release energy.

      1. Process of cellular respiration

      2. Fermentation of sugar to carbon dioxide

      3. Bacteria that carry out fermentation

II. Cells transport materials through membranes.

   A. Some materials move by diffusion.

      1. Particle movement from higher to lower concentrations

      2. Movement of water through membrane (osmosis)

   B. Some transport requires energy.

      1. Active transport

      2. Examples of active transport

Correct Outline Form
Include a title.

Arrange key ideas, subpoints, and details as shown.

Indent the divisions of the outline as shown.

Use the same grammatical form for items of the same rank. For example, if A is a sentence, B must also be a sentence.

You must have at least two main ideas or subpoints. That is, every A must be followed by a B, and every 1 must be followed by a 2.

Concept Map

1. Write an important concept in a large oval.
2. Add details related to the concept in smaller ovals.
3. Write linking words on arrows that connect the ovals.

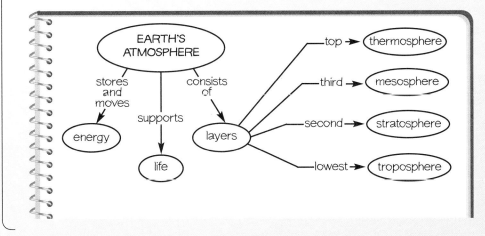

The main ideas or concepts can often be found in the blue headings. An example is "The atmosphere stores and moves energy." Use nouns from these concepts in the ovals, and use the verb or verbs on the lines.

Venn Diagram

1. Draw two overlapping circles, one for each item that you are comparing.
2. In the overlapping section, list the characteristics that are shared by both items.
3. In the outer sections, list the characteristics that are peculiar to each item.
4. Write a summary that describes the information in the Venn diagram.

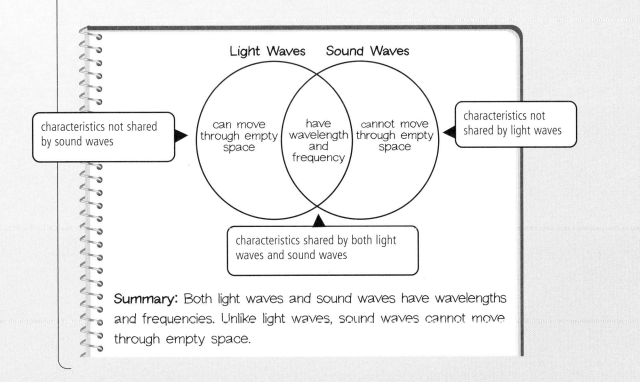

Summary: Both light waves and sound waves have wavelengths and frequencies. Unlike light waves, sound waves cannot move through empty space.

Vocabulary Strategies

Important terms are highlighted in this book. A definition of each term can be found in the sentence or paragraph where the term appears. You can also find definitions in the Glossary. Taking notes about vocabulary terms helps you understand and remember what you read.

Description Wheel

1. Write a term inside a circle.

2. Write words that describe the term on "spokes" attached to the circle.

When studying for a test with a friend, read the phrases on the spokes one at a time until your friend identifies the correct term.

leads to deposition

carries particles long distances

moving water a main agent

wind and ice other agents

first stage: weathering

carries sediment

EROSION

Four Square

1. Write a term in the center.

2. Write details in the four areas around the term.

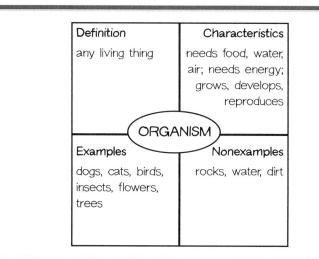

Definition	Characteristics
any living thing	needs food, water, air; needs energy; grows, develops, reproduces
ORGANISM	
Examples	Nonexamples
dogs, cats, birds, insects, flowers, trees	rocks, water, dirt

Include a definition, some characteristics, and examples. You may want to add a formula, a sketch, or examples of things that the term does *not* name.

Frame Game

1. Write a term in the center.
2. Frame the term with details.

> Include examples, descriptions, sketches, or sentences that use the term in context. Change the frame to fit each new term.

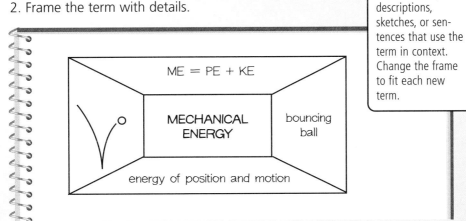

$$ME = PE + KE$$

MECHANICAL ENERGY

bouncing ball

energy of position and motion

Magnet Word

1. Write a term on the magnet.
2. On the lines, add details related to the term.

> You can also use phrases or sentences on the lines.

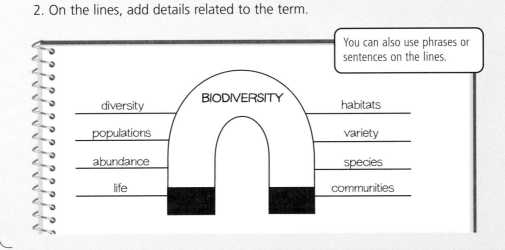

BIODIVERSITY

diversity | habitats
populations | variety
abundance | species
life | communities

Word Triangle

1. Write a term and its definition in the bottom section.
2. In the middle section, write a sentence in which the term is used correctly.
3. In the top section, draw a small picture to illustrate the term.

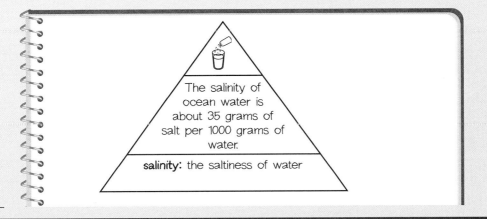

The salinity of ocean water is about 35 grams of salt per 1000 grams of water.

salinity: the saltiness of water

Appendix

Station Symbols

Meteorologists use station symbols to condense the weather data they receive from ground stations. The symbols are displayed on maps. The information in a station symbol can be understood by the meteorologists of any country.

In the symbol, air pressure readings are shortened by omitting the initial 9 or 10 and the decimal point. For numbers greater than 500, place a 9 to the left of the number and divide by 10 to get the air pressure in millibars. For numbers less than 500, place a 10 to the left and then divide by 10.

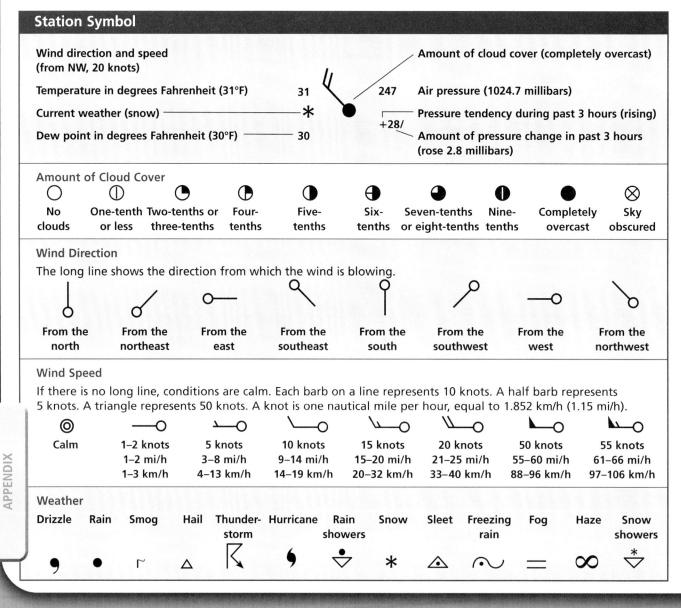

Station Symbol

Wind direction and speed (from NW, 20 knots)

Temperature in degrees Fahrenheit (31°F)   31

Current weather (snow)   *

Dew point in degrees Fahrenheit (30°F)   30

Amount of cloud cover (completely overcast)

247   Air pressure (1024.7 millibars)

+28/   Pressure tendency during past 3 hours (rising)

Amount of pressure change in past 3 hours (rose 2.8 millibars)

Amount of Cloud Cover

| No clouds | One-tenth or less | Two-tenths or three-tenths | Four-tenths | Five-tenths | Six-tenths | Seven-tenths or eight-tenths | Nine-tenths | Completely overcast | Sky obscured |

Wind Direction

The long line shows the direction from which the wind is blowing.

| From the north | From the northeast | From the east | From the southeast | From the south | From the southwest | From the west | From the northwest |

Wind Speed

If there is no long line, conditions are calm. Each barb on a line represents 10 knots. A half barb represents 5 knots. A triangle represents 50 knots. A knot is one nautical mile per hour, equal to 1.852 km/h (1.15 mi/h).

| Calm | 1–2 knots 1–2 mi/h 1–3 km/h | 5 knots 3–8 mi/h 4–13 km/h | 10 knots 9–14 mi/h 14–19 km/h | 15 knots 15–20 mi/h 20–32 km/h | 20 knots 21–25 mi/h 33–40 km/h | 50 knots 55–60 mi/h 88–96 km/h | 55 knots 61–66 mi/h 97–106 km/h |

Weather

| Drizzle | Rain | Smog | Hail | Thunder-storm | Hurricane | Rain showers | Snow | Sleet | Freezing rain | Fog | Haze | Snow showers |

Relative Humidity

You can find the relative humidity by calculating the difference between the two readings on a psychrometer. First look up the dry-bulb temperature in the left-hand column of the relative humidity chart. Then find in the top line the difference between the wet-bulb temperature and the dry-bulb temperature.

Relative Humidity (%)

Dry-Bulb Temperature (°C)	Difference Between Wet-Bulb and Dry-Bulb Temperatures (°C)															
	0	1	2	3	4	5	6	7	8	9	10	11	12	13	14	15
−20	100	28														
−18	100	40														
−16	100	48														
−14	100	55	11													
−12	100	61	23													
−10	100	66	33													
−8	100	71	41	13												
−6	100	73	48	20												
−4	100	77	54	32	11											
−2	100	79	58	37	20	1										
0	100	81	63	45	28	11										
2	100	83	67	51	36	20	6									
4	100	85	70	56	42	27	14									
6	100	86	72	59	46	35	22	10								
8	100	87	74	62	51	39	28	17	6							
10	100	88	76	65	54	43	33	24	13	4						
12	100	88	78	67	57	48	38	28	19	10	2					
14	100	89	79	69	60	50	41	33	25	16	8	1				
16	100	90	80	71	62	54	45	37	29	21	14	7	1			
18	100	91	81	72	64	56	48	40	33	26	19	12	6			
20	100	91	82	74	66	58	51	44	36	30	23	17	11	5		
22	100	92	83	75	68	60	53	46	40	33	27	21	15	10	4	
24	100	92	84	76	69	62	55	49	42	36	30	25	20	14	9	4
26	100	92	85	77	70	64	57	51	45	39	34	28	23	18	13	9
28	100	93	86	78	71	65	59	53	47	42	36	31	26	21	17	12
30	100	93	86	79	72	66	61	55	49	44	39	34	29	25	20	16

Wind Speeds

Descriptive names, such as *fresh gale,* were used by sailors and other people to describe the strength of winds. Later, ranges of wind speeds were determined. The table below lists the wind speeds and conditions you might observe around you on land.

Beaufort Scale of Wind Speeds

Beaufort Number	Wind Speed	Description
0	0 km/h (0 mi/h)	**Calm or Still** Smoke will rise vertically
1	2–5 km/h (1–3 mi/h)	**Light Air** Rising smoke drifts, weather vane is inactive
2	6–12 km/h (4–7 mi/h)	**Light Breeze** Leaves rustle, can feel wind on your face, weather vane moves
3	13–20 km/h (8–12 mi/h)	**Gentle Breeze** Leaves and twigs move around, lightweight flags extend
4	21–30 km/h (13–18 mi/h)	**Moderate Breeze** Thin branches move, dust and paper raised
5	31–40 km/h (19–24 mi/h)	**Fresh Breeze** Small trees sway
6	41–50 km/h (25–31 mi/h)	**Strong Breeze** Large tree branches move, open wires (such as telegraph wires) begin to "whistle," umbrellas are difficult to keep under control
7	51–61 km/h (32–38 mi/h)	**Moderate Gale** Large trees begin to sway, noticeably difficult to walk
8	62–74 km/h (39–46 mi/h)	**Fresh Gale** Twigs and small branches are broken from trees, walking into the wind is very difficult
9	75–89 km/h (47–54 mi/h)	**Strong Gale** Slight damage occurs to buildings, shingles are blown off of roofs
10	90–103 km/h (55–63 mi/h)	**Whole Gale** Large trees are uprooted, building damage is considerable
11	104–119 km/h (64–72 mi/h)	**Storm** Extensive, widespread damage. These typically occur only at sea, rarely inland.
12	120 km/h or more (74 mi/h or more)	**Hurricane** Extreme damage, very rare inland

Tornado Intensities

The Fujita scale describes the strength of a tornado based on the damage it does. The scale is useful for classifying tornadoes even though it is not exact. For example, a tornado can strengthen and then weaken before it dies out. The wind speeds are estimates of the strongest winds near the ground. Most tornadoes are F0 or F1. One-quarter to one-third of tornadoes are F2 or F3. Only a few percent of tornadoes are F4 or F5.

Fujita Scale for Tornadoes

F-Scale	Wind Speed	Type of Damage
F0	64–116 km/h (40–72 mi/h)	**Light Damage** Some damage to chimneys; branches broken off trees; shallow-rooted trees pushed over; sign boards damaged
F1	117–180 km/h (73–112 mi/h)	**Moderate Damage** Surface peeled off roofs; mobile homes pushed off foundations or overturned; moving autos blown off roads
F2	181–253 km/h (113–157 mi/h)	**Considerable Damage** Roofs torn off frame houses; mobile homes demolished; boxcars overturned; large trees snapped or uprooted; light-object missiles generated; cars lifted off ground
F3	254–332 km/h (158–206 mi/h)	**Severe Damage** Roofs and some walls torn off well-constructed houses; trains overturned; most trees in forest uprooted; heavy cars lifted off the ground and thrown
F4	333–418 km/h (207–260 mi/h)	**Devastating Damage** Well-constructed houses leveled; structures with weak foundations blown away some distance; cars thrown and large missiles generated
F5	419–512 km/h (261–318 mi/h)	**Incredible Damage** Strong frame houses leveled off foundations and swept away; automobile-sized missiles fly through the air in excess of 100 meters (109 yds); trees debarked; incredible phenomena will occur

Glossary

A

acid rain
Rain that has become more acidic than normal due to pollution. (p. 70)

    lluvia ácida Lluvia que se ha vuelto más ácida de lo normal debido a la contaminación.

air mass
A large volume of air that has nearly the same temperature and humidity at different locations at the same altitude. (p. 79)

    masa de aire Un gran volumen de aire que tiene casi la misma temperatura y humedad en distintos puntos a la misma altitud.

air pollution
Harmful materials added to the air that can cause damage to living things and the environment. (p. 27)

    contaminación de aire Materiales nocivos añadidos al aire que pueden causar daño a los seres vivos y al medio ambiente.

air pressure
The force of air molecules pushing on an area. (p. 43)

    presión de aire La fuerza de las moléculas de aire empujando sobre un área.

altitude
The distance above sea level. (p. 10)

    altitud La distancia sobre el nivel del mar.

atmosphere
The outer layer of gases of a large body in space, such as a planet or star; the mixture of gases that surrounds the solid Earth; one of the four parts of the Earth system. (p. 9)

    atmósfera La capa externa de gases de un gran cuerpo que se encuentra en el espacio, como un planeta o una estrella; la mezcla de gases que rodea la Tierra sólida; una de las cuatro partes del sistema terrestre.

atom
The smallest particle of an element that has the chemical properties of that element. (p. xvii)

    átomo La partícula más pequeña de un elemento que tiene las propiedades químicas del elemento.

B

barometer
An instrument that measures air pressure in the atmosphere. (p. 46)

    barómetro Un instrumento que mide la presión del aire en la atmósfera.

biosphere (BY-uh-SFEER)
All living organisms on Earth in the air, on the land, and in the waters; one of the four parts of the Earth system. (p. xix)

    biosfera Todos los organismos vivos de la Tierra, en el aire, en la tierra y en las aguas; una de las cuatro partes del sistema de la Tierra.

blizzard
A blinding snowstorm with winds of at least 56 kilometers per hour (35 mi/h), usually with temperatures below –7°C (20°F). (p. 90)

    ventisca Una cegadora tormenta de nieve con vientos de por lo menos 56 kilómetros por hora (35 mi/h), usualmente con temperaturas menores a –7°C (20°F).

C

climate
The characteristic weather conditions in an area over a long period of time. (p. 117)

    clima Las condiciones meteorológicas características de un lugar durante un largo período de tiempo.

climate zone
One of the major divisions in a system for classifying the climates of different regions based on characteristics they have in common. (p. 125)

    zona climática Una de las mayores divisiones en un sistema de clasificación de climas de diferentes regiones, basado en las características que tienen en común.

compound
A substance made up of two or more different types of atoms bonded together.

    compuesto Una sustancia formada por dos o más diferentes tipos de átomos enlazados.

condensation

The process by which a gas changes into a liquid. (p. 56)

condensación El proceso por el cual un gas se transforma en líquido.

conduction

The transfer of heat energy from one substance to another through direct contact without obvious motion. (p. 18)

conducción La transferencia de energía calorífica de una sustancia a otra a través de contacto directo, sin que haya movimiento obvio.

continental climate

A climate that occurs in the interior of a continent, with large temperature differences between seasons. (p. 120)

clima continental El clima que se presenta en el interior de un continente, con grandes diferencias de temperatura entre estaciones.

convection

The transfer of energy from place to place by the motion of heated gas or liquid; in Earth's mantle, convection is thought to transfer energy by the motion of solid rock, which when under great heat and pressure can move like a liquid. (p. 19)

convección La transferencia de energía de un lugar a otro por el movimiento de un líquido o gas calentado; se piensa que en el manto terrestre la convección transfiere energía mediante el movimiento de roca sólida, la cual puede moverse como un líquido cuando está muy caliente y bajo alta presión.

Coriolis effect (KAWR-ee-OH-lihs)

The influence of Earth's rotation on objects that move over Earth. (p. 49)

efecto Coriolis La influencia de la rotación de la Tierra sobre objetos que se mueven sobre la Tierra.

cycle

n. A series of events or actions that repeat themselves regularly; a physical and/or chemical process in which one material continually changes locations and/or forms. Examples include the water cycle, the carbon cycle, and the rock cycle.

v. To move through a repeating series of events or actions.

ciclo s. Una serie de eventos o acciones que se repiten regularmente; un proceso físico y/o químico en el cual un material cambia continuamente de lugar y/o forma. Ejemplos: el ciclo del agua, el ciclo del carbono y el ciclo de las rocas.

D

data

Information gathered by observation or experimentation that can be used in calculating or reasoning. *Data* is a plural word; the singular is *datum*.

datos Información reunida mediante observación o experimentación y que se puede usar para calcular o para razonar.

density

A measure of the amount of matter packed into a unit volume; the density of an object is equal to its mass divided by its volume. (p. 10)

densidad Una medida de la cantidad de materia contenida en una unidad de volumen; la densidad de un objeto es igual a su masa dividida por su volumen.

dew point

The temperature at which air with a given amount of water vapor will reach saturation. (p. 58)

punto de rocío La temperatura a la cual el aire con una cantidad determinada de vapor de agua alcanzará la saturación.

E

element

A substance that cannot be broken down into a simpler substance by ordinary chemical changes. An element consists of atoms of only one type.

elemento Una sustancia que no puede descomponerse en otra sustancia más simple por medio de cambios químicos normales. Un elemento consta de átomos de un solo tipo.

El Niño (ehl NEEN-yoh)

A disturbance of wind patterns and ocean currents in the Pacific Ocean that causes temporary climate changes in many parts of the world. (p. 136)

El Niño Un disturbio en los patrones de viento y las corrientes oceánicas del océano Pacifico que causa cambios climáticos temporales en muchas partes del mundo.

energy

The ability to do work or to cause a change. For example, the energy of a moving bowling ball knocks over pins; energy from food allows animals to move and to grow; and energy from the Sun heats Earth's surface and atmosphere, which causes air to move. (p. xv)

energía La capacidad para trabajar o causar un cambio. Por ejemplo, la energía de una bola de boliche en movimiento tumba los pinos; la energía proveniente de su alimento permite a los animales moverse y crecer; la energía del Sol calienta la superficie y la atmósfera de la Tierra, lo que ocasiona que el aire se mueva.

evaporation

The process by which liquid changes into gas. (p. 56)

evaporación El proceso por el cual un líquido se transforma en gas.

experiment

An organized procedure to study something under controlled conditions. (p. xxiv)

experimento Un procedimiento organizado para estudiar algo bajo condiciones controladas.

F

force

A push or a pull; something that changes the motion of an object. (p. xvii)

fuerza Un empuje o un jalón; algo que cambia el movimiento de un objeto.

fossil

A trace or the remains of a once-living thing from long ago. (p. xxi)

fósil Un rastro o los restos de un organismo que vivió hace mucho tiempo.

fossil fuels

Fuels formed from the remains of prehistoric organisms that are burned for energy. (p. 28)

combustibles fósiles Combustibles formados a partir de los restos de organismos prehistóricos que son consumidos para obtener energía.

freezing rain

Rain that freezes when it hits the ground or another surface and coats the surface with ice. (p. 68)

lluvia helada Lluvia que se congela cuando cae a la tierra o cualquier otra superficie y cubre la superficie con hielo.

friction

A force that resists the motion between two surfaces in contact. (p. xxi)

fricción Una fuerza que resiste el movimiento entre dos superficies en contacto.

front

The boundary between air masses. (p. 82)

frente El limite entre masas de aire.

G

gas

A state of matter different from liquid and solid, with no definite volume and no definite shape.

gas Un estado de la material, que no es sólido ni líquido, en el cual la sustancia se puede expandir o contraer para llenar un recipiente.

geosphere (JEE-uh-SFEER)

All the features on Earth's surface—continents, islands, and seafloor—and everything below the surface—the inner and outer core and the mantle; one of the four parts of the Earth system. (p. xix)

geosfera Todas las características de la superficie de la Tierra, es decir, continentes, islas y el fondo marino, y de todo bajo la superficie, es decir, el núcleo externo e interno y el manto; una de las cuatro partes del sistema de la Tierra.

global winds

Winds that travel long distances in steady patterns over several weeks. (p. 48)

vientos globales Vientos que viajan grandes distancias en patrones fijos por varias semanas.

gravity

The force that objects exert on each other because of their mass. (p. xvii)

gravedad La fuerza que los objetos ejercen entre sí debido a su masa.

greenhouse effect

The process by which certain gases in a planet's atmosphere absorb and emit infrared radiation, resulting in an increase in surface temperature. (p. 24)

efecto invernadero El proceso mediante el cual ciertos gases en la atmósfera de un planeta absorben y emiten radiación infrarroja, resultando en un incremento de la temperatura superficial del planeta.

greenhouse gases

Gases, such as carbon dioxide and methane, that absorb and give off infrared radiation as part of the greenhouse effect. (p. 24)

gases invernadero Gases, como el dióxido de carbono y el metano, que absorben y emiten radiación infrarroja como parte del efecto invernadero.

H

hail

Layered lumps or balls of ice that fall from cumulonimbus clouds. (p. 68)

granizo Trozos de hielo que caen de nubes cumulonimbos.

high-pressure system

A generally calm and clear weather system that occurs when air sinks down in a high-pressure center and spreads out toward areas of lower pressure as it nears the ground. (p. 84)

sistema de alta presión Un sistema climático generalmente claro y calmo que se presenta cuando el aire desciende en un centro de alta presión y se esparce hacia áreas de baja presión conforme se acerca al suelo.

humidity

The amount of water vapor in air. (p. 58)

humedad La cantidad de vapor de agua en el aire.

hurricane (HUR-ih-KAYN)

A tropical low-pressure system with sustained winds of 120 kilometers per hour (74 mi/h) or more. (p. 87)

huracán Un sistema tropical de baja presión con vientos sostenidos de 120 kilómetros por hora (74 mi/h) o más.

hydrosphere (HY-druh-SFEER)

All water on Earth—in the atmosphere and in the oceans, lakes, glaciers, rivers, streams, and underground reservoirs; one of the four parts of the Earth system. (p. xix)

hidrosfera Toda el agua de la Tierra: en la atmósfera y en los océanos, lagos, glaciares, ríos, arroyos y depósitos subterráneos; una de las cuatro partes del sistema de la Tierra.

hypothesis

A tentative explanation for an observation or phenomenon. A hypothesis is used to make testable predictions. (p. xxiv)

hipótesis Una explicación provisional de una observación o de un fenómeno. Una hipótesis se usa para hacer predicciones que se pueden probar.

I

ice age

A period of time during which surface temperatures drop significantly and huge ice sheets spread out beyond the polar regions. (p. 135)

edad de hielo Un período de tiempo durante el cual las temperaturas superficiales disminuyen significativamente y grandes capas de hielo se extienden más allá de las regiones polares.

infrared radiation (IHN-fruh-REHD RAY-dee-AY-shuhn)

Radiation of lower frequencies than visible light. (p. 23)

radiación infrarroja Radiación de frecuencia más baja que la luz visible.

isobar (EYE-suh-BAHR)

A line on a weather map connecting places that have the same air pressure. (p. 101)

isobara Una línea en un mapa climático que conecta lugares que tienen la misma presión de aire.

J, K

jet stream

A wind that flows in the upper troposphere from west to east over vast distances at great speeds. (p. 52)

corriente de chorro Un viento que sopla vastas distancias en la troposfera superior de oeste a este a grandes velocidades.

L

latitude

The distance in degrees north or south from the equator. (p. 118)

latitud La distancia en grados norte o sur a partir del ecuador.

law

In science, a rule or principle describing a physical relationship that always works in the same way under the same conditions. The law of conservation of energy is an example.

ley En las ciencias, una regla o un principio que describe una relación física que siempre funciona de la misma manera bajo las mismas condiciones. La ley de la conservación de la energía es un ejemplo.

low-pressure system

A large and often stormy weather system that occurs when air moves around and into a low-pressure center, then moves up to higher altitudes. (p. 85)

sistema de baja presión Un sistema climático grande y usualmente lluvioso que se presenta cuando el aire se mueve alrededor de y hacia un centro de baja presión, y luego se mueve hacia mayores altitudes.

M, N

marine climate

A climate influenced by a nearby ocean, with generally mild temperatures and steady precipitation. (p. 120)

clima marino El clima influido por un océano cercano, y que generalmente tiene temperaturas moderadas y precipitación poco variable.

mass

A measure of how much matter an object is made of.

masa Una medida de la cantidad de materia de la que está compuesto un objeto.

matter

Anything that has mass and volume. Matter exists ordinarily as a solid, a liquid, or a gas. (p. xvii)

materia Todo lo que tiene masa y volumen. Generalmente la materia existe como sólido, líquido o gas.

meteorologist (MEE-tee-uh-RAHL-uh-jihst)

A scientist who studies weather. (p. 98)

meteorólogo Un científico que estudia el clima.

microclimate

The climate of a smaller area within a subclimate. (p. 128)

microclima El clima de un área más pequeña dentro de un subclima.

molecule

A group of atoms that are held together by covalent bonds so that they move as a single unit.

molécula Un grupo de átomos que están unidos mediante enlaces covalentes de tal manera que se mueven como una sola unidad.

monsoon

A wind that changes direction with the seasons. (p. 54)

monzón Un viento que cambia de dirección con las estaciones.

O

ocean current

A stream of water that flows through the ocean in a regular pattern. (p. 121)

corriente oceánica Un flujo de agua que se mueve a través del océano de una forma regular.

ozone

A gas molecule that consists of three oxygen atoms. (p. 23)

ozono Una molécula de gas que consiste en tres átomos de oxígeno.

P, Q

particulates

Tiny particles or droplets, such as dust, dirt, and pollen, that are mixed in with air. (p. 28)

particulados Diminutas partículas o gotas, como por ejemplo de polvo, tierra o polen, que están mezcladas con el aire.

precipitation

Any type of liquid or solid water that falls to Earth's surface, such as rain, snow, or hail. (p. 57)

precipitación Cualquier tipo de agua líquida o sólida que cae a la superficie de la Tierra, como por ejemplo lluvia, nieve o granizo.

R

radiation (RAY-dee-AY-shuhn)

Energy that travels across distances as certain types of waves. (p. 17)

radiación Energía que viaja a través de la distancia en forma de ciertos tipos de ondas.

rain shadow

An area on the downwind side of a mountain that gets less precipitation than the side that faces the wind. (p. 129)

sombra de lluvia Un área viento abajo de una montaña que recibe menos precipitación que el lado de la montaña que hace frente al viento.

relative humidity

The comparison of the amount of water vapor in air with the maximum amount of water vapor that can be present in air at that temperature. (p. 58)

humedad relativa La comparación entre la cantidad de vapor de agua en el aire y la cantidad máxima de vapor de agua que puede estar presente en el aire a esa temperatura.

S

saturation

A condition of the atmosphere in which the rates of evaporation and condensation are equal. (p. 58)

saturación Una condición de la atmósfera en la cual las tasas de evaporación y condensación son iguales.

seasons

Periods of the year associated with specific weather conditions. (p. 122)

estaciones Los períodos del año asociados a condiciones climáticas específicas.

sleet

Small pellets of ice that form when rain passes through a layer of cold air and freezes before hitting the ground. (p. 68)

aguanieve Pequeñas bolitas de hielo que se forman cuando la lluvia pasa a través de una capa de aire frío y se congela antes de caer al suelo.

smog

The combination of smoke and fog; a type of air pollution that occurs when sunlight causes unburnt fuels, fumes, and other gases to react chemically, often seen as a brownish haze. (p. 28)

smog La combinación de humo y neblina; un tipo de contaminación de aire que se presenta cuando la luz solar provoca la reacción química de combustibles no consumidos, humos y otros gases, que a menudo se ve como una bruma parda.

storm surge

A rapid rise in water level in a coastal area that occurs when a hurricane pushes a huge mass of ocean water, often leading to flooding and widespread destruction. (p. 89)

marea de tormenta Un rápido aumento del nivel del agua en un área costera que ocurre cuando un huracán empuja una gran masa de agua oceánica, muchas veces provocando inundaciones y destrucción extensa.

system

A group of objects or phenomena that interact. A system can be as simple as a rope, a pulley, and a mass. It also can be as complex as the interaction of energy and matter in the four parts of the Earth system.

sistema Un grupo de objetos o fenómenos que interactúan. Un sistema puede ser algo tan sencillo como una cuerda, una polea y una masa. También puede ser algo tan complejo como la interacción de la energía y la materia en las cuatro partes del sistema de la Tierra.

T

technology

The use of scientific knowledge to solve problems or engineer new products, tools, or processes.

tecnología El uso de conocimientos científicos para resolver problemas o para diseñar nuevos productos, herramientas o procesos.

theory

In science, a set of widely accepted explanations of observations and phenomena. A theory is a well-tested explanation that is consistent with all available evidence.

teoría En las ciencias, un conjunto de explicaciones de observaciones y fenómenos que es ampliamente aceptado. Una teoría es una explicación bien probada que es consecuente con la evidencia disponible.

thunderstorm

A storm with lightning and thunder. (p. 92)

tormenta eléctrica Una tormenta con relámpagos y truenos.

tornado

A violently rotating column of air stretching from a cloud to the ground. (p. 95)

tornado Una columna de aire que gira violentamente y se extiende desde una nube hasta el suelo.

tropical storm (TRAHP-ih-kuhl)

A low-pressure system that starts in the tropics with winds of at least 65 kilometers per hour (40 mi/h) but less than 120 kilometers per hour (74 mi/h). (p. 87)

tormenta tropical Un sistema de baja presión que inicia en los trópicos con vientos de por lo menos 65 kilómetros por hora (40 mi/h) pero menores a 120 kilómetros por hora (74 mi/h).

U

ultraviolet radiation (UHL-truh-VY-uh-liht RAY-dee-AY-shuhn)
Radiation of higher frequencies than visible light, which can cause sunburn and other types of damage. (p. 23)

radiación ultravioleta Radiación de frecuencia más alta que la luz visible que puede causar quemaduras de sol y otros tipos de daño.

urban heat island
The warmer body of air over a city. (p. 128)

isla de calor urbana La masa de aire más cálida que se encuentra sobre una ciudad.

V

variable
Any factor that can change in a controlled experiment, observation, or model. (p. R30)

variable Cualquier factor que puede cambiar en un experimento controlado, en una observación o en un modelo.

volume
An amount of three-dimensional space, often used to describe the space that an object takes up.

volumen Una cantidad de espacio tridimensional; a menudo se usa este término para describir el espacio que ocupa un objeto.

W, X, Y, Z

weather
The condition of Earth's atmosphere at a particular time and place. (p. 47)

estado del tiempo La condición de la atmósfera terrestre en un lugar y momento particular.

wind
The horizontal movement of air caused by differences in air pressure. (p. 47)

viento El movimiento horizontal de aire provocado por diferencias en la presión de aire.

Index

Page numbers for definitions are printed in **boldface** type.
Page numbers for illustrations, maps, and charts are printed in *italics.*

INDEX

L

laboratory equipment
  beaker, R12, *R12*
  double-pan balances, R19, *R19*
  force meter, R16, *R16*
  forceps, R13, *R13*
  graduated cylinder, R16, *R16*
  hot plates, R13, *R13*
  meniscus, R16, *R16*
  microscope, R14–R15, *R14*
  spring scale, R16, *R16*
  rulers, metric, R17, *R17*
  test-tube holder, R12, *R12*
  test-tube rack, R13, *R13*
  test tubes, R12, *R12*
  triple-beam balances, R18, *R18*
Labrador Current (ocean), *121*
labs, R10–R35. *See also* experiments.
  equipment, R12–R19
  safety, R10–R11
lakes
  acid rain and, 70
  snow and, 90
land. *See also* continent.
  air masses formed over, *80*
land breezes, *53*
latitude, **118**
  climate and, 117, *118, 140*
  global wind patterns and, *48*, 48–52, *51, 52*
lava, xiv, *xiv, xxiii*
laws, physical, xvi
light, visible, xv, 16–17, 22–23
lightning, *xxiv, 71*, 92, 94
London, England, climate of, *121*
low-pressure systems, *84*, **85**, *100, 101*, 106
  storms associated with, 85, 87–91
lung disease, air pollution and, 29

M

magnetic field, xvii
manatee, 5
manufacturing
  contribution to air pollution, *28*
  contribution to greenhouse gases, *30*
marine west coast subclimate, *126, 127*

mass, xvii, 10
math skills
  adding measurements, *55*
  area, **R43**
  decimal, **R39**, R40
  describing a set of data, R36–R37
  equations, 26
  formulas, **R42**
  fractions, **R41**
  line graphs, *139*
  mean, **R36**
  median, **R36**
  mode, **R37**
  percents, **R41**
  proportions, **R39**
  range, **R37**
  rates, 86, **R38**
  ratios, **R38**
  scientific notation, **R44**
  significant figures, **R44**
  volume, **R43**
matter, xvi–xix, **xvii**
Mauna Loa Observatory, 112, *112*
mean, **R36**
median, **R36**
Mediterranean subclimate, *126, 127*
mercury, inches of (unit of air pressure), 101
mesosphere, *20,* 21, 36
meteorite, xxiv
meteorologists, **98**, 98–99, *103*, 106, 117
meteorology, 98–103, *99, 100, 101, 102*, 106
  Internet career link, 5
  tools used in, 46, *99*, 100–103, *106*
meteors, 21
methane, greenhouse effect and, 24, 28, *30*
metric system, R20–R21
  changing metric units, R20, *R20*
  converting between U.S. customary units, R21, *R21*
  temperature conversion, R21, *R21*
Mexico City, air quality in, *29*
microclimates, **128**, *128*, 140
microscope, R14–R15, *R14*
  making a slide, or wet mount, *R15*
  viewing an object, R15
millibar (unit of air pressure), *100, 101. See also* isobars.
minerals, xix

mode, **R37**

moist mid-latitude climate zones, 125, *126, 127*

monsoons, 53, **54,** *54*

Montana, precipitation patterns in, 123

Montreal Protocol (international agreement), 33.
    See also chlorofluorocarbons; ozone layer.

mountain breezes, 53

mountains, xv
    climates of, *119*
    global warming effects on, 137
    Himalayan, xxi
    rain shadows caused by, *129*

Murcutt, Glenn (architect), 124

N

Natashquan, Canada, climate of, *121*

National Hurricane Center (U.S.), 89

National Oceanic and Atmospheric
    Administration (U.S.), 100

National Weather Service (U.S.), 90, 96

nimbostratus clouds, *61*

nitric acid, 70

nitrogen, 24. *See also* nitrogen cycle.
    atmospheric, *11,* 12
    plants and, 12, *13, 15*

nitrogen cycle, 12, *13*
    role of bacteria in, 12, *13*
    role of decay in, 12, *13*

nitrogen oxide, 28, 70
    greenhouse effect and, 24, *30*

North America
    average annual temperatures in, *118*
    tornado frequency in, 95
    weather during El Niño years, 136

North Atlantic Current (ocean), *121*

North Carolina, hurricane damage to, *89*

North Equatorial Current (ocean), *121*

Northern Hemisphere
    global warming's effect on, 137
    seasons in, 122
    wind patterns in, *49, 51, 52, 84, 85*

Norwegian Current (ocean), *121*

note-taking strategies, **R45–R49**
    combination notes, 42, R45, *R45*
    concept map, R49, *R49*

content frame, R45, *R45*

main idea and detail notes, 116, R46, *R46*

main idea web, 78, R46, *R46*

mind map, R47, *R47*

outline, R48, *R48*

supporting main ideas, 8, R47, *R47*

Venn diagram, R49, *R49*

O

observations, **xxiv, R2,** R5, R33
    qualitative, R2
    quantitative, R2

ocean, xix. *See also* Atlantic Ocean; Indian
        Ocean; Pacific Ocean.
    air masses formed over, *80*
    hurricane formation over, *88,* 106

ocean currents, xv, xix, **121,** *121*
    climate and, 117, *121,* 140
    cold-water, *121*
    role in El Niño events, *136*
    warm-water, *121*

oil. *See* fossil fuels.

operational definition, **R31**

opinion, **R9**
    different from fact, R9

orbit, xvii

outer space, altitude of, 10

oxygen. *See also* ozone.
    animals' use of 12, *13, 15*
    atmospheric (gas), *11,* 14, *15,* 23, 24, 32
    elemental, 23
    life processes and, 12, *13, 15*

ozone, *20,* 21, **23,** *23,* 32. *See also* ozone layer.
    absorption of ultraviolet radiation by, *20,* 21,
        23, 32, *36*
    chlorine reaction with, 32
    as pollutant, 28
    smog formation and, 28
    stratosphere and, *20,* 21, *23, 23*
    troposphere and, 28

ozone alert, *29*

ozone layer, *20,* 21, *23,* 28
    absorption of ultraviolet radiation by, *20,* 21,
        23, 23, 32, *36*
    destruction of, by human activities, 32–33, *33, 36*

INDEX

S

safety, R10–R11
  animal, R11
  chemical, R11
  clean up, R11
  directions, R10
  dress code, R10
  electrical, R11
  fire, R10
  glassware, R11
  heating, R10
  hurricanes, *89*
  icons, R10–R11
  lab, R10–R11
  sharp object, R11
  thunderstorms, *94*
  tornadoes, *96*
  winter storms, *91*
salt, in atmosphere, 11, *28*
satellite
  images, 3, *4,* 5, *14, 102*
  weather data collection, *99, 102, 103*
  weather forecasting and, 112
saturation, **58**
science, nature of, xxii–xxv
Scientific American Frontiers, 2, 4
scientific notation, **R44**
scientific process, xxiii–xxv
  asking questions and, xxiii
  determining what is known and, xxiii
  interpreting results and, xxv
  investigating and, xxiv
  sharing results and, xxv
sea breezes, *53,* 128
  thunderstorms and, *93*
sea fan, *4,* 4–5
sea level
  air density at, 10, *44*
  global warming effects on, 138
seasons, xv, **122,** 140
semiarid subclimate, *126, 127*
Shinn, Gene, 4
ships
  weather data collection and, *99*
  wind pattern use and, 52

shorelines
  hurricane damage to, *89*
  winds along, *53*
siesmograph, *xxii*
significant figures, **R44**
SI units. *See* International System of Units.
skin cancer, 23
sleet, 57, **68,** *69, 72*
slides, making, R15, *R15*
Smith, Garriet, 4
smog, **28,** *28,* 29
smog alert, 29
smoke, 27, 28
  smog formation and, 28
snow, 57, 68, *69, 72*
  formation of, 67, 68, *69*
  lake-effect, 90
  measurement of, 67
snow line, *118*
snow storms, 90. *See also* winter storms.
soil
  eroded, 14
  nitrogen cycle and, 12, *13*
solar radiation, xiv–xv, 17, *36*
  absorption of, 16, *17, 20,* 21, 22–25, *26,* 29, *36*
  air movement and, 47–48, *48*
  energy of different types of, 23
  heating effect of, 16, *18,* 18–19, *20,* 21, 23, *48*
  infrared, **23,** 24, *25, 36*
  reflection of, 16, *17, 20,* 22–25, *26, 29*
  ultraviolet, **23,** 32, *36*
  visible, 16, *17,* 22, *102*
solar system, xvii
South America, weather during El Niño years, 136
Southern Hemisphere
  seasons in, 122
  wind patterns in, *49, 51, 52*
South Pole, *33*
space objects, effect on global climate, 133
spring, 122
standardized test practice, 39, 75, 109, 143
  analyzing data, 143
  analyzing diagrams, 75
  analyzing maps, 109
  interpreting graphs, 39
Stanley, Mount (central Africa), climate of, 118

T

Acknowledgments

Photography

Cover © Bill Ross/Corbis; **i** © Bill Ross/Corbis; **iii** *left (top to bottom)* Photograph of James Trefil by Evan Cantwell; Photograph of Rita Ann Calvo by Joseph Calvo; Photograph of Linda Carnine by Amilcar Cifuentes; Photograph of Sam Miller by Samuel Miller; *right (top to bottom)* Photograph of Kenneth Cutler by Kenneth A. Cutler; Photograph of Donald Steely by Marni Stamm; Photograph of Vicky Vachon by Redfern Photographics; **vi** © Catherine Karnow/Corbis; **vii** AP/WideWorld Photos; **ix** Photographs by Sharon Hoogstraten; **xiv–xv** Doug Scott/age fotostock; **xvi–xvii** © AFLO FOTO Agency; **xviii–ix** © Tim Fitzharris/Masterfile; **xx–xxi** AP/WideWorld Photos; **xxii** © Vince Streano/Corbis; **xxiii** © Roger Ressmeyer/Corbis; **xxiv** top University of Florida Lightning Research Laboratory; *center* © Roger Ressmeyer/Corbis; **xxv** *center* © Mauro Fermariello/Science Researchers; *bottom right* © Alfred Pasieka/Photo Researchers; **xxvi–xxvii** © Stocktrek/Corbis; **xxvi–xxvii** NOAA; **xxvii** © Alan Schein Photography/Corbis; **xxvii** Vaisala Oyj, Finland; **2–3** © Bruce Byers/Getty Images; **3** *top* The Chedd-Angier Production Company; *bottom* © D. Faulkner/Photo Researchers; **4** *top left* Luiz C. Marigo/Peter Arnold, Inc.; *top center* Image courtesy Norman Kuring, SeaWiFS Project/NASA; *top right* Norbert Wu; *bottom center* © The Chedd-Angier Production Company; **6–7** © Peter Griffith/Masterfile; **7** *top, center* Photographs by Sharon Hoogstraten; **10** *top* © Didrik Johnck/Corbis Sygma; *bottom* Photograph by Sharon Hoogstraten; **11** NASA; **13** © Michael K. Nichols/NGS Image Collection; **14** *top left, top right* Provided by the SeaWiFS Project, NASA/Goddard Space Flight Center, and ORBIMAGE; **15** M. Thonig/Robertstock.com; **16** David Young-Wolff/PhotoEdit; **17** Photograph by Sharon Hoogstraten; **19** © Gerald and Buff Corsi/Visuals Unlimited, Inc.; **22, 24** Photographs by Sharon Hoogstraten; **26** *top, bottom* PhotoDisc/Getty Images; *background* © Pulse Productions/SuperStock/PictureQuest; **27** Photograph by Sharon Hoogstraten; **28** © P.G. Adam/Publiphoto/Photo Researchers; **29** AP/WideWorld Photos; **30** *background, center left* PhotoDisc/Getty Images; *center right* © Corbis/PictureQuest; **32** © Mug Shots/Corbis; **33** *top left, bottom left* NASA/Goddard Space Flight Center; **34** *top left* © Still Pictures/Peter Arnold, Inc.; *left, right* Photographs by Sharon Hoogstraten; **36** NASA; **37** © Tom Branch/Photo Researchers; **40–41** © Catherine Karnow/Corbis; **41, 45, 47** Photographs by Sharon Hoogstraten; **54** *top left, top right* Earth Vistas; **55** *top* NASA/Corbis; *background* © Lester Lefkowitz/Corbis; **56** *center right* Photograph by Sharon Hoogstraten; *bottom right* © Japack Company/Corbis; **57** © Kristi Bressert/Index Stock Imagery/PictureQuest; **59** Photograph by Sharon Hoogstraten; **60** Grant Heilman/Grant Heilman Photography, Inc.; **62** *top* © John Mead/Photo Researchers; *center* © Royalty-free/Corbis; *bottom* Fred Whitehead/Animals Animals/Earth Scenes; **63** © Tom Till; **64** *top* © Gunter Marx Photography/Corbis; *bottom left, bottom right, center* Photographs by Sharon Hoogstraten; **66** © Stockbyte/PictureQuest; **67** Photograph by Sharon Hoogstraten; **69** *bottom left* © Larry West/Photo Researchers; *bottom right* © Astrid & Hanns-Frieder Michler/Photo Researchers; **70** © Will McIntyre/Photo Researchers; **71** © 1990 Warren Faidley/Weatherstock; **74** © Dorling Kindersley; **76–77** AP/WideWorld Photos; **77, 81** Photographs by Sharon Hoogstraten; **83** © PhotoDisc/Getty Images; **86** © Stephen J. Krasemann/Photo Researchers; **87** Photograph by Sharon Hoogstraten; **88** Image by Marit Jentoft-Nilsen/NASA GSFC; **89** *top, center* Courtesy of U.S. Geological Survey; **90** Photograph by Sharon Hoogstraten; **91** AP/WideWorld Photos; **92, 94** *top* Photographs by Sharon Hoogstraten; *bottom left* © PhotoDisc/Getty Images; **95** *left, center, right* © David K. Hoadley; **96** © Reuters/New Media/Corbis; **97** *background* © Waite Air Photos, Inc.; *top left, top right* © Fletcher & Baylis/Photo Researchers; **98** Used with permission © January 9, 2003 Chicago Tribune Company, Chicago, Illinois. Photograph by Sharon Hoogstraten; **101** Provided by Space Science & Engineering Center, University of Wisconsin-Madison; **102** WSBT-TV, South Bend, Indiana; **104** *top left* Mary Kate Denny/PhotoEdit, Inc.; *center left, bottom right* Photographs by Sharon Hoogstraten; **105** Photograph by Sharon Hoogstraten; **106** Image by Marit Jentoft-Nilsen/NASA GSFC; **108** Used with permission © January 9, 2003 Chicago Tribune Company, Chicago, Illinois. Photograph by Sharon Hoogstraten; **110** *top right* © Joel W. Rogers/Corbis; *bottom* © Dorling Kindersley;

111 *top left* © Snark/Art Resource, New York; *top right* Matthew Oldfield, Scubazoo/Photo Researchers; *bottom* National Museum of American History, Smithsonian Institution; **112** *top left* © Mark A. Schneider/Photo Researchers; *top right* © Bettmann/Corbis; *right center* © Roger Ressmeyer/Corbis; *bottom* © Corbis; **113** *top left* NASA; *top right* Photograph courtesy of the University Corporation for Atmospheric Research (UCAR) **114–115** © Ferrero-Labat/Auscape International; **115** *top, center,* **117, 119** Photographs by Sharon Hoogstraten; **120** *left* Tony Freeman/PhotoEdit, Inc.; *right* © Duomo/Corbis; **123** *top left, top right* Steve McCurry/Magnum Photos; **124** *top left* © Dave G. Houser/Corbis; *center right* AP/WideWorld Photos; *center left, bottom* Glenn Murcutt; **125** © The Image Bank/Getty Images; **127** *center left* © Rick Schafer/Index Stock Imagery/PictureQuest; *top left* © Gerald D. Tang; *bottom* © Photodisc/Getty Images; *center right* © Willard Clay; *top right* © Bill Ross/Corbis; *bottom left* © John Conrad/Corbis; **130** *top left* © Mark Lewis/Pictureque/PictureQuest; *center left* Photograph by Sharon Hoogstraten; **132** Johner/Photonica; **133** *top right* © Photodisc/Getty Images; *bottom right* Photograph by Sharon Hoogstraten; **137** Lonnie G. Thompson, Ohio State University; **139** Simon Fraser/Mauna Loa Observatory/Photo Researchers; **140, R28** Photodisc/Getty Images.

Illustrations and Maps

Accurate Art Inc. **75, 109**
Argosy **46, 119**
Richard Bonson/Wildlife Art Ltd. **44, 72**
Peter Bull/Wildlife Art, Ltd. **99, 106**
Stephen Durke **17, 18, 25, 36**
Chris Forsey MCA **129**
Gary Hincks **20, 36, 48, 51**
MapQuest.com, Inc. **3, 14, 49, 52, 54, 55, 80, 83, 84, 85, 86, 88, 89, 93, 97, 118, 120, 121, 123, 126, 133, 134, 135, 136, 140, 143**
Precision Graphics **53, 59, 72**
Mike Saunders **61, 69, 72**
Dan Stuckenschneider **R11–R19, R22, R32**
Space Science and Engineering Center, University of Wisconsin-Madison **84, 100, 101, 102, 106**
Raymond Turvey **83, 106**